AMERICAN CROSSROADS

Edited by Earl Lewis, George Lipsitz, George Sánchez, Dana Takagi, Laura Briggs, and Nikhil Pal Singh

Why Busing Failed

The publisher gratefully acknowledges the generous support of the Anne G. Lipow Endowment Fund for Social Justice and Human Rights of the University of California Press Foundation, which was established by Stephen M. Silberstein.

Why Busing Failed

RACE, MEDIA, AND THE NATIONAL
RESISTANCE TO SCHOOL DESEGREGATION

Matthew F. Delmont

UNIVERSITY OF CALIFORNIA PRESS

University of California Press, one of the most distinguished university presses in the United States, enriches lives around the world by advancing scholarship in the humanities, social sciences, and natural sciences. Its activities are supported by the UC Press Foundation and by philanthropic contributions from individuals and institutions. For more information, visit www.ucpress.edu.

University of California Press
Oakland, California

Library of Congress Cataloging-in-Publication Data

Delmont, Matthew F., author.
  Why busing failed : race, media, and the national resistance to school desegregation / Matthew F. Delmont.
    pages cm. — (American Crossroads ; 42)
  Includes bibliographical references and index.
  ISBN 978-0-520-28424-1 (cloth : alk. paper)
  ISBN 978-0-520-28425-8 (pbk. : alk. paper)
  ISBN 978-0-520-95987-3 (ebook)
  1. Busing for school integration—United States—History—20th century.
2. School integration—Massive resistance movement—United States—
History—20th century. I. Title. II. Series: American crossroads ; 42.
  LC214.52.D45 2016
  379.2′63—dc23
  2015031885

25 24 23 22 21 20 19 18 17 16
10 9 8 7 6 5 4 3 2 1

CONTENTS

AT WWW.WHYBUSINGFAILED.COM

Ways to Teach "Busing" Differently
Video Clips
Images
Selected Research Materials

ILLUSTRATIONS

ACKNOWLEDGMENTS

I am fortunate to have received encouragement from family, friends, mentors, and colleagues for as long as I can remember. My mom, Diane Delmont, did an amazing job of raising me, and I am eternally thankful for her love and support. After researching this book, I also appreciate the work she did to navigate the open enrollment system in Minneapolis and the fact that she drove me to Burroughs Elementary School every day.

Thank you also to Frank Bowman, Bobbie and Lindy Stoltz, Katie Stoltz, Leari Jean and Jewel Anderson, and my late grandmother Kaye Henrikson, for their love and support.

I've found at Arizona State University a wonderful place to teach history and American studies. Thank you to Matt Garcia, Desiree Garcia, Bambi Haggins, Aaron Bae, Karen Leong, Calvin Schermerhorn, Michael Stancliff, Mark Tebeau, Chris Jones, Sujey Vega, Rudy Guevarra, Brianna Theobald, Lee Bebout, Don Fixico, Victoria Thompson, Don Critchlow, Gayle Gullet, Lauren Harris, Laurie Manchester, Anna Holian, Pen Moon, Catherine O'Donnell, Katherine Osburn, Jim Rush, Paul Hirt, Phil Vandermeer, and my other colleagues in history and American studies at Arizona State University for discussing my research and helping me strengthen my arguments. Thank you to Alexus Stewart and Corrigan Vaughan for working as research assistants on this project.

Thank you to Dean George Justice, Dean Patrick Kenney, Provost Mark Searle, and President Michael Crow for welcoming me to Arizona State University and for supporting my research.

Niels Hooper, my editor at University of California Press, supported this project from the earliest proposal and encouraged me to frame the book more broadly. Thank you to Bradley Depew and Rachel Berchten for guiding this book through production and to Elizabeth Berg for her careful copy editing. Thank you to Cynthia Savage for preparing the book's index. And thank you to Alex Dahne, Elizabeth Shreve, and Kate Pinnick for publicizing the book.

This project started at Scripps College, where I was also fortunate to have excellent colleagues and students. Thanks to Julie Liss, Rita Roberts, Sheila Walker, Bill Anthes, Nancy Neiman Auerbach, Hal Barron, Stu McConnell, Lily Geismer, Damien Sojoyner, Chris Guzaitis, Frances Pohl, Dan Segal, Diana Selig, Victor Silverman, and Claudia Strauss for their collegiality and support. This research benefited from research support at Scripps, for which I would like to thank Dean Amy MarcusNewhall, Associate Dean Gretchen Edwalds-Gilbert, and former President Lori Bettison-Varga. Thank you also to the Scripps students who worked with me as research assistants on this project: Theresa Iker, Jessica Warren, Laurel Schwartz, Emily Horne, Faye Jones, Laura Kent, Ann Kirkpatrick, Alexa Kopelman, Elizabeth McElvein, Kaitlin Morris, Aly Monroe, Claire Pompetti, Laura Rossiter, Ariel Saland, Elisabeth Salzberg, and Colleen Syms.

Thank you to Ed Oetting and Bee Gallegos at ASU library for helping me track down important sources. Thank you to the archivists, librarians, and staff members at the Vanderbilt Television News Archive, University of Georgia Peabody Awards Collection, Lyndon Baines Johnson Presidential Library, Richard Nixon Presidential Library, and State of Florida Archives. Thank you to the Center on the American Governor, Eagleton Institute of Politics at Rutgers University for grant support.

This book has benefited immensely from the feedback of colleagues who read rough drafts of the chapters or heard conference presentations. Jeanne Theoharis, George Lipsitz, and an anonymous reader for University of California Press encouraged me to expand the book's scope and to deepen my analysis. Thanks also to Aniko Bodroghkozy, Steve Classen, Phil Ethington, Gillian Frank, Herman Gray, Matthew Lassiter, Victoria Johnson, Lynne Joyrich, Allison Perlman, and Gayle Wald, for offering useful suggestions in different venues.

Thanks to my friends from the Jackal club: Shawn Anderson, Tim Arnold, Victor Danh, Jessie Davis, Jake Ewart, Kara Hughes, Jake Lentz, Ken Miller, and Cabral Williams.

Thank you to Marcia Chatlain and Mario Sifuentez for being friends since graduate school. Seeing you at the American Studies Association conference each fall is one my favorite things about this profession.

Finally, thank you to Jacque Wernimont, Xavier, and Simone for their love.

Introduction

"Busing has been a failure in Boston," the *Boston Globe* informed readers in 1994, on the twentieth anniversary of the start of court-ordered desegregation in the city. "It achieved neither integration nor better schooling."[1] Speaking to a group of Chicago educators in 1981, assistant United States attorney general for civil rights William Bradford Reynolds offered a similar assessment: "Forced busing has, in the final analysis, largely failed in two major respects. It has failed to gain needed public acceptance and it has failed to translate into enhanced educational achievement."[2] Reynolds, who played a central role in articulating and carrying out the Reagan administration's civil rights policies, found company from across the political spectrum in describing "busing" for school desegregation as a misguided policy. Running unsuccessfully for president in 1976, Ronald Reagan told voters that "school busing has failed miserably. It has created bitterness, not eliminated it."[3] A year earlier, Democratic senator Joe Biden described busing as a "bankrupt concept" that violated "the cardinal rule of common sense," and introduced two successful "antibusing" amendments in the Senate.[4] Biden's perspective on "busing" unintentionally echoed that of the 1972 National Black Political Convention resolution that characterized "busing" as "a bankrupt, suicidal method of desegregating schools, based on the false notion that black children are unable to learn unless they are in the same setting as white children."[5] President Nixon welcomed the National Black Political Convention's "antibusing" resolution and that same year told a group of white parents in Philadelphia, "Busing of school children has failed to meet either of its intended purposes—failed to promote quality education for all and to end the racial isolation which we all agree must be ended."[6] Despite the work of civil rights advocates in every region of the country, the chorus of voices insisting that "busing" was a failed experiment dominated the debate on school desegregation. The certainty with which so many politicians, parents, and writers described "busing" as a failure has obscured the history of one of the nation's most controversial civil rights issues.

Why Busing Failed reconsiders the history of "busing" for school desegregation and shows that "busing" failed to more fully desegregate public schools because school officials, politicians, courts, and the news media valued the desires of white parents more than the rights of black students. This argument requires rethinking the history of "busing" in three key ways. First, we have to understand how "busing" became the common-sense way to describe school desegregation. As civil rights advocates continually pointed out, "busing" was a fake issue. Students in the United States had long ridden buses to school, and the number of students transported to school at public expense in the United States expanded from 600,000 in 1920 to 20,000,000 in 1970.[7] In concert with rural to urban migration, school buses made it possible for multigrade elementary schools to replace one-room schoolhouses and for comprehensive high schools to become commonplace. School buses, in this era, were among the educational privileges enjoyed by white students. "The white rode buses, the Negro walked long weary miles in all kind of weather, cold, wind and rain, as well as the scortching [sic] heat of summer," Rosa Parks remembered of her childhood in Montgomery, Alabama.[8] Reverend Theodore Hesburgh, president of University of Notre Dame and a member of the Commission on Civil Rights, said, "I remember Medgar Evers saying that his first recollection of busing was the new school buses passing him and other black children on the way to school . . . splashing them with mud as the white children on their way to a good school yelled out the window, 'Nigger! Nigger!' No objections to busing then."[9] In other parts of the South, as well as New York, Boston, and many other northern cities, students rode buses past closer neighborhood schools to more distant schools to maintain segregation. Linda Brown, the plaintiff in *Brown v. Board of Education of Topeka,* rode a bus over twenty miles to attend a black school, when the white school was only four blocks from her family's home.[10] In 1959 the National Association for the Advancement of Colored People (NAACP) ran a fund-raising advertisement in the *New York Times* to call attention to the use of "busing" to maintain segregated schools after *Brown.* The advertisement features a six-year-old girl asleep on a school bus, cradling her schoolbooks. The young girl in the image is a first-grade student in Yancey County, North Carolina, where she and other black children were bused past all-white schools in their home county to segregated black schools forty miles away in Asheville. "The situation in Yancey County has scores of parallels throughout the South," the advertisement informs readers. "It's been more than 5 long years since the Supreme Court decision of May 17, 1954—and yet the segregated school with its callous long-hauls and its myriad inferiorities continues to cheat Negro children of their right to equal training for life."[11] With the growing use of school buses in most school districts, white parents did not raise a fuss or wax nostalgic for "neighborhood schools." In Boston, more than 50 percent of middle-school students and 85 percent of high-school students were bused before court-ordered "busing" with no objection until and unless it was linked to desegregation.[12] Put more starkly, then, school buses were fine for the majority of white families; "busing" was not.

White parents and politicians framed their resistance to school desegregation in terms of "busing" and "neighborhood schools." This rhetorical shift allowed them to support white schools and neighborhoods without using explicitly racist language. As early as 1957, white parents in New York rallied against "busing." In Detroit in 1960, thousands of white parents organized a school boycott to protest the "busing" of three hundred black students from an overcrowded school to a school in a white neighborhood.[13] In Boston, Louise Day Hicks made opposition to "busing" a centerpiece of her political campaigns. "It was Mrs. Hicks who kept talking against busing children when the NAACP hadn't even proposed busing," the *Boston Globe* noted in 1965.[14] "I have probably talked before 500 or 600 groups over the last years about busing," Los Angeles assemblyman Floyd Wakefield said in 1970. "Almost every time someone has gotten up and called me a 'racist' or a 'bigot.' But now, all of the sudden, I am no longer a bigot. Now I am called 'the leader of the antibusing' effort."[15] With "busing," northerners found a palatable way to oppose desegregation without appealing to the explicitly racist sentiments they preferred to associate with southerners.

Describing opposition to "busing" as something other than resistance to school desegregation was a choice that obscured the histories of racial discrimination and legal contexts for desegregation orders. In covering school desegregation in Boston and other northern cities, contemporary news media took up the "busing" frame, and most histories of the era have followed suit. Our understanding of school desegregation in the North is skewed as a result, emphasizing innocent "de facto" segregation over the housing covenants, federal mortgage redlining, public housing segregation, white homeowners' associations, and discriminatory real estate practices that produced and maintained segregated neighborhoods, as well as the policies regarding school siting, districting, and student transfers that produced and maintained segregated schools. I use "busing" in quotation marks throughout this book to emphasize that this term developed as a selective way to label and oppose school desegregation.

"Busing" for school desegregation was about the constitutional rights of black students, but the story of "busing" has been told and retold as a story about the feelings and opinions of white people. The violent resistance that greeted school desegregation in mid-1970s Boston engraved that city's "busing crisis" into school textbooks and cemented the failure of "busing" in the popular imagination. One reason Boston's "busing crisis" continues to resonate for so many readers and viewers is that it serves as a convenient end point for the history of civil rights, where it is juxtaposed with *Brown v. Board of Education* (1954) or the Little Rock school integration crisis (1957). In this telling, the civil rights movement, with support from federal officials and judges, took a wrong turn in the North and encountered "white backlash." The trouble with this story is that journalists and pundits identified a "white backlash" not only in 1974, but also in 1964. A more important issue with the "backlash" story is that the perspectives of white parents who opposed school desegregation figured prominently in the very civil rights legislation against which they later rebelled. In drafting the 1964 Civil Rights Act, for example, the bill's northern sponsors drew a sharp distinction between segregation by law in the South and so-called racial imbalance in the North, amending Title IV, section 401b, to read: "'Desegregation' means the assignment of students to public schools and within such schools without regard to their race, color, religion, or national origin, but 'desegregation' shall not mean the assignment of students to public schools in order to overcome racial imbalance."[16] This "antibusing" language was directly designed to keep federal civil rights enforcement of school desegregation focused away from the North, and white politicians and parents in cities like Boston, Chicago, and New York regularly pointed to the 1964 Civil Rights Act to justify the maintenance of white schools. Politicians across regional lines, including both Democrats and Republicans, reflected and fed their constituents' fears of "busing." Local, state, and national politicians argued for white "neighborhood schools" and railed against "forced busing" and "massive busing." Despite claims of judicial activism, moreover, federal courts were slow to act on school desegregation, especially outside the South. By the mid-1970s, the Supreme Court's rulings on school desegregation made it exceedingly difficult to prove that school districts had intentionally discriminated on the basis of race and had the result of protecting white suburbs from "busing." Rather than focusing on "white backlash," this book shows how preemptive white protests shaped "antibusing" legislation and slowed the pace of school desegregation.

The battle over "busing" was never primarily a debate over policy. Social scientists published hundreds of articles on "busing" in the 1960s and 1970s, but these experts were working with piecemeal data to try to make sense of school desegregation plans that were still unfolding. In 1975, sociologist James Coleman, who published widely read and cited reports on race and educational opportunity, lamented that "there has not been . . . any systematic and continuous and comparable gathering of data initiated at the Federal level on the variety of consequences of school desegregation." Without national data, Coleman continued, "it has been left to a variety of partly poorly- and partly well-conceived studies done at the local level for us to attempt to infer something about those consequences."[17] United States Civil Rights Commission vice chairman Stephen Horn echoed Coleman's sentiments in 1979. "Because the Federal Government has been negligent in establishing a systematic program of analysis which would aid policymakers in judging the effectiveness and the intended and unintended consequences of desegregation," Horn argued, "currently policymakers can pick an isolated social science study completed on one school or a district and use it to support or oppose a particular course of action."[18] Politicians and parents looked to the latest studies from policy analysts like Thomas Pettigrew, David Armor, and Gary Orfield to support their already established views on "busing," but these reports did not reach as many people or convey the emotional charge of media coverage of "antibusing" protests.[19]

Rather than being a policy debate, the battle over "busing" was about how school desegregation would be defined in media and public discourse, and about how much actual desegregation would take place in the nation's schools, especially in schools outside the South. Understanding the history of "busing" for school desegregation requires paying attention not only to court cases and desegregation policies, but also to how television and print news media framed "busing" for national audiences. These media representations were particularity important because, even at its peak in the 1970s, court-ordered busing applied to less than 5 percent of public school students nationally.[20] "Antibusing" parents and politicians also borrowed media strategies from the civil rights movement to thwart "busing" for school desegregation. "Busing" emerged as a hot-button national political issue not because the majority of American families experienced it, but rather because television and print news helped establish "busing" as the common-sense way to describe, debate, and oppose school desegregation.

The second way this book rethinks the history of "busing" is to discard the myth that so-called de facto residential and school segregation in the North was innocent. The history of "busing" for school desegregation is crucial to understanding how "de facto" segregation developed as a cultural and political construct.[21] While civil rights advocates initially promoted this distinction between "southern-style" and "northern-style" segregation to build a political consensus against Jim Crow laws in the South, the de jure–de facto dichotomy ultimately made it possible for public officials, judges, and citizens in both North and South to deny legal responsibility for the visible realities of racial segregation. As black writer James Baldwin observed in 1965, "De facto segregation means Negroes are segregated, but nobody did it."[22] Over the past two decades scholars have revealed the vast web of governmental policies that produced and maintained racially segregated neighborhoods and schools in the North, as well as highlighting the civil rights activists who fought against these structures of racial discrimination.[23] These studies provide overwhelming evidence that, in every region of the country, neighborhood and school segregation flowed from intentional public policies, not from innocent private actions or free-market forces. Among the most important aspects of this body of scholarship is that it shows the distinction between de jure segregation and de facto segregation to be false.[24]

In hearing school desegregation cases in the 1960s and 1970s, several federal and state court judges also cast a critical light on the de jure–de facto framework. In *Taylor v. New Rochelle* (1961), Judge Irving Kaufman found the New Rochelle school board's "neighborhood school" plan had intentionally gerrymandered the attendance zone to maintain a black elementary school. "It is of no moment whether the segregation is labeled by the defendant as 'de jure' or 'de facto,' as long as the Board, by its conduct, is responsible for its maintenance," Kaufman ruled. "Constitutional rights are determined by realities, not by labels or semantics."[25] In Los Angeles in 1970, Judge Alfred Gitelson found that the Los Angeles Unified School District "Board has, since at least May of 1963, by and through its actual affirmative policies, customs, usages and practices, doings and omissions, segregated, de jure, its students." Gitelson continued, "The court finds that [the] Board's separate but allegedly equal schools were not equal in fact, either as to plant or facilities or teachers and curriculum, and that Board has not made available to all its students equal educational opportunity."[26] In *Davis v. School District of City of Pontiac* (1970), Judge Damon Keith ruled, "Where a Board of Education has contributed and played a major role in the development and growth of a segregated situation, the Board is guilty of de jure segregation. The fact that such came slowly and surreptitiously rather than by legislative pronouncement makes the situation no less evil."[27] Similarly, Judge W. Arthur Garrity's decision in *Morgan v. Hennigan* (1974) made it clear that the Boston School Committee and superintendent "took many actions in their official capacities with the purpose and intent to segregate the Boston public schools and that such actions caused current conditions of segregation in the Boston public schools."[28]

The "crisis" in Boston and in other cities that faced court-ordered school desegregation was about unconstitutional racial discrimination in the public schools, not about "busing." Judges ordered "busing" as a remedy in northern school districts such as Boston, Denver, Detroit, Kansas City, Las Vegas, Los Angeles, and Pontiac that were found guilty of intentional de jure segregation in violation of *Brown v. Board* and the Fourteenth Amendment.[29] U.S. Department of Health, Education, and Welfare chief Leon Panetta, whose advocacy of investigating school segregation in the North got him fired from the Nixon administration, said in late 1969, "It has become clear to me that the old bugaboo of keeping federal hands off northern school systems because they are only de facto segregated, instead of de jure segregated as the result of some official act, is a fraud. . . . There are few if any pure de facto situations. Lift the rock of de facto and something ugly and discriminatory crawls out from under it."[30]

The challenge for civil rights lawyers and activists was that it was extraordinarily difficult to lift all of the rocks of "de facto" to expose the illegal discrimination underneath. Sixty years after the *Brown* decision, June Shagaloff, who led NAACP efforts to challenge school segregation outside the South, said, "I've never really come to terms with whether we made a mistake or not. The reason we called them de facto segregated schools was we didn't have the manpower to examine the histories of so many individual school systems to prove intent. So we took the position that segregated schools were harmful educationally for all children psychologically, in every way, and that it was the responsibility of school officials, local and state, to reorganize public school systems to eliminate the existence of segregation in fact."[31] School desegregation lawsuits took months of research and cost hundreds of thousands of dollars. Obtaining evidence of discriminatory actions required first extracting information from often obstructionist school officials and then sifting through decades of meeting minutes, memos, and school board policies. Each lawsuit, moreover, risked alienating donors and politicians who supported school desegregation in Mississippi, Georgia, and Alabama, but not in New York, Illinois, or California. Civil rights lawyers and activists had to overcome enormous barriers to get a northern school district into the courtroom, much less persuade a judge to find a school district guilty of unconstitutional discrimination.

If the framework of "de facto" segregation placed a difficult evidentiary burden on civil rights advocates, it provided "antibusing" politicians and parents with material and psychic benefits. By upholding the myth of "de facto" segregation, residents of white neighborhoods could profit from public policies that funneled resources to their communities and pass on appreciating assets to future generations, while also claiming to be free from the ugly stain of racism. The battles over "busing" showed that this faith in white racial innocence with regard to residential and school segregation was largely immune to evidence. When courts found school boards in Boston, Detroit, Los Angeles, and other cities guilty of intentional and unconstitutional racial discrimination, politicians and parents insisted that their cities could not possibly be segregated and decried the court-ordered desegregation remedies, such as "busing," as unjust and inconvenient infringements on the rights of white families. The myth of "de facto" segregation has persisted for decades because for many people no amount of evidence to the contrary could upset the bedrock belief that unlawful segregation and racism were exclusively a southern phenomenon.

The national news media bears much of the responsibility for perpetuating the myth of "de facto" segregation and the idea that racism was unique to the South. In *An American Dilemma* (1944), Swedish social scientist Gunner Myrdal's landmark study of race in the United States, Myrdal noted, "The Northerner does not have his social conscience and all his political thinking permeated with the Negro problem as the Southerner does. Rather, he succeeds in forgetting about it most of the time. The Northern newspapers help him by minimizing all Negro news, except crime news. The Northerners want to hear as little as possible about the Negroes. . . . The result is an astonishing ignorance about the Negro on the part of the white public in the North."[32] In the two decades after Myrdal's work, black people continued to migrate to northern cities, and television became the nation's dominant news source, but little changed in terms of media attention to racism outside the South. In 1968, the National Advisory Commission on Civil Disorders, chaired by Illinois governor Otto Kerner, highlighted the media's lack of attention to everyday black lives in cities like Chicago, Newark, or Watts. "The news media have failed to analyze and report adequately on racial problems in the United States and, as a related matter, to meet the Negro's legitimate expectations in journalism," the Kerner Commission argued. "By and large, news organizations have failed to communicate to both their black and white audiences a sense of the problems America faces and the sources of potential solutions. The media report and write from the standpoint of a white man's world. The ills of the ghetto, the difficulties of life there, the Negro's burning sense of grievance, are seldom conveyed. Slights and indignities are part of the Negro's daily life, and many of them come from what he now calls 'the white press'—a press that repeatedly, if unconsciously, reflects the biases, the paternalism, the indifference of white America."[33] The Kerner Commission report went on to describe the "enforced confinement [of black people] in segregated housing and schools" as one of "the most bitter fruits of white racial attitudes."[34] Writing in 1970, Federal Communications Commission (FCC) commissioner Nicholas Johnson noted that while media coverage of the civil rights struggle in the South "seared the nation's conscience" and "opened up the 'closed society' in the Deep South . . . now the racial crisis has moved North and West, and the editors and producers may have lost some of their enthusiasm for pointing out the threadbare parts of the nation's social fabric." Referring to the Kerner Commission's report on civil disorders, Johnson continued, "In my judgment, the extent of surprise in each community measured precisely the failure of its news media."[35] The news media played a crucial role in establishing white racial attitudes regarding segregated schools and neighborhoods as both unremarkable and incontestable. The maintenance of northern school segregation was premised on a willful ignorance of clear and consistent policies of racial discrimination, which the news media promoted daily and nightly.[36]

The third and final way this book rethinks the history of "busing" is by questioning the cherished idea that the news media supported the goals of civil rights advocates. The news media's support for the southern civil rights movement is one of the iconic stories we tell about race in America, but it is a limited and limiting story. This story is powerful and widely accepted because both civil rights leaders and television journalists who covered civil rights in the South declared the medium's importance to the movement.

"Had it not been for TV I do not think the civil rights movement could have succeeded as quickly," said Julian Bond, who cofounded the Student Nonviolent Coordinating Committee (SNCC) and served as that civil rights organization's communications director. "I think it would have won out in the end but television brought it home just so quickly."[37] Robert Schakne, who covered the Little Rock school integration crisis for CBS News, said, "We had no idea that our form of journalism would essentially change the way the country thought."[38] William Monroe, NBC's Washington bureau chief, described television as "the chosen instrument of the revolution," and argued that "network-television newscasts brought in the message day after day that integration was overtaking other Southern cities and that it could not be prevented."[39] "The Negro revolution of the 1960's could not have occurred without the television coverage that brought it to almost every home in the land," said *CBS Reports* producer William Peters. "Those who have tried with the written word to make the facts of Mississippi come alive to the people of Minnesota, as I have, probably applaud with me the success of television in accomplishing this difficult feat."[40]

One of the reasons the southern civil rights movement resonated so powerfully through television and photojournalism was that it presented a stark distinction between good and evil. Virtuous black demonstrators withstood verbal harassment and physical violence from nasty white segregationists.[41] Images of confrontations in Little Rock, Birmingham, and Selma framed racism in stark detail. Wallace Westfeldt, a Nashville newspaper reporter who went on to work as an executive producer of NBC's *Huntley-Brinkley Report,* said, "Even without any commentary, a shot of a big white man spitting and cursing at black children did more to open up the national intellect than my [newspaper] stories ever could."[42] Both the civil rights movement and the news media were invested in exposing these acts of excessive violence to audiences outside the South. In the midst of the voting rights marches in Selma, Alabama, in 1965, Martin Luther King told marchers and the news media, "We are here to say to the white men that we no longer will let them use clubs on us in the dark corners. We're going to make them do it in the glaring light of television."[43] This strategy successfully exposed physical acts of violence, but it worked less well to reveal other forms of racism and discrimination. While police and private citizens certainly perpetrated acts of physical violence against black people in the North as well, it was far more difficult to expose to the "glaring light of television" the policies and actions that produced and maintained segregated neighborhoods and schools. These structural dimensions of racial segregation often worked subtly and developed over decades, which made them difficult to capture and make visible in a photograph or television broadcast.

If television was successful in framing the southern civil rights struggle as a moral imperative, the news media did not present civil rights activity in the North with the same moral clarity. Analysis of the coverage of "busing" for school desegregation reveals how mainstream media personnel based mostly in the North covered civil rights in the North differently than it did in the South. *New York Times* managing editor Turner Catledge recognized that his and other northern papers brought a different scrutiny to civil rights stories and the "race beat" in the South. "We've had open season on the South here now for some time," Catledge remarked to a conference of editors and publishers in 1963, "and it seems to me that, especially when you read the editorial pages in the North, some people are too much concerned about what's going on somewhere else and too little concerned about what's going on right at their own door."[44] While Catledge recognized that the *Times* covered civil rights stories "at their own door" timidly, the paper's editorial positions on school desegregation in New York did little to change this dynamic. The *New York Times,* like the *Montgomery Advertiser* and many other southern newspapers, framed civil rights activists' demands for school desegregation as equivalent to white protestors' demands to maintain school segregation.[45] Some city dailies, like the *Chicago Tribune,* were openly hostile to the civil rights movement and calls for school desegregation in their cities. National television news broadcasts framed protest marches for and against school desegregation using similar camera angles, shot sequencing, and interview questions. Whereas news media helped underscore the urgency of the black civil rights movement in the South in the 1950s and 1960s, by the mid-1960s and 1970s white "antibusing" protestors received the vast bulk of media attention. Television and print news helped establish "busing" as the common-sense way of discussing school desegregation. By overemphasizing white parents' and politicians' resistance to "busing," news media contributed to the perspective that desegregation was moving too fast and was unrealistic.

For their part, "antibusing" activists were careful students of the civil rights movement and the movement's media strategies. White "antibusing" demonstrators purposefully modeled their protests on civil rights marches, and television news' production techniques heightened these similarities, shaping the protests into segments that looked very similar. "Martin Luther King walked all over and he got a lot of things done," Irene McCabe announced at an "antibusing" rally in Pontiac in 1971. "This is our civil rights movement."[46] At a March 1964 rally against school desegregation and "busing," a white mother freely acknowledged to an NBC television reporter that civil rights activists inspired the parents' choice of strategies. "We feel like we can prove as much as our opponents [using] the same tactics," she said. "We have as much right as they do. These are our civil rights and we're taking advantage of them."[47] Framed in this way, the white defense of school segregation in the North looked much more reasonable and justified than similar efforts in the South. "TV didn't determine the outcome, but it did aid and abet those motivated to destroy integration in any form," Los Angeles Superior Court judge Paul Egly said in 1981. "That [busing resistance] was the story TV could understand. TV didn't understand the story that was going on in court. They didn't understand the minority side. There was no story for them there because there were no riots, no pickets, nothing whatsoever but poor education and segregation."[48] As historian Nathan Irvin Huggins noted in 1978, television cameras "broadcast the sentiments of the white, Pontiac, Michigan, housewife [Irene McCabe] protesting 'forced busing' as earnestly as they had the achievement of Mrs. Rosa Parks in the Montgomery bus boycott."[49] It is impossible to understand the longevity and intensity of "busing" as a political issue without understanding how news media framed the subject and how parents and politicians made savvy use of television and print news to oppose "busing."

Television reporting on controversial political issues like civil rights and the war in Vietnam created a lively debate among politicians, policymakers, and citizens regarding what counted as balanced news coverage. In *Red Lion Broadcasting Co. v. Federal Communications Commission* (1969), the U.S. Supreme Court affirmed the constitutionality of the Fairness Doctrine, "the requirement that discussion of public issues be presented on broadcast stations, and that each side of those issues must be given fair coverage."[50] Four years later, in *CBS v. Democratic National Committee,* the Supreme Court found that "since it is physically impossible to provide time for all viewpoints ... the broadcaster, therefore, is allowed significant journalistic discretion in deciding how best to fulfill the Fairness Doctrine obligations."[51] Beyond these court cases, a broad public debate swirled around the balance and fairness of television news, with dozens of books and articles arguing that television news was politically biased in favor of either liberals or conservatives.[52] (The Vanderbilt Television News Archive, one of the key archives for my research, was founded in 1968 in part to monitor whether network news broadcasts were presenting one-sided coverage of Vietnam.)[53] The Nixon administration figured prominently in these debates over political bias, as the president, Vice President Spiro Agnew, and advisers like Pat Buchanan sparred constantly with the news media and looked for ways to get the president's message directly to the American people without being filtered and criticized by broadcasters.[54]

These debates over balanced coverage often overlooked the fact that the stories television networks defined as newsworthy had little to do with political beliefs of anchors like Walter Cronkite or John Chancellor and much more to do with producers and assignment editors who determined where to assign correspondents and camera crews. Once a story like "busing" was identified as newsworthy, it continued to receive regular coverage. Producing the news required anticipating the news, and at each network the majority of stories were assigned in advance in order to have the stories shot, transmitted to New York, edited, and narrated in time for the nightly broadcast. "We have the whole country to cover, and we can't just set up cameras and wait for news to happen somewhere," an NBC producer told journalist Edward Jay Epstein. "We have to plan it out in advance."[55] To cover national news in the late 1960s, NBC national news had regular camera crews only in New York, Chicago, Los Angeles, Washington, DC, and Cleveland, as well as camera operators who could form ad hoc crews in Boston, Houston, and Dallas (CBS and ABC had similar operations).[56] Covering the "antibusing" protests in Pontiac, for example, meant dispatching the Chicago- or Cleveland-based camera crew and then transmitting the news report electronically over an AT&T closed-circuit "long line" connection from an affiliate station in Detroit to broadcasting facilities in New York. These "long line" connections were expensive. In his 1973 study of the television news industry, Epstein described an NBC executive rejecting a story about a new Boeing passenger plane because "I just didn't think it was worth four thousand dollars [for a long line] to go to Seattle."[57] These economic and technological factors meant television producers favored stories that were sure to deliver compelling visuals, connect to establish story lines, and resonate with national audiences. "Antibusing" protests fit all three of these criteria of newsworthiness. Once television producers had identified "antibusing" protests in cities like Boston, Louisville, and Pontiac as newsworthy, these cities were more likely to be covered (and overcovered) in future news plans.

When viewing the relationship between television news and civil rights over a longer time frame, it is clear that production decisions regarding what makes for compelling visual news and the cost of securing this footage outweighed any moral or political commitments television personnel brought to their work. For a time, these production dynamics favored civil rights stories that developed at a safe distance from the North. During the late 1950s and early 1960s, television producers deemed the southern civil rights movement to be worthy of allocating camera crews and correspondents, and the images produced in Little Rock, Birmingham, and Selma repaid the high financial cost of gathering the news and transmitting the footage back to New York. Just a few years later, however, "antibusing" protests replaced the civil rights movement in the calculus of producing television news. Whatever praise television news personnel deserve for advancing civil rights in the South must be tempered by the fact that television news advanced the resistance to "busing" for school desegregation as a national story with the same vigor.

Television news broadcasts were not designed to produce deeply researched reports, and they were particularly ill equipped to present complex stories like school desegregation, which involved law, education, politics, social science, and history. Despite the enormous audience for national television news and the political and cultural influence of these broadcasts, the networks devoted very little money to research departments. "At NBC News . . . there have been no adequate facilities for backgrounding a story," former anchorman Robert MacNeil noted in 1967. "An index or morgue or clipping service which collects and files information from day to day for instant retrieval is the most elemental part of a news organization. Broadcasters, however, have to rely on their memories, on what recent newspapers they can find, or on what makeshift files they are able to patch together in the midst of very busy lives." A research director noted similar limitations at CBS. "The Evening News, our network flagship, has only one researcher to handle queries on everything from Viet Nam to multiple birth. And for the hectic, final half-hour before air, our main CBS News reference library is closed." Without extensive research departments, network news programs in this era relied on Associated Press (AP) and United Press International (UPI) wire services for the majority of their story assignments and background.[58] In this vein, TV news producer Av Westin described the network evening news as "an illustrated headline service . . . not a broadcast of record."[59] The wire services, in turn, produced more stories on the subjects that television broadcasts elevated as newsworthy. This dynamic meant that once "busing" became identified as newsworthy, television news and wire service editors continued to look for stories that connected with this news hook.

The United States Commission on Civil Rights complained in 1972 that "somehow the busing-for-desegregation debate has become clouded in its own language and expressions, in which the word 'busing' almost always follows such labels as 'massive' and 'forced.' . . . [S]omehow a pattern of fears and myths has become fixed in the minds of the public, making it hard to sort out the facts and determine what is true and what is false."[60] The Commission on Civil Rights did not have the public relations budget or expertise to challenge the "fears and myths" prompted in the battle over "busing." "Antibusing" parents and politicians were able to turn the news media to their advantage because they organized media-ready protests, and speeches simplified the complex issue of school desegregation into an easily legible news hook, "busing."

Why Busing Failed begins in the hub of national media, New York, where the battle over "busing" first emerged in the late 1950s and early 1960s. Like in Montgomery and Jackson, many New York politicians and citizens did not want the *Brown* decision to come to their schools. Black parents and civil rights advocates, including Ella Baker, Kenneth Clark, and Reverend Milton Galamison, thought otherwise and pressed for desegregation plans in the city. Indeed, the largest civil rights demonstration of the era occurred in New York in February 1964, when more than 460,000 students and teachers stayed out of school to protest the lack of a comprehensive plan for desegregation. White resistance grew as well, with white parents and politicians first objecting to rumored plans to bus students between Harlem and Staten Island and then organizing rallies to oppose plans to transfer students between predominantly black and Puerto Rican schools and white schools. These white protests attracted national attention from the news media and from the United States congressmen who were debating the Civil Rights Act in the spring of 1964. The Civil Rights Act included an "antibusing" provision that sought to address the demands of white parents and politicians in New York and other northern cities.

The second chapter examines how limited resources and weak political will for federal enforcement of school desegregation guidelines enabled school segregation to flourish in cities like Chicago. Title VI of the Civil Rights Act gave the U.S. Department of Health, Education, and Welfare (HEW) authority to withhold funds if school districts failed to comply with rules against school segregation. In 1965, HEW briefly withheld $30 million in federal funds from Chicago, finding the city's schools to be in "probable noncompliance" with Title VI's antidiscrimination provision. Facing pressure from Mayor Richard J. Daley, Senator Everett Dirksen, Illinois congressmen, and President Lyndon Johnson, HEW's case in Chicago quickly unraveled, despite overwhelming evidence that Chicago school officials were not innocent bystanders to the creation and maintenance of racially differentiated schools. HEW's surrender in Chicago encouraged school officials and politicians in other cities to maintain positions of resistance and noncompliance with regard to "busing" and school desegregation.

Chapter 3 examines the fights over "busing" and school desegregation in 1960s Boston. Black civil rights activists like Ruth Batson and Ellen Jackson organized against educational inequality in Boston over a decade before the city's "busing crisis" in the mid-1970s. Boston's schools were resolutely segregated, with vast differentials in funding, school resources, and teacher quality. Boston's schools grew more segregated in the decades after *Brown,* as the district bused white children to white schools. Like their counterparts in New York and Chicago, civil rights activists, parents, and students in Boston were organized, creative, and persistent in their protests. In their efforts to desegregate Boston's schools, the black community encountered white school officials and politicians like Louise Day Hicks who rose to power on the promise that they would never let this happen. "Busing" helped Hicks emerge as a national icon of white resistance to civil rights, and by opposing school desegregation throughout the 1960s, Hicks and her fellow Boston School Committee members postponed dealing with the structural problems that emerged in the mid-1970s as Boston's "busing crisis."

The fourth chapter highlights the bipartisan and interregional political opposition to "busing." From Arizona senator and Republican presidential candidate Barry Goldwater, U.S. Attorney General Robert Kennedy, and Vice President Hubert Humphrey in the 1960s to Mississippi segregationist Senator John Stennis, Oregon Democratic congresswoman Edith Green, and New York Republican congressman Norman Lent in the 1970s, a chorus of politicians opposed "busing." At the state level, several governors voiced opposition to "busing," including most notably Florida governor Claude Kirk, who protested court-ordered "busing" by suspending a local school board in Manatee County (Bradenton, Florida) and appointing himself school superintendent. For politicians like Kirk who aspired to the national stage, "busing" offered a recognizable issue on which to take a stand. Elected officials' widespread opposition to "busing" sowed confusion and led many Americans to believe that school desegregation was moving much faster than it actually was. Reflecting and feeding their constituents' fears of school desegregation, politicians helped make "busing" into a recognizable issue that was easily vilified.

Chapter 5 examines how President Richard Nixon leveraged the presidency's unique political power and media platform to limit "busing" for school desegregation. Through television addresses, policy statements, and press releases, the Nixon administration shaped the debate over "busing" and normalized resistance to federal courts' school desegregation orders. In addition to the Nixon administration's skillful use of media to communicate opposition to "busing," the president reined in the lawyers and officials working in the Justice Department and HEW who were on the frontline of enforcing (or not enforcing) school desegregation policies. Nixon also worked to bend the judiciary to his views on school desegregation and "busing," appointing a record number of federal judges and four Supreme Court justices. Nixon's appointees were in the majority in *Milliken v. Bradley* (1974), which overturned a lower court and blocked a metropolitan desegregation plan that would have involved Detroit and its suburbs. "I fear," Supreme Court justice Thurgood Marshall argued in his dissenting opinion in *Milliken,* that "[today's holding] is more a reflection of a perceived public mood that we have gone far enough in enforcing the Constitution's guarantee of equal justice than it is the product of neutral principle of law."[61] *Milliken* placed a nearly impossible burden of proof on those seeking school desegregation across city and suburban lines by requiring evidence of deliberate segregation across multiple school districts. *Milliken* meant that most suburbs were untouched by school desegregation, while city schools grew more segregated by race and class.

The sixth chapter analyzes the "antibusing" campaign led by Pontiac mother Irene McCabe. While thousands of parents across the nation raised their voices against "busing," none received the same level of national television attention as McCabe. Though McCabe did not have any formal media training, she proved skillful at making her National Action Group protests into television-friendly events. More than simply an example of white backlash to civil rights, McCabe learned from other protest movements, creating television-ready scenes that garnered attention and framed her cause in a favorable light. Most notably, McCabe led a group of "marching mothers" on a 620-mile march from Pontiac to Washington, DC, in support of an "antibusing" constitutional amendment. McCabe cultivated a multifaceted television persona, combining political acumen, sexuality, and especially during the march to Washington, a calculated vulnerability that made local "antibusing" politics into national news.

The seventh chapter examines what "busing" meant to black communities. Rather than accepting "busing" as the logical frame for debating school desegregation, black people argued that white opposition to "busing" was simply a new way of expressing antiblack racism, that "busing" was a phony issue which obscured the causes of educational inequality, and that school buses had long been used to maintain segregated schools. School desegregation plans frequently led to negative outcomes for black students and teachers, including the closure of formerly black schools and the loss of employment for black teachers. In addition, black students in recently desegregated schools were disproportionately suspended and pushed out of school. Each of these themes illuminates reasons why black communities were often ambivalent regarding "busing." The various responses and alternatives black people offered were largely ignored by white media and politicians, who instead focused on more adamantly "antibusing" black viewpoints, such as the National Black Political Convention in Gary, Indiana, or Clay Smothers, who called himself "the most conservative black man in America" and appeared at "antibusing" rallies across the country. Rather than adapting their coverage to present the multiple and often conflicting black opinions on "busing," national media preferred black voices that did not disrupt the predetermined "busing" frame.

The eighth and final chapter returns to Boston to examine how television news defined the start of court-ordered school desegregation as a "crisis." People outside Boston came to know and care about the city's "busing crisis" because television news featured the story regularly. Footage of confrontations between protestors and law enforcement provided television producers with compelling visuals to illustrate "forced busing" but said little about the students or schools ostensibly at the center of the story. Television news' emphasis on the white ethnic neighborhoods of South Boston and Charlestown, moreover, obscured the ordinariness of the racial attitudes in these neighborhoods and focused attention away from resistance to school desegregation in middle-class areas like Hyde Park or West Roxbury. Like media coverage of "busing" over the prior two decades, television news coverage of Boston's "busing crisis" framed the story in terms of white anger and rendered black Bostonians as bit players in their own civil rights struggle.

Why Busing Failed focuses on the places and people that played the most important roles in shaping the national debate over "busing" for school desegregation. This national perspective on the history of "busing" is important because it connects an array of civil rights, educational, and political issues across local and regional lines. This national perspective, moreover, provides a framework for understanding the dozens of cities that had either court-ordered or voluntary desegregation plans.[62]

To reconsider the history of "busing" for school desegregation, *Why Busing Failed* draws on an array of sources, including congressional records, letters, memos, speeches, court decisions, desegregation plans, civil rights commission reports, magazines, oral histories, and photographs. To understand how the news media presented "busing" for national and local audiences, I have examined dozens of hours of archived television news coverage at the Vanderbilt Television News Archive, the University of Georgia's Walter J. Brown Media Archives and Peabody Award Collection, as well as the NBC and ABC archives. In addition to these televisual sources, I have collected and analyzed over ten thousand newspaper reports related to "busing" and school desegregation from the *New York Times, Boston Globe, Chicago Tribune, Detroit Free Press, Los Angeles Times, Washington Post,* and *Wall Street Journal,* as well as black newspapers, including the *Atlanta Journal Constitution, Baltimore Afro-American, Bay State Banner, Chicago Defender, Cleveland Call and Post, Los Angeles Sentinel, New York Amsterdam News, Norfolk Journal and Guide, Pittsburgh Courier,* and *Philadelphia Tribune.* This mix of sources makes it possible to trace how "busing" plans developed in different cities, how legislation and court decisions aided or limited school desegregation, and how television and print news framed "busing" for viewers and readers.

· · ·

As I have talked with people over the past six years about my research, the book that comes up most frequently is J. Anthony Lukas's *Common Ground: A Turbulent Decade in the Lives of Three American Families* (1985). Lukas's best-selling, Pulitzer Prize– and National Book Award–winning story, more than any other work, has shaped popular views of the history of "busing." Lukas's book examined Boston's "busing crisis" by tracing the experiences of three local Boston families—the working-class black Twymons, the working-class Irish McGoffs, and the middle-class Yankee Divers—from 1968 to 1978. These family stories are woven together with profiles of five white public figures—politicians Louise Day Hicks and Kevin White, Judge Arthur Garrity, *Boston Globe* editor Thomas Winship, and archbishop of Boston Humberto Cardinal Medeiros. "Busing," in Lukas's telling, was a foolhardy plan that was destined to fail. Despite their demographic differences, each of the families in his story shared a dislike of "busing," a "common ground" shared, the book suggests, by millions of other Americans. David Halberstam described *Common Ground* as "a bittersweet book on the end of an American dream."[63] In his *New York Times* review, sociologist Kai Erickson praised the book as a "huge and marvelous work. . . . Every family in the book has its genealogy, every community its history, every event its context—and Mr. Lukas seems to trace all of them back as far as his data will permit."[64] Sociologist Robert Dentler, a court-appointed expert who worked on deseg-regation plans for Boston and over a dozen other cities, was much more criti-cal of *Common Ground.* "Dramatically engaging as the story of each family may be, no evidence from them explains at all adequately the story of school desegregation," Dentler argued. "The thousands of filings in *Morgan v. Hennigan* go unexamined. . . . There is no review, and there are no quotations from the public records of the litigation except for a sentence or two from the federal court's liability opinion. . . . Lukas serves as the chronicling outsider who collects, sifts, and weaves a more complete fabric of exculpation out of the stuff of . . . local legends."[65]

Black civil rights activists in Boston greeted *Common Ground* with anger and frustration akin to Mississippi civil rights activists' criticisms of *Mississippi Burning* (1988) (a film that ignored the role of black activists while glorifying the FBI's role in the civil rights movement in Mississippi).[66] Black Bostonians disputed Lukas's favorable presentation of white resistance to school desegregation, his emphasis on black family dysfunction, and his selection of a black family with no ties to the decades-long campaign to secure educational equality for black children (he found the black family he profiled through a social worker). Describing Lukas as a "faulty historian," longtime Boston civil rights activist Ruth Batson lamented the seduction of Lukas's narrative and the difficulty of dislodging it. It's "like swimming against a strong tide," Batson wrote, "like being in a large crowd, trying to reach a destination, advancing twenty steps and being pushed back forty steps."[67] Batson and other black Boston community members organized a conference in 1994 at Northeastern University to document the history of community struggle for racial equality and educational justice. Batson researched, solicited questionnaires and primary documents from conference participants, and subsequently published a nine-hundred-page memoir/chro-nology of the black educational movement in Boston from 1638 to 1975, to ensure that black activism would be part of the historical record. Batson, like other civil rights advocates, understood that how we remember the history of "busing" for school desegregation matters.

Getting the history of "busing" right is important because it enables us to see more clearly how school segregation and educational inequality continued in the decades after *Brown*. The majority of white Americans never supported civil rights if it meant confronting or overturning the structures of racial discrimination that created and maintained segregated schools and neighborhoods. The battle over "busing" exposed this truth. The news media, lauded for its coverage of civil rights in the South, described civil rights advocates who called for school desegregation in the North "extremists" and shored up the myth that segregation in the North was innocent rather than the product of decades of local, state, and federal policies.

For over half a century, parents, school officials, politicians, and writers from across the political spectrum have described "busing" as unrealistic, unnecessary, and unfair. "Busing" is so routinely described as having failed that we have lost sight of what this equation—"busing failed"—asks us to believe about the history of civil rights in the United States. Agreeing that "busing failed" makes it possible to dismiss the educational goals which were a pillar of the civil rights movement and the constitutional promise of equality endorsed by, but never fully realized after, *Brown*. The "busing failed" narrative is comforting because it authorizes people to accept the continuing racial and socioeconomic segregation of schools in the United States as inevitable and unchangeable. *Why Busing Failed* shows that national resistance to school desegregation was immense but not inevitable. My hope is that dislodging the "busing failed" narrative and understanding the specific choices Americans made to thwart school desegregation leads to a more honest understanding of the history of civil rights.

ONE

The Origins of "Antibusing" Politics

FROM NEW YORK PROTESTS TO
THE CIVIL RIGHTS ACT

There is a pressing need for a liberalism in the North that is truly liberal, that firmly believes in integration in its own community as well as in the deep South.

—DR. MARTIN LUTHER KING JR., *speaking to Urban League of New York City, 1960*

I do not blame the two distinguished Senators from New York, for they desire to protect New York City, as well as Chicago, Detroit, and similar areas.... In my opinion the two Senators from New York are, at heart, pretty good segregationists; but the conditions in their State are different from the conditions in ours.

—MISSISSIPPI SENATOR JAMES O. EASTLAND, *1964*

ON A SNOWY MARCH DAY in 1964, over ten thousand white parents walked from the Board of Education Building in Brooklyn to city hall in Manhattan to protest against school desegregation in New York City. Carrying signs reading, "We oppose voluntary transfers," "Keep our children in neighborhood schools," "I will not put my children on a bus," and "We will not be bused," the marchers called their coalition of local organizations "Parents and Taxpayers." They hoped to persuade the school board to abandon a school pairing plan that called for students to be transferred between predominantly black and Puerto Rican schools and white schools. "Most of the demonstrators were taking their case into the streets for the first time," the *New York Times* reported, noting that more than 70 percent of the demonstrators were women.[1] "For every mother who's here, there's another one sitting at home with both her children, wishing she could be here," said Joan Adabo, a mother from Jackson Heights, Queens.[2] While the protestors sought to influence policy at the city level, television news captured the scope

FIGURE 1. "Fifteen thousand white mothers" march across Brooklyn Bridge to protest "busing." *NBC News,* March 12, 1964.

of the march for a national audience. On NBC and ABC, rooftop camera shots showed a long line of protestors snaking through the wet streets of the city, while another camera angle depicted marchers, ten abreast, emerging from the fog as they crossed the Brooklyn Bridge. A street-level shot panned down to capture the marchers' reflection in the curbside puddles, an artistic image emphasizing that the protestors braved inclement weather to be heard and seen. Television news, as well as newspaper coverage and photographs, gave the protestors national visibility. One mother spoke frankly to an NBC reporter about why Parents and Taxpayers opted for a public protest march: "We feel like we can prove as much as our opponents to use the same tactics. We have as much right as they do. These are our civil rights and we're taking advantage of them."[3]

The white protestors were borrowing tactics from the African American and Puerto Rican protestors in New York who organized a school boycott a month earlier that kept over 460,000 students out of school to demand that the school board create a plan for desegregation. This pro-desegregation boycott was, in 1964, the largest civil rights demonstration in the history of the United States (bigger than the 1963 March on Washington), but the event is

FIGURE 2. A white mother explains to a television journalist, "These are our civil rights and we're taking advantage of them." *NBC News,* March 12, 1964.

largely absent from histories of civil rights. The *New York Times,* which insisted that there was "no official segregation in the city," criticized the boycott as "misguided."[4] Given this climate, New York's civil rights activists recognized that the white protestors, while much fewer in number, would command much more attention from politicians. Civil rights veteran Bayard Rustin, recruited by Reverend Milton Galamison to organize the pro-desegregation boycott, planned a second rally at city hall in response to the white parents' march and said, "We will be successful if we can top the anti-integration people by one person. . . . I'll be happy with 15,000 and one Negroes, Puerto Ricans, and whites."[5] Doris Innis, a member of Harlem's Congress of Racial Equality (CORE), later reflected, "When 10,000 Queens white mothers showed up to picket city hall against integration, it was obvious we had to look for other solutions."[6]

These civil rights activists understood that the white "antibusing" marchers conveyed a powerful message visually and rhetorically. By 1964, the public protest march was a tactic closely identified with African American civil rights demonstrators. This made the white protestors particularly newsworthy, because they offered television and print reporters a new angle on a familiar story line. The newness of the white protest march also helped emphasize the view that white citizens were entering the school fight for the first time, after being pushed too far by school board officials. In reality, school officials and politicians structured housing and school policies around the expectations of white citizens. What these white "antibusing" marchers were making public was their fear and frustration that this settled expectation was being disturbed.[7]

By calling themselves Parents and Taxpayers, these white protestors made an implicit claim that they occupied a higher level of citizenship than black and Puerto Rican New Yorkers, who were also parents and taxpayers. Parents and Taxpayers advanced a similar argument to the hundreds of segregationists in the South and North who, in the years after the *Brown* decision, wrote to the Supreme Court to complain that the court was violating their rights as taxpayers.[8] The news media and politicians paid special attention to Parents and Taxpayers because they were white, while also affirming the group's assertion that their resistance to "busing" for school desegregation was about their rights as parents, taxpayers, or homeowners, not about race. The simultaneous assertion and disavowal of white political power made it difficult for civil rights advocates to counter Parents and Taxpayers and similar "antibusing" groups.

Perhaps no one took more notice of the white "antibusing" march than the legislators who were debating the Civil Rights Act in the spring of 1964, where several United States senators mentioned the New York protest. Senator Absalom Robertson of Virginia read to his colleagues directly from the news ticker the day of the protest: "Nearly 15,000 parents opposed to planned busing of their children for public school integration descended on city hall today in the largest civil demonstration there in years."[9] Later in March, Louisiana's Russell Long said to Indiana's Birch Bayh, "I presume the Senator noticed that on a cold, snowy day in New York City 15,000 white mothers got out and protested. I have heard that half a million whites have joined in a counter protest to the mobs marching and taking over. It could happen even in Indiana."[10] South Carolina senator Strom Thurmond returned to this talking point in April: "In New York, where students were 'bused' around, such a howl went up that 15,000 people assembled in protest against the practice."[11] "Fifteen thousand white mothers," Georgia's Richard Russell reiterated in June, "walked in the snow to protest any action to correct [racial] imbalance by the assignment of children to schools outside their residential areas."[12]

FIGURE 3. The white New Yorkers who protested against "busing" drew the attention of United States congressmen and were mentioned repeatedly in the debates over the 1964 Civil Rights Act. *ABC News,* March 12, 1964.

For southern senators who opposed the Civil Rights Act, the white parents' protests against school desegregation in New York highlighted what they saw as the hypocrisy of the Civil Rights Act's different treatment of school segregation in different regions. In addition to recognizing New York's standing as a cosmopolitan city and international media hub, southern senators stressed the New York protests because U.S. congressman Emanuel Celler, who represented Brooklyn, had played an important role in drafting the legislation and shepherding it through the House of Representatives. Celler, as the southern senators repeatedly pointed out, oversaw the bill as one amendment stripped federal power to investigate and remedy "racially imbalanced" schools and another amendment drew a line between desegregation of schools in the South ("'Desegregation' means the assignment of students to public schools and within such schools without regard to their race, color, religion, or national origin") and desegregation of so-called de facto segregated schools ("'Desegregation' shall not mean the assignment of students to public schools in order to overcome racial imbalance"). Illinois senator Everett Dirksen and Montana senator Mike Mansfield successfully proposed another "antibusing" amendment to Title IV, section 407: "Nothing herein shall empower any official or court of the United States to issue any order seeking to achieve a racial balance in any school by requiring the transportation of pupils or students from one school to another or one school district to another in order to achieve such racial balance, or otherwise enlarge the existing power of the court to insure compliance with constitutional standards."[13] Regarding this amendment, Mississippi's James Eastland argued, "It appears that the draftsmen of the Dirksen-Mansfield substitute are so zealous to protect the States of New York, Illinois, Indiana, Ohio, Pennsylvania, Michigan, Missouri, and California, where de facto segregation is now such an important factor in life, that they go so far as to deny the court itself the power to enlarge its existing decisions regarding the achievement of racial imbalance."[14]

While they vehemently opposed the Civil Rights Act, these southern politicians saw clearly that the legislation's "racial imbalance" loophole would allow school segregation to exist and expand in northern cities like New York, Chicago, and Detroit. For these southern politicians, the "15,000 white mothers" were a symbol of how resistance to school desegregation in the North was accorded more political respect than similar efforts in the South. Seeing the white parent protests against "busing" as a "white backlash" to civil rights, as the news media and scholars would later describe them, obscures the fact that these protests encouraged northern congressmen to exempt northern schools from the Civil Rights Act's desegregation provisions.

This chapter examines how New York emerged as the focal point for the battle over "busing" for school desegregation in the late 1950s and early 1960s, how "busing" developed as shorthand for politicians and parents to describe and oppose school desegregation in polite terms that distinguished them from the South, and how protests in New York shaped the wording of the Civil Rights Act. These early demonstrations against school desegregation in the North offer an example of how local protests worked their way into national debates and how, in turn, the resulting national policies shaped what kinds of changes were possible at the local level. These early "busing" protests and the resulting "antibusing" provision in the Civil Rights Act limited the federal authority and political will to uproot school segregation in the North, and encouraged local, state, and national politicians to take up "busing" as a way to oppose civil rights. At the same time, early "busing" protests emboldened northern school boards to delay taking action to address school segregation. "Fifteen thousand white mothers" marched in New York a decade before Boston's "busing crisis" garnered national attention, and these early "busing" protests help explain both why Boston and other northern cities were able to postpone desegregating until ordered to do so by a federal court and why "busing" resonated so powerfully as a way to oppose school desegregation. Taking a long view of the "busing" battles makes clear the important role that anticipation and fear played in motivating opposition to "busing." White parents in New York and elsewhere organized to stop "busing" even before school boards or courts ordered that buses be used for school desegregation and despite the fact that most cities had used buses to maintain segregated schools. News media coverage of "busing" protests and plans played an important role in fostering this anticipation and fear. Desegregation plans designed for a handful of schools in two neighborhoods could become citywide stories via newspapers, or national stories via magazines or television broadcasts. Parents in Seattle, Pontiac, and Los Angeles, like the senators in Washington, DC, watched and read about the "fifteen thousand white mothers" protesting "busing" in New York, and this news contributed to existing local fears that "busing" might soon come to their cities. The white parents who took to the streets to protest school desegregation on a wet and cold day in March 1964 walked less than three miles, but their protest rippled across the country, and their opinions shaped civil rights for years to come.

NEW YORK AFTER *BROWN V. BOARD*

In 1954, New York City had the nation's largest black population. New York's black population had grown from 60,000 (under 2 percent of the total city population) to 750,000 (over 9 percent of the total city population) in the prior five decades, as migrants from southern states and immigrants from the Caribbean joined African Americans who had lived in the city for generations.[15] Significant black neighborhoods developed in Harlem, Bedford-Stuyvesant, and Brownsville, with people drawn by the vibrant cultural life in these areas but also restricted by racially discriminatory housing policies and a lack of affordable housing in other parts of the city. The majority of black students in New York attended segregated schools, but school officials maintained they were not to blame for this situation. "We did not provide

Harlem with segregation," insisted New York City school superintendent William Jansen in 1954. "We have natural segregation here—it's accidental."[16] Counter to Jansen's suggestion, in New York as in other northern cities, school zoning policies worked in concert with housing discrimination to segregate schools.[17] Black parents and their white allies had protested the New York schools in the twenty years before *Brown,* calling for equal education, an end to teachers' corporal punishment of students, and removal of textbooks with racist text and imagery.

Ella Baker and Dr. Kenneth Clark, two of the most important African American thinkers and activists in the twentieth century, played central roles in pushing for educational equality in New York. Baker, best known for her grassroots organizing in the South for the Southern Christian Leadership Conference (SCLC) and Student Nonviolent Coordinating Committee (SNCC), had lived in New York City since 1927. Baker traveled across the country in the 1940s organizing black communities as the director of branches of the National Association for the Advancement of Colored People (NAACP), and served as the president of the New York NAACP in the early 1950s. Baker grew frustrated both by the poor condition of education for black students in New York and the NAACP's reluctance to prioritize racial discrimination in New York and other northern cities. "They were always talking about the poor people down South," Baker later recalled. "And so the question was, what do you do about the poor children right here?"[18]

Kenneth Clark, famed for the doll experiments that would be cited in the *Brown* case, was also well aware of the racism and educational inequality black children faced, having founded the Northside Center for Child Development with his wife Dr. Mamie Clark to provide mental health care to Harlem's children.[19] In the summer of 1952, Baker and the Clarks organized meetings of black civic leaders and parents at the Clarks' suburban home in Hastings-on-the-Hudson to discuss educational issues in the city. The following summer the ad hoc group formally became the Committee on New York Public Schools, with Kenneth Clark serving as chairman and Baker leading the organizing effort. This committee was the foundation for the Intergroup Committee on New York's Public Schools, an interracial coalition of twenty-eight social, welfare, civic, labor, and religious organizations. Formed in April 1954, the Intergroup Committee included Clark as chairman and Baker on the steering committee.

In the months before the *Brown* decision, Clark and Baker worked to make school segregation in New York an issue that school officials and politicians could no longer ignore. In a February 1954 speech at the Urban League's Negro History Week dinner, Clark surveyed the problems of gerrymandered school zones and overcrowded and deteriorating black schools, and called on the board of education to study the conditions of the city's public schools and racially segregated schools "where they exist in fact, but not by law."[20] Clark repeated this call at the Intergroup Committee's April 1954 conference on New York City's Public Schools and gained the endorsement of over forty organizations that attended, including the United Parents Associations of New York City, the NAACP, and the Urban League.[21] New York Superintendent William Jansen strongly disagreed with Clark's statements, and he tasked his assistant superintendents with providing evidence to refute Clark's assertions.[22] The U.S. Supreme Court's May 1954 ruling in *Brown v. Board of Education,* which held that state school segregation laws were unconstitutional, buoyed Clark and the Intergroup Committee, as did the important role the landmark case assigned to Clark's research on the negative psychological impact of school segregation on black children. Facing local and national pressure, Arthur Levitt, the president of the board of education, asked the Public Education Association (PEA) to "test by impartial inquiry the validity of the appellation 'Jim Crow,'" an announcement that received front-page coverage in the *New York Times.*[23] In other words, New York's school officials praised the *Brown* decision but wondered if it applied to them.

The *New York Amsterdam News,* one of the city's leading black newspapers, continued to press the issue in the summer and fall of 1954, encouraging the PEA to conduct a "real study and not a whitewash" and reminding school officials that they were "duty bound to see to it that educational services and facilities in no community fall below those in any other community."[24] The *Amsterdam News* also ran an editorial cartoon titled "Siamese Twins" that featured two figures wearing academic caps and gowns, joined at the hip, labeled "New York City's School System" and "The South's Jimcro [sic] tradition."[25] To counter what he called the *Amsterdam News'* "calculated campaign of opposition to the Board of Education," the school board's public relations assistant advised Jansen to make a "good faith" effort to implement the PEA report's recommendations and establish a Commission on Integration, made up of board members and civic leaders. Accompanying the formation of the Commission on Integration in December 1954, the board of education passed a resolution that took note of the Supreme Court's *Brown* ruling against segregated schools, and tasked the commission with recommending "whatever further action is necessary to come closer to the ideal, viz., the racially integrated school."[26] While this amounted to little more than a promise for additional study, Clark praised the move as a necessary starting point.

Thanks to regular newspaper coverage, the debate over school segregation in the months before and after the *Brown* decision reached a large audience among white New Yorkers. June Shagaloff, who had worked with Clark to conduct historical and social science research for the *Brown* case and later led NAACP efforts to challenge school segregation outside the South, recalled that "the word 'desegregation' was a new word" for white citizens, school officials, and the white press. "These were issues that were new to them."[27] Clark also saw public awareness as the first goal of the Intergroup Committee's work: "To focus public attention on the fact of *de facto* segregated schools in New York City [was] an important goal, because we felt that the people of New York City were not aware of public school segregation as an issue which faced the city itself."[28]

For their part, school officials remained cautious about the legal ramifications of school segregation receiving wider attention. Following a press release on the PEA's school study, schools superintendent Jansen wrote to Rose Shapiro, who was directing the zoning portion of the PEA's report, to ask her to avoid using *segregation* in relation to New York schools. "The use of the word 'segregation' in releases is always unfortunate," Jensen wrote. "Segregation means a deliberate act of separating. In Kenneth Clark's allegation, he alleges that we deliberately segregate children which is false. . . . The statement of principles also implies that racial segregation exists in our schools. There is no justification for charging this to our schools."[29] Many other northern school officials, politicians, and parents shared Jansen's distaste for the word *segregation,* preferring words like *separation* and *racial imbalance.* These word choices emphasized that northern-style school segregation was innocent, natural, and lawful, while perpetuating the myth that racism structured spaces and opportunities in the South but not the North.

The PEA report, released in October 1955, found that 71 percent of elementary schools enrolled either 90 percent or more black and Puerto Rican students or over 90 percent white students. While describing this as "a state of affairs which we should all deplore," the report also insisted that this issue "cannot be placed at the doorstep of the Board of Education" and drew a clear distinction between "separation" and "segregation": "Many conditions conspire to promote such a separation of children in schools but in a strictly legal sense of the word there is no such thing as segregation in the school system of New York City."[30] While the report did not make a formal recommendation regarding integration, it recommended that information on school district lines be made publicly accessible and that "whenever a superintendent can further integration by drawing district lines he should so do."[31]

Despite these modest recommendations, the report became a subject of controversy among white parents and teachers, and it was here that the term *busing* first appeared in news reports, public hearings, and rumors as a way to describe and discourage school desegregation. The *Wall Street Journal* was the first major newspaper to sound alarms over "busing" by overstating the scale of the school board's zoning plan. After describing two hundred black children who were bused to PS 93 in the Bronx, journalist Peter Bart warned, "This is only the beginning. A 'master plan' to speed up the integration process for New York's 925,000 public school pupils has been drawn up by the subcommittee on zoning of the Board's Commission on Integration. If approved, the plan will take effect next September. It proposes extensive use of city-financed buses to create racially balanced schools and suggests that racial integration should be the sole objective of school zoning." Describing what he called an "enforced mass migration of school children," Bart alerted readers that white children were already being "bused": "Hundreds of New York students are already criss-crossing the city by bus and subway to schools far from home. . . . Not only are children from Negro sections of Harlem traveling to hitherto all-white schools; in some instances, white pupils are crossing regular school zones to enter all-Negro schools."[32] The Associated Press also picked up the story in spring 1957, noting that "five words: 'Selective use of bus transportation'" had sparked "fiery protests" in New York. While the AP's report was less alarmist than the *Wall Street Journal,* the AP story made clear the national implications of the New York case: "The nation's biggest city has gone beyond legal requirements that all races be admitted to schools on an equal basis, and is taking additional direct action to foster interracial student bodies. The move could set a trend."[33] In addition to these news reports, white residents in East Queens and other neighborhoods received reprints, sent anonymously, of pamphlets such as "The Ugly Truth about the NAACP" and "The Red Hand in New York Schools," which attacked the NAACP and school integration as communist.[34] These publications stoked existing fears in the white community and fueled rumors that the school board was calling for extensive cross-city "busing" for school desegregation.

In their letters to the board of education, many parents were unambiguous in listing the reasons they feared and opposed school desegregation. One father asked, "Do you gentleman honestly believe that you can then ship our children back to some slum school . . . to spend their lunch hours in streets that are civic cesspools . . . without a fight on your hands?"[35] An "Irate Parent" framed opposition in the language of homeowners' rights: "Do you think that I and so many others like me moved to this neighborhood so that our [children] would be uprooted and have to travel to a place at an uncomfortable distance!"[36] The racism in other letters was explicit. "The Negro is emerging from ignorance, savagery, disease and total lack of any culture," one letter stated. "Is it necessary to foist the Negro on the White Americans for fair play?"[37] Another letter simply said, "We don't want our children integrated with Blacks."[38] These letters offer a snapshot of the feelings that underscored opposition to school desegregation and suggest how, in the privacy of homes and neighborhood spaces, such sentiments propelled rumors that "busing" was imminent.

Well aware of the growing public sentiment on desegregation, Superintendent Jensen and his colleagues held public meetings in white neighborhoods and issued statements to newspapers in an attempt to quell these widespread "busing" rumors. "We have no intention whatsoever of long-distance bussing or bussing of children simply because of their color," Jansen told the *New York Times* in response to a report on the more than two thousand letters the board of education had received criticizing the integration plan.[39] "These rumors are completely false," Jansen later said to a gathering of seven hundred parents, teachers, and principals in Queens. "No such action is planned."[40] True to his word, Jansen's report on zoning, issued in July 1957, reflected the concerns of parents who had rallied against the potential of "busing." The report identified "the neighborhood school concept" as the heart of the school's zoning policy and stated, "Pupils should not be transported by bus from one school to another solely for the purpose of integration." Jensen also reasserted that the issue of school segregation was largely beyond the control of the school board: "The homogenous character of some school neighborhoods is an effect of segregated residential patterns, a condition which the schools cannot deal with directly."[41] While Jansen's report may have placated the desires of white parents and teachers, it drew the ire of Commission on Integration members like Ella Baker who worked on the preliminary zoning report. "There is a unanimous revolt of the Integration Commission against Dr. Jansen's position," Kenneth Clark told the *New*

York Times. "We feel that the Superintendent is deliberately confusing, delaying, distorting, and sidetracking the reports of our commission. He is no more likely to implement our reports than he was two years ago.... The people of the city will not tolerate this sabotage."[42]

Clark was frustrated not only that Jansen had delayed and watered down the zoning report but that "busing" came to dominate the public discussion over school desegregation in New York. Clark argued that the Commission on Integration's zoning report

> became the basis for a tremendous amount of local and national distortion. Before we knew it, it was rumored that this subcommittee was recommending that children from all white neighborhoods should be taken by bus to schools in the heart of Negro ghettoes. It was even stated children would be brought from Staten Island to attend schools in Harlem. Those of us who had worked for two years with the Commission on Integration, and who were in constant touch with the activities of each subcommittee, were first shocked and then alarmed at what we were reading in some areas of the press. It was not long before we became aware of the fact that these distortions and rumors were not accidental. They seemed to have been planted and they received wide circulation throughout the city and the nation.... Systematic study of the report on zoning revealed that at no place in the report is there a suggestion that young children be "bussed" any considerable distance in order to facilitate integration.... I should like to add one other fact not found in this report: namely, there were until last year instances in which buses were used by the Board of Education to transport white children away from a near Negro school to a more distant non-Negro school. It is fascinating, in the observation of this whole process, to note that there were no national press alarms about this fact.[43]

Writing in 1958, Clark identified how making "busing" the frame for the debate could derail school desegregation. In addition to eliding the earlier use of buses to transport students to maintain segregated schools, "busing" made school desegregation less about the constitutional rights of black children and more about the desires and fears of white parents. Fears of "busing" in New York outpaced the numerical reality of students transferred for school desegregation, a pattern that would be repeated nationally. Focusing on "busing" also gave equal weight to black protests against segregated schools and white protests to maintain these segregated conditions.

Superintendent Jansen, for example, described integration and "busing" as issues that had "stirred extremists on both sides," some who wanted to "build Rome in a day" and others who "resist every step."[44] Jansen's framing of the "busing" issue borrowed from President Dwight Eisenhower, who answered a question regarding violence against school integration in Clinton (Tennessee), Mansfield (Texas), and Sturgis (Kentucky) by comparing "extremists" who "are so filled with prejudice that they even resort to violence" with those "on the other side . . . who want to have the whole matter settled today." [45] (President Richard Nixon expressed a similar sentiment in 1969, arguing for a "middle course" on school desegregation between "two extreme groups . . . those who want instant integration and those who want segregation forever.")[46] Like Eisenhower before him and Nixon after him, Jansen's use of "extremists on both sides" allowed him to present official inaction as a fair middle ground rather than as the maintenance of an educational status quo that benefited white students and harmed black students. Instead of seeing school desegregation as an issue that necessarily involved changing structures of racial discrimination, "busing" enabled parents, school officials, politicians, and the media to frame the story around the preferences and demands of white parents.

CIVIL RIGHTS PRESSURE

As black parents and civil rights advocates escalated their demands for quality education and achieved an important legal victory, white parents organized simultaneously to restrict desegregation measures. White protests and the threat of such protests influenced school policy preemptively, throttling the school board's already slow movement on school desegregation. In the mid- and late 1950s, several parent and community groups organized to address the school conditions faced by black students. One group was a coalition of black and Jewish parents and community members, led by educational activist Annie Stein, Brooklyn NAACP branch education committee chair Winston Craig, and Reverend Milton Galamison, minister at Bedford-Stuyvesant's Siloam Presbyterian Church. This group called for zoning changes to integrate JHS 258 in Bedford-Stuyvesant. The school opened in the fall of 1955 with an enrollment of over 98 percent black students despite the school board's promise earlier that year to end "racially homogenous" schools.[47] Two years of community rallies, petitions, and calls on the school board to zone for desegregation were not enough to overcome the board's concerns about how white parents would respond to rezoning. "It is known that the Board of Education members are deeply concerned by the issues involved in desegregating the school," the *New York Times* reported. "Several members said privately that if white children were forced to attend, violence among the parents might break out."[48] The NAACP's national leadership also factored the potentially violent responses of white parents into its thinking: "If zoning is so conducted as to arouse substantial resistance in some part of the school community, and if the resistance should in fact have a violent outcome (or be susceptible to depiction as such) the consequences to the overall desegregation program, North as well as South, could be incalculably damaging."[49] Concerned about alienating supportive donors in New York and other northern cities, the NAACP's national leadership made their decision to not support the Brooklyn branch's protest of JHS 258.

In Harlem, a concurrent school boycott resulted in an important legal victory and ultimately pushed the school board to establish an "open enrollment" policy. A group of Harlem mothers organized in 1956 to protest school conditions in their neighborhood, forming the Parents Committee for Better Education and enlisting young black attorney Paul Zuber.[50] The committee expanded quickly and joined forces with local chapters of the NAACP, the Negro Teachers Association, Harlem's Parents Committee for Better Education, and other local organizations to form Parents in Actions Against Education Discrimination.[51] The coalition worked to organize parents across the city throughout 1957, culminating with a protest and rally at city hall at the start of the school year that drew several hundred people.[52] The *Amsterdam News'* headline, "Don't Forget N.Y. Has Its Own School Problem," connected the rally to the ongoing school integration crisis in Little Rock, as did a protester's sign that asked, "Is Brooklyn, New York above the Mason Dixon Line?"[53] While the protest did not result in any immediate changes in the schools, the group continued to organize parents. The following year parents of twenty-one black children in Harlem and Brooklyn kept their children home in a boycott aimed at forcing the school board to allow their children to transfer to integrated schools with better resources and more experienced teachers.[54] The *Amsterdam News* dubbed the Harlem mothers the "Little Rock Nine of Harlem," and the six-month boycott was a clear indication of the resolve of black activists to fight school segregation in the North.[55] The school board took the parents to Children's Court. Judge Nathanial Kaplan found four of the parents guilty of violating the compulsory attendance law, while two other mothers appeared before Judge Justine Wise Polier, who dismissed the charges.

Judge Polier's ruling in the *Skipwith* case validated many of the black parents' critiques of the school board. Judge Polier found that half the teachers at majority–black and Puerto Rican schools were unlicensed, compared to only 30 percent at majority-white schools. "So long as non-white . . . schools have a substantially smaller proportion of regularly licensed teachers than white . . . schools, discrimination and inferior education, apart from that inherent in residential patterns, will continue," Polier wrote. "The Constitution requires equality, not mere palliatives. Yes the fact remains that more than eight years after the Supreme Court ruling in *Sweatt v. Painter* and more than four years after its ruling in *Brown v. Board of Education,* the Board of Education of the City of New York has done substantially nothing to rectify a situation it should never have allowed to develop, for which it is legally responsible, and with which it has had ample time to come to grips, even in the last four years." As a result, Polier ruled the parents should not be bound by the compulsory attendance law: "The Board of Education has no moral or legal right to ask that this Court shall punish parents, or deprive them of custody of their children, for refusal to accept an unconstitutional condition which exists in the schools to which the Board has assigned their children."[56] After initially appealing Polier's decision, the board of education ultimately reached an agreement with the parents for their children to trans-fer to a different junior high school in Harlem that had a pilot project to provide enhanced guidance and counseling services and cultural programs.[57] Judge Kaplan, who had convicted the mothers who were in his court on the same charges, followed Judge Polier's lead and declined to sentence the moth-ers if they enrolled their children at the new junior high school.[58] It took six months, but the parents successfully forced the school board to transfer their children to better schools.

While *Skipwith* did not set state or federal legal precedents, parents and civil rights activists viewed the decision optimistically in their fight against school segregation in the North. The *Amsterdam News* praised the decision and published the ruling in serial form over four issues of the newspaper.[59] "The Polier decision," Kenneth Clark said, "was the initial and dramatic first step in a series of tests to see whether it is possible to get relief from de facto segregated schools."[60] Over the next half dozen years, groups of New York City parents used school boycotts in an effort to get their children trans-ferred to better schools.[61] Influenced by the Harlem parents he represented in the *Skipwith* case, attorney Paul Zuber encouraged parents in New Rochelle, New York, to keep their children out of school, protests that resulted in *Taylor v. Board of Education of City School District of City of New Rochelle* (1961), the first ruling against school segregation in a northern city after *Brown*. In Brooklyn, Reverend Milton Galamison, who had left the NAACP to form the Parents' Workshop for Equality in New York City Schools with Annie Stein, threatened a large-scale boycott of schools in the fall of 1960.[62] Under continual pressure from black parents and civil rights advocates, in 1960 the board of education formalized an "open enrollment" or "permissive zoning" policy, allowing students to transfer to schools with empty seats outside their districts. This "open enrollment" plan resembled the "freedom of choice" plans southern school districts utilized to evade complying with the *Brown* decision.[63] These plans, in both the North and the South, advanced a color-blind ideology that allowed communities to avoid integration without publicly supporting segregation.

White communities who had raised alarms two years earlier over "busing" and proposed zoning changes saw the expansion of open enrollment in the city as a threat to the neighborhoods and schools they sought to protect, despite the fact that white students had benefited disproportionately from the permissive zoning that functioned on an ad hoc basis. In the summer and fall of 1959, white parents in the Glendale-Ridgewood section of Queens organized to protest the transfer of four hundred black and Puerto Rican students from overcrowded elementary schools in the Bedford-Stuyvesant section of Brooklyn. Days after the board announced the transfer, the Glendale-Ridgewood parents marched outside city hall on a rainy morning, carrying signs reading "Neighborhood Schools for All," "Bussing Creates Fussing," "We Have Just Begun to Fight," and "When We Are Right We Fight." A small group of black mothers and children held a counterprotest, with signs reading, "This Is N.Y.C. not Little Rock" and "Are These the 'J.D.s' [juvenile delinquents] That Glendale fears?"[64] As the opening of school neared, "blockbusting" real estate agents used the transfer plan to stoke homeowners' fears that integrated schools would lower property values.[65] After trying unsuccessfully to sue the board of education to block the transfer, the Glendale parents organized a one-day school boycott that kept over 40 percent of white students home.[66] While these protests did not thwart the transfer plan, the students bused into Glendale faced racial harassment. Students found the message "Blacks Go Home" scrawled on the front and side of one Queens elementary school.[67] At another elementary school, the principal ordered all the black students to be searched for weapons, based on rumors circulating among white parents.[68]

The controversy over this student transfer plan highlights the predicament that faced the board of education and the way white concerns over

FIGURE 4. White parents from Queens (NY) protest the proposed transfer of four hundred black and Puerto Rican students from the Bedford-Stuyvesant section of Brooklyn. This was a one-way "busing" plan that would not have transferred any white students. Associated Press photo, June 25, 1959.

"busing" figured in how school officials addressed school desegregation. On the one hand, the school board expanded its open enrollment policy to make themselves appear compliant and as a concession to the increasingly vocal demands of black parents for better schooling options. On the other hand, white protests of even small-scale desegregation efforts led school officials to downplay school integration as a policy goal. The Bedford-Stuyvesant to Glendale-Ridgewood transfer plan, for example, involved only four hundred students across five schools, and it was a one-way transfer that did not bus any white Queens students. That even a modest one-way "busing" program could spark months of organized protests speaks to the level of resistance to school desegregation that shadowed every school board decision. School officials characterized the transfers as temporary emergency measures to deal with school overcrowding rather than part of a larger school desegregation policy.

In explaining the Glendale transfers, Charles Silver, president of the school board, said, "The purpose of these transfers is not based on the integration program but on the policy of providing full and equal educational opportunities for all children."[69] Superintendent Theobald agreed, promising that the board was "firmly committed to the concept of neighborhood schools."[70] In trying to neutralize protests from two vocal constituencies, the school board adopted modest desegregation policies to appease black parents and advocated "neighborhood schools" to satisfy white parents. These political calculations did not result in a middle point between the demands of black and white parents, but rather were doubly negative for supporters of school desegregation. The school board's desegregation policies were small scale and defended half-heartedly because they already factored in the expected white community response regarding how much desegregation was realistic or acceptable. Modest desegregation programs fell short of the expectations of black parents and civil rights activists but still managed to lead to significant white protests. These white protests in turn served to caution the school board against taking bolder steps to desegregate schools.

The school board's open enrollment policy reflected these limitations. Facing protests from parents and civil rights organizations, the board formalized its open enrollment policy in 1960 and expanded the policy over the next three years to include more schools. The program represented a compromise that failed to meet activists' citywide desegregation demands, but many viewed it as an important intermediary step toward school desegregation. The *New York Times* praised "free choice in city schools" and saw a school board adopting "a new policy that will no longer regard neighborhood boundaries as immovable barriers."[71] The *Amsterdam News* also applauded the open enrollment policy as a sign that school board members "[have] rounded the turn on the road to integration and are coming down the home stretch under full steam. We do not hesitate to say that we are happy about this."[72] The school board, however, did little to publicize or explain the program to parents, and in some cases school personnel actively discouraged parents from participating. "In almost every school I have anything to do with, Open Enrollment was not only not pushed but talked against," remarked one civil rights activist. "Parents got lectures about how hard it is to travel and go to a school far away."[73] A school official noted that "field sabotage" undercut the program: "Principals and teachers often did not inform parents about Open Enrollment options.... Some principals told parents about the plan in ambiguous or technical language that they could not understand. . . . Another technique was to discourage parents by telling them of all the difficulties involved—from bussing their children to segregated classes in receiving schools."[74] The language of "open enrollment" and "freedom of choice" was rhetorically powerful because this option purported to offer all students, regardless of race, equal access to the school system's educational resources. In practice, these "openings" or "choices" were very difficult to access. Open enrollment policies placed the burden of school desegregation on black and Puerto Rican families and led to little actual integration. In light of the school board's limited publicity, groups like Brooklyn's Parents' Workshop distributed fact sheets to parents with information on receiving schools, reading scores in the schools, and the distance between schools.[75] Despite these efforts to spread the word about open enrollment, after five years less than 5 percent of eligible students were applying for transfers annually and the 22,000 students who did transfer made up less than 3 percent of black and Puerto Rican students.[76]

Beyond offering minimal support to open enrollment, the school board also fanned rumors in white neighborhoods that the open enrollment policy would lead to citywide "busing."[77] New York schools superintendent Dr. Calvin Gross responded to a sit-in protest at the board of education headquarters by describing Reverend Milton Galamison and the two dozen other demonstrators as "extremists" who want "instant racial balances." "The things they apparently want," Gross continued, "can only be achieved by the involuntary bussing of children over a long distance."[78] "'Busing' is not the issue," the NAACP's June Shagaloff argued, "but it has been used and misused to justify the status-quo of school segregation. It has been used and misused to cloak the basic question: What plan can most effectively achieve meaningful desegregation throughout the city?"[79] In a radio interview days after he was arrested for the sit-in protest at the board of education, Galamison said, "Dr. Gross' remarks about instant integration and his remarks about busing in my opinion have been designed to . . . incite . . . the white community. It's been like waving a red flag and it's designed, I feel, to bring opposition to what we want to achieve and the thing to which he committed himself."[80] Responding to Gross's characterization of civil rights advocates as "extremists" demanding "instant integration" (which reprised remarks made seven years earlier by President Eisenhower and Gross's predecessor, William Jansen), Galamison responded drily, "It's my personal opinion that three years is a reasonable period of time in which to . . . provide a plan."[81]

By 1964, the black community's frustration with the glacial pace of change in the schools led to a boycott that was the largest civil rights demonstration in the history of the United States. The boycott was a high point for the New York Citywide Committee for Integrated Schools. For a brief period, this committee brought together relatively moderate local chapters of the NAACP with more militant local chapters of CORE, as well as the Parents' Workshop and Harlem Parent Committee.[82] Led by Brooklyn minister Milton Galamison and organized by Bayard Rustin, the civil rights stalwart who organized the 1963 March on Washington, over 460,000 students stayed out of school on February 3, 1964.[83] Groups of students, parents, and some teachers marched in front of three hundred schools and the board of education headquarters, chanting "Jim Crow must go" and singing "We Shall Overcome."[84] Rustin was particularly encouraged that in addition to hundreds of thousands of black students, the boycott had support from over one hundred thousand Puerto Rican students.[85] "I think we are on the threshold of a new political movement—and I do not mean it in the party sense—that is going to change the face of New York in housing, in jobs and in schools," Rustin remarked.[86] At a rally on the eve of the boycott, Puerto Rican community leader Irma Vidal Santaella declared, "This is the beginning of the partnership between the Puerto Ricans and our sisters and brothers."[87] Tina Lawrence, a black college student who helped organize the boycott, saw the massive protest as a challenge to New York City's white residents. "They thought it was all right when it was happening in Jackson, Miss., but now it's happening here," she said. "The people are going to wake up."[88] The boycott, however, did not draw significant support from white liberals and moderates. Organizations that supported school integration, like the United Parents Association, Public Education Association, Anti-Defamation League, Catholic Interracial Council, and American Jewish Congress, opposed the school boycott as an inappropriate tactic.[89]

The *New York Times,* which had supported modest zoning changes for school desegregation, described the boycott as a "violent, illegal approach of adult-encouraged truancy." The *Times* raised the specter of "busing" to explain why the civil rights demands were "unreasonable and unjustified." "Given the pattern of residence in New York City, the Board of Education can do just so much to lessen imbalance in the schools," the editorial argued. "To ask more is to ignore the facts and figures of school population and pupil distribution. You can bus children just so far. You can hire bus drivers when you ought to be hiring teachers. You can put children into buses for an hour and a half or more each day—as the board plans to do for some—but what do they learn in the bus?"[90] The *Times'* position sounded strikingly similar to James Donovan, president of the New York City School Board, who a month earlier said, "Everyone in the City of New York has rights . . . and there is *[sic]* simply limits of feasibility that arise. . . . You simply cannot put one million children on wheels and send them all over the city of New York."[91] Donovan wildly overstated the number of children who would have been reassigned to desegregate New York's schools. New York in 1964 was transporting annually fewer than ten thousand students, mostly black and Puerto Rican children, through open enrollment and programs to aid integration and lessen overcrowding.[92] Even a tenfold increase in this number would still have been only 10 percent of Donovan's "one million children" figure. Opposition to "busing," of course, was never really tied to empirical evidence. The *Times,* like Donovan and "antibusing" parents and politicians, argued from a gut belief that "busing" for school desegregation was unrealistic.

This *Times* editorial illustrates how the news media covered civil rights developments in the North with much less moral clarity than similar stories in the South. Speaking to a conference of editors and publishers in 1963, *New York Times* managing editor Turner Catledge recognized that his and other northern papers brought a different scrutiny to civil rights stories in the South. "We've had open season on the South here now for some time," Catledge remarked,

> and it seems to me that, especially when you read the editorial pages in the North, some people are too much concerned about what's going on somewhere else and too little concerned about what's going on right at their own door. . . . There seems to be a disposition, especially on our editorial pages, to demand that the Southerners accept some sort of an emotional change in this matter, which they're not going to do. Integration is coming to the South . . . but it's not wanted. Is it wanted any more in Minnesota or in New York? I think this is the question our readers are entitled to have us explore.[93]

While Catledge recognized that the *Times* covered civil rights stories "at their own door" timidly, the paper's editorial positions on school desegregation in New York did little to change this dynamic. The *Times* was critical of civil rights advocates in New York and reluctant to ask white readers to confront the emotional, legal, and political issues raised by school desegregation.

Hodding Carter III, managing editor of the *Delta Democrat-Times* in Greenville, Mississippi, argued that "most newspapers in America today, no matter where they are... are in a large sense representatives of the *status quo*... and geography and history make a vast difference in the attitude of the editor toward his society."[94] While Carter was discussing small-town southern newspapers, on the question of civil rights in New York, the *Times* was no less parochial. Writer Margaret Halsey criticized the *Times* and other white newspapers for failing to recognize this parochial quality. "It is within 'the power of the press' to make Negroes feel less like voices crying in the wilderness and more like people who are being listened to," Halsey argued. "It is within the power of the press to open the eyes of white people to their own insularity."[95] In their coverage of "busing," the *Times* failed on both counts.

This *Times* editorial also highlights how the school board's failure to clearly explain or defend their desegregation policies made it possible for "busing" to dominate the discussion. Reflecting on the board's poor communications, a city official recalled asking the board to make a public statement endorsing a specific desegregation plan. "You have a series of possible integration measures," he said. "You have a policy position on integration. Use these measures. Use them sensitively. Use them combined. Use them one after another. Use them however you want to, but make clear where you stand." The official recalled being rebuffed and misunderstood. "They heard us saying that we wanted them to bus large numbers of children for miles and miles, which we never said. That wasn't even relevant."[96]

While the boycott succeeded as a public demonstration of unity among blacks and Puerto Ricans, these alliances began to fray shortly after the boycott. Eager to build on the success of the boycott and to keep applying pressure on the school board, Galamison planned a second boycott for March 16. Galamison's plan failed to draw support from the national leadership of the NAACP, CORE, or the Urban League, who worried that another boycott would only alienate white moderates and hamper potential negotiations with school officials and city politicians.[97] The National Association of Puerto Rican Rights withdrew from the boycott coalition, and local Puerto Rican organizers shifted their emphasis to community control of schools, including bilingual education.[98] Bayard Rustin, whose organizing skills had proved crucial to the success of the first boycott, also did not support the second boycott because he felt that Galamison was moving in a militant direction that would result in an all-black protest and foreclose the possibility of interracial organizing for school desegregation.[99] The Brooklyn and Bronx chapters of CORE, the Parents' Workshop, and the Harlem Parents Committee supported the second boycott, as did Malcolm X, who told a local television news reporter that he had come to "see the successful exposé of the New York City school system, it proves you don't have to go to Mississippi to find a segregated school system, we have it right here in New York City."[100]

Galamison's decision to go forward with the second boycott despite limited support from former civil rights allies reflected both his frustration with the school board's slow pace of change and his belief that grassroots protests would be more likely than boardroom negotiations to force the school officials to take action. Among those influenced by the grassroots civil rights protests were Parents and Taxpayers, a coalition of white neighborhood groups who had organized protest marches and a boycott against school desegregation in 1964. Building on over eight years of white parents' complaints and demonstrations over proposed zoning plans and "busing," the Parents and Taxpayers rally on March 13 drew over ten thousand parents. The protestors called on the board of education to abandon the "Princeton Plan," a school-pairing plan that called for predominately black and Puerto Rican schools to be paired with predominately white schools and for students to be transferred between the schools. Marchers held signs reading, "Keep Our Children in Neighborhood Schools" and "I Will Not Put My Children on a Bus."

Media coverage helped frame these protests against school desegregation and "busing" as equivalent to earlier civil rights protests in the city. Television news established this equivalency in two ways. First, television producers presented pro–civil rights and anti–civil rights protest marches using similar camera angles, shot sequencing, and interview questions. The white demonstrators purposely modeled their protests on civil rights marches, and television news production techniques heightened these similarities, shaping the protests into segments that looked very similar. Second, television news featured representatives for the different movements in brief point-counterpoint segments. Segments, for example, would cut between Parents and Taxpayers leader Rosemary Gunning and boycott leader Milton Galamison answering questions regarding school desegregation. NBC likely opted for this point-counterpoint structure as a way to comply with the Federal Communication Commission's (FCC) Fairness Doctrine. The FCC emphasized the "balanced presentation of opposing viewpoints" in outlining the Fairness Doctrine in 1949.[101] The agency sent all licensees a notice in July 1963 about their obligation

FIGURES 5 AND 6. Television news featured school boycott leader Milton Galamison and Parents and Taxpayers' leader Rosemary Gunning in short, point-counterpoint interview segments. This suggested an equivalency between the demands of civil rights activists and the demands of white parents who opposed school desegregation. *NBC News,* March 6, 1964.

to comply with the Fairness Doctrine, indicating that "when the licensee permits ... the presentation of views regarding an issue of current importance, such as racial segregation, integration or discrimination ... he must offer spokesmen for all responsible groups within the community similar opportunities for expression of the viewpoints of their respective group."[102] While this point-counterpoint structure worked well to highlight areas of disagreement between Gunning and Galamison, it rendered demands to maintain school segregation as equivalent to demands to desegregate schools. Framed in this way, the white defense of school segregation in the North looked much more reasonable and justified than similar efforts in the South.

Conversely, viewing the movements as equivalent made it possible to argue that both were too extreme. After Parents and Taxpayers organized a "white boycott" in September 1964 that kept over 275,000 students out of school to protest the school board integration plans, the *New York Times* editorialized, "When this current demonstration is over, we hope there will be no more of these boycotts, whether sponsored by white or black. They succeed in nothing except to make a good many New Yorkers a little ashamed of their city."[103] Unstated in the *Times* editorial was that an end to demonstrations, "white or black," would maintain a segregated school system and only benefit the white communities who wanted the school board to stop additional efforts to desegregate schools. Whether framed as equally valid or equally extreme, media coverage benefited Parents and Taxpayers more than New York's civil rights activists.

A week after the white student boycott of schools, the *Times* ran a story headlined, "Poll Shows Whites in City Resent Civil Rights Drive," regarding a survey commissioned to study the extent of "white backlash" sentiment in the city. "While denying deep-seated prejudice against Negroes," Fred Powledge wrote, the majority of white New Yorkers surveyed "said they believed the Negro civil rights movement had gone too far" and "spoke of Negroes' receiving 'everything on a silver platter' and of 'reverse discrimination' against whites."[104] The article, one of the first to use the term *white backlash,* pointed to several developments that had led to white resentment, including the 1964 Civil Rights Act, civil rights protests in New York over schools, jobs, and housing, and riots that summer in New York, Rochester, Chicago, and Philadelphia. While the story presented "white backlash" as a new development, Powledge need only have looked at his own paper's archives to see that white resistance to civil rights had developed alongside black protests for years before 1964.

The "white backlash" story line failed to capture how white resistance to "busing" and school desegregation set policy limits at the local and national level. In New York City, the school board took years to adopt modest desegregation programs in deference to white parents' fears of "busing," and then undercut these programs when white communities organized protests. At the national level, politicians shaped the 1964 Civil Rights Act to protect school segregation in the North so as not to offend the sentiments of white voters in the North, whose protests against "busing" were fresh in the congressmen's minds.

When President John F. Kennedy sent civil rights legislation to Congress in the summer of 1963, the "Desegregation of Public Education" section called for the commissioner of education to, on request from local school boards, "render technical assistance in the preparation, adoption, and implementation of plans for desegregation of public schools or other plans designed to deal with problems arising from racial imbalance in public school systems."[105] The administration's bill referenced "racial imbalance," the phrase preferred by northerners to describe their own school segregation, eight times.[106] When it reached Congress, House Judiciary Committee chairman Emanuel Celler assigned the administration's bill to Subcommittee No. 5, which he also chaired and which had a majority of northern Democrats who were likely to support strong civil rights legislation. Celler, a Democrat from Brooklyn, Ohio Republican William McCulloch, the ranking minority party member on the subcommittee, and deputy attorney general Nicholas Katzenbach played important roles in crafting a subcommittee bill that would have enough support from northern Democrats and moderate Republicans to overcome opposition in the House and Senate from southern Democrats and conservative Republicans. At McCulloch's suggestion, the education section of the bill was amended to delete references to "racial imbalance," thereby making the law applicable only to de jure school segregation in the South.[107] When the subcommittee bill came to the House floor in February, Florida Republican William Cramer expressed concern that a recently decided case, *Blocker v. Board of Education on Manhasset* (1964), which found unconstitutional school segregation in Long Island, New York, could expand the scope of the bill. If the subcommittee had been able to consider this case, he argued, "I think . . . we would have taken another look at the bill and probably put something specific in it saying that it is not the intention of Congress to include racial imbalance or de facto segregation."[108] To remedy this, on February 6, 1964, Cramer introduced an amendment to section 401b so that the section's existing definition of *desegregation* ("'Desegregation' means the assignment of students to public schools and within such schools without regard to their race, color, religion, or national origin") was followed by a clarification: "'Desegregation' shall not mean the assignment of students to public schools in order to overcome racial imbalance."[109] In introducing the amendment, Cramer made clear that it aimed to prevent "busing" for desegregation: "The purpose is to prevent any semblance of congressional acceptance or approval ... [for] any balancing of school attendance by moving students across school district lines to level off percentages where one race outweighs another."[110] Celler accepted the amendment without discussion, and this wording was enshrined in the 1964 Civil Rights Act.

Southern senators, who already opposed civil rights legislation, were incensed by the blatant hypocrisy of the bill's education section and the way the amendment so clearly catered to white northerners' concerns. "I do not blame the two distinguished Senators from New York, for they desire to protect New York City, as well as Chicago, Detroit, and similar areas. But why should they attempt to penalize our part of the country?" Mississippi senator James Eastland asked. Referring to New York senators Jacob Javits and Kenneth Keating, Eastland continued, "In my opinion the two Senators from New York are, at heart, pretty good segregationists; but the conditions in their State are different from the conditions in ours."[111] Eastland's fellow Mississippian John Stennis and Alabama senator John Sparkman made the most explicit connection among Celler, the white parent protests in New York, and the "racial imbalance" loophole to protect segregated Northern schools in an exchange on the Senate floor on May 1, 1964:

> STENNIS: As the bill came to the Senate, it contained a provision
> prohibiting the busing of children from one part of a city to another, in
> an attempt to achieve racial balance in the schools. Was not that amend-
> ment agreed to by Representative Celler of New York, the manager of the
> bill in the House? Did not he agree to it, on the floor of the House,
> rather than make a fight to keep the other provision in the bill? Is not
> that true?
>
> SPARKMAN: Yes. I do not know what motivated the Representative from
> New York; but he is from New York, and undoubtedly he had received
> many protests. In fact, probably he read in the *New York Times,* as we

did, about 15,000 white mothers who protested against the busing of their children. Does the Senator from Mississippi remember that incident?

STENNIS: Oh, yes.

SPARKMAN: At one time the busing of schoolchildren was done; and 15,000 mothers in New York—in Westchester County and the adjoining areas—vigorously protested against it. I do not know whether their protests had any influence on Representative Celler. . . . I do not know what motivated him to do that; but . . . when the bill was brought up in the House, a provision was written into it by someone who wished to make certain that the ghettos . . . remain just as they are; and Representative Celler accepted the amendment. . . . By the way, the administration did not ask for that provision.[112]

Stennis, Sparkman, and the other senators who criticized Celler were not invested in desegregating New York's schools; rather they wanted southern states to have the same latitude to define and largely ignore school segregation that New York, Ohio, Illinois, and other northern states enjoyed and would continue to enjoy under the bill.

Still, the senators' repeated references to the New York protest speak to the imprint these parents left on the bill and the actual double standard the bill enshrined. The timing of the New York protest, coming days after the Senate opened debate on the Civil Rights Act, made the "fifteen thousand white mothers" representative of like-minded white parents who protested against school desegregation in other cities in the prior months. Surveying "recent school and residential troubles in New York City, in Philadelphia, in Cleveland, in Chicago, in Detroit, and elsewhere," Florida senator Spessard Holland argued that these protests "make it completely clear that millions of people in our Northern States prefer de facto segregation, or something very much like that, or at least do not want to adopt any program of compulsory mingling of the races."[113]

While northern senators disagreed with their southern colleagues' charges of hypocrisy, they agreed that the civil rights legislation was amended to prohibit "busing" for school desegregation. New Jersey senator Harrison Williams described how "segregationist propaganda" had created confusion among his constituents and had led many to write to him that "busing should be forbidden." Williams received these letters, he said, "despite the fact that section 401(b) in title IV of H.R. 7152 specifically prohibits the busing of students across town, in order to achieve racial balance in the public schools.

That provision clearly related to busing, and legislatively prohibits busing in order to achieve racial balance in the public schools."[114]

. . .

The legacy of New York's school desegregation battles in the 1950s and 1960s is threefold. First, New York City schools were amply and intentionally segregated, but in the wake of the *Brown* decision, white parent protests warned New York City's school officials against taking substantial steps to address school desegregation. In the mid- and late 1950s, desegregating New York's schools was demographically possible, if politically controversial. By 1964, however, white flight to the suburbs and suburban school districts and long-standing white protest meant that there were over two hundred segregated schools in New York, compared to fifty-two in 1954.[115] Second, the white parents' protests influenced the amendments ensuring that the Civil Rights Act would not apply to school segregation and "busing" in the North. Finally, the white parents' protests and the Civil Rights Act debates and legislation codified "busing" as the way to discuss and oppose school desegregation. This framing appeased northern sensitivities and distinguished their protests from those occurring in the South.

New York continued to play a leading role in "antibusing" politics for the next several years. Parents and Taxpayers paid a political lobbyist in Albany to encourage state legislators to pass regulations prohibiting "busing" for school desegregation in the state, and politicians proposed such legislation every year from 1964 to 1969. In 1969, an "antibusing" bill sponsored by state senators Norman Lent of Long Island and Joseph Kunzeman of Queens passed the New York House and Senate and was signed into law by Governor Nelson Rockefeller, before being found unconstitutional by a federal court the following year.[116] The Lent-Kunzeman "neighborhood schools" bill generated national interest among integration opponents and became a model for similar "freedom of choice" school legislation in several southern states, including Georgia, South Carolina, Tennessee, Louisiana, and Alabama.[117] New York's "antibusing" bill also influenced U.S. senator John Stennis of Mississippi, who in 1970 introduced an amendment calling for a uniform national school desegregation policy, with the hope of sparking more national opposition to "busing" and desegregation.[118] As a U.S. congressman representing Long Island in 1972, Lent proposed a highly publicized constitutional amendment, H.J. Res. 620, to bar "busing."

In explaining the series of protests for and against civil rights in New York, Senator Jacob Javits told his colleagues, "New York is a great center of communications, and when people demonstrate in New York, they are not demonstrating for the New York Senators alone. It is fair to say that they are demonstrating for the Nation and the world."[119] As Javits understood, parents in New York were engaged in neighborhood battles with implications that reached well beyond New York. New York's fights over "busing" were both intensely local disputes that contested neighborhood boundaries on a block-by-block basis and national disputes that shaped the ways school desegregation would be debated and defeated for years to come.

TWO

Surrender in Chicago

CITIES' RIGHTS AND THE LIMITS OF FEDERAL ENFORCEMENT OF SCHOOL DESEGREGATION

In New York and Chicago, you don't have separate but equal schools. You have integration.

—U.S. REPRESENTATIVE EMANUEL CELLER, *1964*

When the United States Office of Education was pressured into restoring Federal funds to Chicago's segregated public school system, it represented the first abject surrender to the principle that separate but equal is wrong in the South, but acceptable in the North—particularly if a city can muster enough Northern politicians and educators with a segregationist mentality to practice this shameful hypocrisy.

—ADAM CLAYTON POWELL, *1965*

ON JULY 4, 1965, AFTER months of school protests and boycotts, civil rights advocates in Chicago filed a complaint with the U.S. Office of Education charging that the Chicago Board of Education violated Title VI of the Civil Rights Act of 1964. The implications of the charges were extremely serious. If Chicago had violated Title VI, which gave the U.S. Department of Health, Education, and Welfare (HEW) authority to withhold funds if school districts failed to comply with rules against school segregation, the city stood to lose $30 million in federal money. Drawing on evidence from an array of published reports and their own investigations, the Coordinating Council of Community Organizations (CCCO) told federal officials that 81 percent of elementary schools and 73 percent of high schools were racially segregated, with 90 percent of black students attending segregated schools. These blacks schools were more acutely overcrowded, had a higher percentage of noncertified teachers, and offered fewer honors classes than white schools.

The CCCO presented its case in no uncertain terms. "The Chicago Board of Education has deliberately segregated the city's public school system," a CCCO report began. "Neither segregation nor integration just 'happens.' Each is deliberately stalled or prevented. The school board, acting under advice of its general superintendent, pursues a deliberate policy of segregation."[1] In its letter to the Office of Education, the civil rights coalition argued that Chicago's schools were unconstitutionally segregated: "When a public body such as the school board draws boundary lines such as it has in the past, and is likely to do again, that produce segregation, then what we have is not *de facto* segregation—it is *de jure* segregation."[2] In addition to calling the innocence of Chicago's school segregation into question, the complaint correctly predicted that Chicago's evasion of school desegregation could have a national influence. "We are further persuaded that the ways and means of creating and perpetuating segregation in Chicago may become the handbook for southern communities seeking to evade the 1954 Supreme Court ruling. We are confident that federal intervention in this matter, through the withholding of funds, will help underline the high fiscal cost, as well the immeasurable social cost, of segregation to Chicago and to the rest of the nation."[3]

When HEW received the Chicago complaint, the agency was focused on school segregation in the South. When HEW's Title VI enforcement guidelines were announced in the *Saturday Review* in March 1965, the magazine made this southern focus clear: "*[Saturday Review]* hopes that Southern school authorities will find these guidelines helpful in making the fateful decisions that confront them. And Northern readers will find, in the calm words and careful analysis of the memo, a clear view of the issues as they have evolved to date."[4] Titled "Title VI: Southern Education Faces the Facts," this introduction to Title VI addressed northerners as innocent readers following a story taking place elsewhere, suggesting the disbelief that greeted the prospect of federal funds being withheld from Chicago for violating the Civil Rights Act.

HEW briefly withheld $30 million in federal funds from Chicago in fall 1965, finding the city's schools to be in "probable noncompliance" with Title VI's antidiscrimination provisions. Facing pressure from Mayor Richard J. Daley, Senator Everett Dirksen, Illinois congressmen, and President Lyndon Johnson, HEW's case in Chicago quickly unraveled, exposing the limits of federal authority in the face of school segregation in the North. "Mayor Daley ostensibly supported the Civil Rights Act and all the Democratic

Congressmen from Illinois . . . voted for it," CCCO leader Al Raby said after the federal funds were restored just five days later. "Yet they are the first to squeal like stuck pigs when the bill is enforced in the North."[5] What Raby saw as a contradiction was actually a logical outcome of the decision to include an "antibusing" provision in the Civil Rights Act that excluded desegregation to correct "racial imbalance" in the North. The *Chicago Tribune,* which staunchly opposed school desegregation in the city, regularly quoted Title IV, section 401b, of the Civil Rights Act of 1964 ("'Desegregation' means the assignment of students to public schools and within such schools without regard to their race, color, religion, or national origin, but 'desegregation' shall not mean the assignment of students to public schools in order to overcome racial imbalance") to support their case against school desegregation.[6] If New York's "antibusing" protests encouraged northern congressmen to exempt northern schools from the Civil Rights Act, HEW's surrender in Chicago encouraged school officials and politicians to maintain positions of resistance and noncompliance with regard to school desegregation.

"DOWN WITH WILLIS"

Civil rights activists and parents in Chicago, like those in New York, investigated school policies across a massive school system with the goal of making school segregation an issue that could not be ignored. In December 1956, after several months of research, the Chicago branch of the NAACP released a survey charging that "school district boundaries . . . follow and reinforce racial segregation," that the percentage of inexperienced teachers "in the predominantly Negro districts is shockingly and disproportionately higher than in predominantly white districts," "that the wide spread belief that Chicago's residential segregation pattern prevents integration within the public schools is a myth, and that the Chicago public schools can be substantially integrated within a short period of time if there is the will to do so." The NAACP hoped the survey would force the school board to acknowledge the existence of school segregation and make a commitment to foster integration. Pointing to New York's approval of a policy of school desegregation, Chicago NAACP president Willoughby Abner said, "It is our firm opinion that nothing short of the adoption and implementation of a forthright policy of racial integration within the Chicago public schools can correct this situation."[7]

In the absence of a reply from the school board, the Chicago branch tried unsuccessfully to get the state's school construction bonds to require new schools to be placed to encourage desegregation and asked the school board to bus students from overcrowded black schools to white schools with empty seats.[8] A February 1958 article in *Crisis,* the national NAACP journal, highlighted many of the Chicago NAACP's statistics regarding educational inequality in the city. They estimated that over 90 percent of black elementary students and 70 percent of black high-school students attended segregated schools. Noting that black students made up 80 percent of students in overcrowded schools with "double shifts," the article asked "whether the school time lost to [the] Negro child is not almost as great in Chicago as it is in Mississippi."[9] These statistics buttressed the argument that school segregation was not accidental and was not out of the control of the school board: "In cost and quality of instruction, school time, districting and choice of sites, the Chicago Board of Education maintains in practice what amounts to a racially discriminatory policy."[10] The school board promised to study the issue but refused to adopt a policy regarding school desegregation or make any substantive policy changes.[11]

Civil rights activists continued to press their case in the early 1960s through community organizing, lawsuits, and public protests. "The NAACP is recruiting allies all over the city . . . in its war against the Chicago Board of Education," the *Chicago Defender* reported in April 1961. Parents from Southside neighborhoods Chatham, Park Manor, and West Avalon gathered for a mass meeting where they heard NAACP executive secretary Reverend Carl Fuqua urge the parents to organize to demand that the school board address school segregation.[12] "As long as Superintendent Benjamin Willis and the board of education take the attitude of ignoring any positive action to integrate Chicago public schools," Fuqua told the parents, "they are assuming the roles of 'protectors of a segregated system' in Chicago. They are in fact acting as segregationists whether they are or not."[13] One outcome of this community organizing was "Operation Transfer," a plan where 160 black parents went to eleven white schools with open seats to request that their children be transferred.[14] The parents were refused, as they expected, but they demonstrated black parents' increasingly public frustration with school conditions.

In September 1961, days after "Operation Transfer," a group of black parents sued the Chicago Board of Education. Paul Zuber, who had represented the New York parents in the *Skipwith* case, also represented the Chicago parents in *Webb v. Board of Education of the City of Chicago.* Fresh off a victory in *Taylor v. Board of Education, New Rochelle,* where the court found that the school board had gerrymandered school boundaries to maintain segregated schools, Zuber was optimistic about the Chicago case. "You've got a segregated school system," he told parents at an overflowing community meeting. "It is planned and perpetuated by your Board of Education, it is administered by your superintendent of schools. What are you waiting for?"[15] The parents in the *Webb* case asked the court to enjoin the school board from assigning black students to overcrowded schools, to assign black students in overcrowded schools to white schools with open space, and to declare the "neighborhood school" policy illegal and unconstitutional.[16] School officials adamantly denied the parents' charges. In his affidavit in the *Webb* case, Superintendent Willis blamed overcrowding on black migration into Chicago and argued, "I know of no attendance area that has been gerrymandered, no construction site that has been selected, no double or overlapping shift program that has been instituted, no classrooms that have been allowed to remain vacant, no upper grade center, elementary or high school branch that has been established for the purpose of creating or maintaining 'Negro elementary schools' or 'white elementary schools' in Chicago, as charged by the plaintiffs' affidavit."[17] Federal district judge Julius Hoffman dismissed the *Webb* case in July 1962 because the parents had not exhausted Illinois's state administrative procedures before going to federal court. The *Webb* case was later reopened and settled out of court in August 1963 with an agreement that the board would adopt a policy of integration and that an independent panel, chaired by University of Chicago sociologist Philip Hauser, would examine the school situation.[18]

With legal options uncertain and unpromising, civil rights activists and parents employed a range of protest tactics. A group of black mothers with the Woodlawn Organization, a Saul Alinsky community organization that favored direct action protests, staged uninvited visits to white schools to search for empty classrooms. Four of the "truth squad" mothers, as the *Defender* called them, were arrested and charged with trespassing and disorderly conduct.[19] Another group of parents staged a two-week-long "study-in," with parents and volunteer tutors teaching students in school hallways and basements, to protest a transfer order that sent students from the overcrowded Burnside Elementary School to another black school rather than a nearby white school. Outside the school, black and white parents and ministers carried signs reading "Schools Factually Segregated" and "No Double

Shifts," and twenty-six demonstrators were arrested for trespassing and unlawful assembly.[20] "The situation calls for a showdown," the *Defender* editorialized. "The community cannot continue to have its rights brazenly flaunted [sic] by irresponsible school officials. The battle line must be drawn somewhere in the struggle to democratize the Chicago schools; Burnside is just as good a place to start the fight."[21] Leading the school battle was the Coordinating Council of Community Organizations (CCCO), formed in spring 1962 as a civil rights coalition including the NAACP, the Urban League, Teachers for Integrated Schools, the Woodlawn Organization, CORE, Chatham-Avalon Park Community Council, and Englewood Council for Community Action.[22]

Parents and activists directed much of their anger at Superintendent Benjamin Willis. In addition to condemning Willis's refusal to acknowledge or address school segregation, civil rights advocates were upset with Willis's policy decisions regarding school overcrowding. Willis ordered the purchase of over one hundred mobile classrooms, called "Willis Wagons" by his detractors, to relieve overcrowding at black schools without transporting black students to white schools with open seats.[23] While school officials contended that mobile classrooms addressed the black communities' complaints about overcrowding, the *Defender* saw the policy as the last straw for black Chicagoans: "It is bad enough to deny us membership on the Mayor's School Board Nominating Committee; it is frustrating enough to prevent us from having a responsible spokesman on the Board. On the top of all this come ... mobile classrooms, aptly dubbed Willis Wagons, to cram down our throats Mr. Willis' segregative school policy. ... On the eighth anniversary of [*Brown v. Board*], Chicago is witnessing a display of defiance of the Court's order undreamed of even in Alabama and Georgia."[24] Fed up with Willis's resistance, civil rights advocates called for the superintendent to be fired. CORE circulated petitions across the city calling for Willis's resignation. "Dr. Willis yields immediately to the protest of white parents, while the complaints of dozens of Negro groups ... go without any comment from the superintendent," Chicago CORE chairmen Milton Davis said.[25] The *Defender* dedicated their front page on August 15, 1963, to a series of accusations about Willis. "WE ACCUSE him of gerrymandering school districts for the primary purpose of 'containing' Negro children in predominantly Negro schools. ... He is an emblem of racial segregation. Dr. Willis must go."[26] Protestors picketed outside Willis's Lakeshore Drive apartment, carrying signs reading "Willis-Wallace, What's the Difference?"—comparing Chicago's superintendent to

DAILY

Chicago 🦅 Defender

Vol. VIII — No. 108 THURSDAY, AUGUST 15, 1963 Price 3 Cents

WE ACCUSE!

Benjamin C, Willis.

Supt. Of Chicago Public Schools

...of perpetuating racial segregation in the public schools of America's second largest city, Chicago, Illinois through the use of mobile classrooms which have been derisively labelled "Willis Wagons."

WE ACCUSE him of gerrymandering school districts for the primary purpose of "containing" Negro children in predominantly Negro schools.

WE ACCUSE him of following an administrative policy which has caused almost one-third of Chicago's population — 925,000 Negroes — to lose confidence in him.

WE ACCUSE him of contemptuously ignoring the very valid and real complaints of both Negro and white parents who believe that his attitude fails to inspire confidence in the Board of Education.

WE HAVE repeatedly accused him—as we did back in February 25, 1962 in a front page editorial. "Willis Must Go"—of failing to declare publicly and forcefully that integration in education is most conducive to the flowering of American democracy, that Negro and white children must learn together if they are going to learn how to live together.

WE HAVE repeatedly accused him of betraying his trust as a public servant by refusing to answer his critics or adequately defend his policies. And we are happy that some of our white sister newspapers have begun to finally "join the club"—the fastest growing club in America, the "Willis Must Go Club." We have missed them during the last year when we were out there all by ourselves, calling for Dr. Willis' departure. Said the Chicago Sun-Times Wednesday in a editorial: "We assume that he has good reasons for doing many of the things for which he is criticized. He does neither

See BENJAMIN WILLIS, Page 2

BENJAMIN C. WILLIS

FIGURE 7. The *Chicago Defender* accused Superintendent Benjamin Willis of segregating Chicago's schools. Willis became the focal point of the black community's protests against educational inequality in the city. *Chicago Defender*, August 15, 1963.

Alabama's segregationist governor George Wallace—and "Whitson Votes Good Like a Segregationist Should," referring to school board member Frank Whitson.[27] Chicagoans at the March on Washington in August 1963 chanted "Down with Willis."[28]

While Willis drew the ire of civil rights advocates, his resistance to school desegregation garnered support from many white parents, business leaders, and the *Chicago Tribune*. Parents of students at all-white Bogan High School, for example, protested the transfer of a small number of gifted black and white students in September 1963. The students, who were eligible to change schools under a new policy that allowed high-school students in the top 5 percent of their class to transfer to schools with honors courses. Twenty-five hundred white parents and community members protested the planned transfer, carrying signs reading, "We Support Dr. Willis and Neighborhood Schools."[29] White students chanted, "Two! Four! Six! Eight!—We don't want to integrate!"[30] A delegation of Bogan parents met with Willis and found him receptive to their concerns, as did white parents who objected to Austin High School and Washington High School being on the transfer list. Without consulting the school board, Willis removed over twenty schools from the transfer list (including Bogan, Austin, and Washington), leaving only nine schools where academically talented students could transfer.[31] Parents of the gifted Hirsch High School students who had attempted to transfer to Bogan obtained a court order directing Willis to abide by the board's stated transfer policy. Willis resigned rather than obey the court order, but three days later, the board voted not to accept his resignation and worked to reconcile with Willis.[32] The *Chicago Tribune* found the news of Willis's resignation "distressing" and wrote, "All things considered he has done an outstandingly good job."[33] Willis also received votes of support from business leaders, including Frederick Bertram, president of the National Home and Property Owners Foundation, who wrote the board of education to praise Willis and condemn civil rights protestors: "On behalf of the great majority of school children, parents, and taxpayers of Chicago, we demand that you seek the reinstatement of Benjamin C. Willis as superintendent. The school board's abdication to the demands of small pressure groups of disorderly demonstrators is disgraceful. . . . Rule of government by pressure of demonstration is anarchy."[34]

As this letter suggests, by 1963 Willis had become a proxy for expressing opposition to or support for civil rights and school desegregation. Sociologist Philip Hauser, whom Willis asked to chair the committee evaluating the schools, told Congress that Willis "has become the symbol of segregated schools not only to his detractors, white and Negro but, also, to his supporters. His recent under-the-table reappointment was heralded by many as a great victory for white supremacy. His refusal to integrate the schools and his silence on the subject . . . [have] made him the champion of racists in Chicago as well as the devil of the civil rights movement."[35] White parents, community leaders, and media who valued Willis's resistance to school desegregation inevitably outweighed whatever pressure civil rights activists were able to apply.

The board's peaceful reconciliation with Willis, combined with years of frustration over overcrowding, temporary teachers, and inadequate resources at schools attended by black children, led CCCO to organize a massive "Freedom Day" school boycott. Similar to school boycotts in cities like Boston, Cleveland, Milwaukee, New York, and Seattle, the Chicago boycott was designed to force the school board to take action to address school segregation.[36] Led by Lawrence Landry, a Chicago native with two degrees from the University of Chicago, the CCCO published a list of thirteen demands in advance of the boycott.[37] The list included demands that the school board remove Willis as superintendent; publish an inventory of school population, classroom availability, and racial demographics for students and teachers in each school; and fully use all available space before using mobile classroom units.[38] Over 220,000 students (47 percent of total enrollment) stayed away from public schools on October 22, 1963, with many attending Freedom Schools at churches and community centers.[39] Ten thousand people marched around city hall and the board of education building, including students carrying signs reading "Willis Must Go" and "No More Little Black Sambo Read in Class."[40] Boycott leaders said the boycott exceeded expectations and threatened to hold one-day boycotts every month until their demands were met. The *Defender*'s headline sprawled over half of the front page: "Boycott a Thumping Success! 225,000 Kids Make Willis Eat Jim Crow."[41] The *Chicago Tribune* saw the boycott in a different light. "No government can permit such a reign of chaos," the *Tribune* editorial page read. "Chicagoans as a whole have been patient with the civil rights demonstrations and generally sympathetic with the aims of Negroes to achieve equality of opportunity. Much of the public's patience vanished Tuesday when the reckless men at the head of the civil rights movement ordered thousands of children out of the public schools. The patience that remains will disappear if the tactics of obstructing government and business are continued."[42]

A second school boycott on February 25, 1964, further revealed the gulf between civil rights advocates and the city's white officials. The *Defender* declared Freedom Day II a success, with 175,000 students staying out of school.[43] The February boycott and protest march around city hall was also designed to impress on Mayor Daley and other politicians that they could not sit on the sidelines of the school fight. Alderman Charles Chew, the only black alderman who supported the boycott, said, "The Democratic machine is no longer oiled." "It is clear that we won today," Lawrence Landry declared regarding the boycott and protest march. "We walked thru the City Hall this time. Next time we will walk over it."[44] Mayor Daley was unimpressed with the boycotts. "What do they prove?" he asked. "Education should never be a political issue and it should never be used by either party to take advantage in politics."[45]

Schools officials linked their opposition to the boycotts and civil rights demands to concerns about "busing." Speaking days before the second school boycott, school board president Clair Roddewig said he strongly opposed "busing kids all over town to integrate schools." Roddewig saw civil rights demands as triggering a dismal chain of events. "First, civil rights leaders demand that Negroes be bused out of all-Negro districts to all-white schools," he said. "Then, as during the recent New York boycott, they demand that white students be bused to all-Negro schools that still remain in the Negro residential districts. Next, when white parents begin sending their children to private schools, they will demand that parents be told where to send their children to school. When in America the day arrives that the state assigns all children to schools, we are finished."[46] For Roddewig, as for many of his peers in other cities, this dire forecast justified school officials' opposition to school desegregation. Framing this as a resistance to "busing" rather than resistance to school desegregation was more than simply a choice of words. Describing civil rights leaders as asking that "Negroes be bused out of all-Negro districts to all-white schools" focused attention on "busing" rather than on the educational rights black students were denied in the "all-Negro districts" perpetuated by school officials. Roddewig's fear that "the state" might someday assign all children to schools overlooked the role school boards, as state agencies, already played in assigning children, and presented school officials as innocent bystanders to questions about school zoning and assignment. Finally, presenting civil rights demands as the trigger for this grim educational future made the movement seem unreasonable and ultimately un-American.

FIVE DAYS IN CHICAGO

By 1965, Chicago's civil rights advocates had engaged in nearly a decade of organized efforts to uproot school segregation but saw little movement from school officials. A series of external reports—Northwestern University law professor John Coons studied the schools for the U.S. Commission on Civil Rights in 1962, and University of Chicago professors Philip Hauser and Robert Havinghurst led committees that published reports in 1964—corroborated and extended the research on school segregation in Chicago that civil rights groups had been conducting since the mid-1950s.[47] Neither these

FIGURE 8. Flyer for Freedom Day school boycott sponsored by the Coordinating Council of Community Organization. Over 220,000 students stayed out of school to protest school segregation and educational inequality in Chicago. Civil rights activists organized similar school boycotts in cities like Boston, Cleveland, Milwaukee, New York, and Seattle on October 22, 1963. Chicago Urban League Records, University of Illinois at Chicago Library, Special Collections.

reports nor the school boycotts were enough to force Willis and the school board to take action on school desegregation. Meyer Weinberg, chairman of the CCCO's Education Committee and editor of the journal *Integrated Education,* expressed frustration at how school officials offered only watered-down proposals in response to civil rights demands. "The civil rights movement always loses because we let Willis define the problem and make the proposals—to which we only react," Weinberg told his colleagues. School officials would face more pressure, he suggested, if the schools were con-

FIGURE 9. Thousands of Chicagoans marched in support of the Freedom Day school boycott, October 22, 1963. Film still used with permission of Kartemquin Films.

fronted with the loss of federal funds due to violations of the Civil Rights Act.[48] To this end, on July 4, 1965, the CCCO filed a complaint with the U.S. Office of Education charging that the Chicago Board of Education had violated Title VI of the Civil Rights Act of 1964.

Chicago presented the first test of Title VI in schools outside the South. Title VI had received relatively little attention in the lengthy debates over the Civil Rights Act of 1964, but quickly emerged as one of the most important and controversial aspects of the legislation. In requiring compliance with antidiscrimination provisions to receive federal funds, Title VI gave the federal government a new weapon to compel school districts to end school segregation.[49] And as federal funds came to constitute a larger share of local school budgets, the threat of withholding significant sums of money added a material cost to resisting school desegregation. In Chicago, for example, federal aid to schools had increased from $372,000 in 1954 to $47.5 million in 1966.[50] Like Title IV, however, which differentiated between southern school segregation and northern "racial imbalance," Congress did not intend Title VI to apply outside the South. In the floor debate of the Civil Rights Act, Senator Hubert H. Humphrey of Minnesota reassured Senator Robert Byrd of West Virginia that "there is no case in which the thrust of the statute under which the money would be given would be directed toward restoring or bringing about a racial balance in the schools."[51] Humphrey also referenced *Bell v. School City of Gary, Indiana,* a 1963 federal court decision upholding "neighborhood schools," arguing, "This case makes it quite clear that while the Constitution prohibits segregation, it does not require integration."[52] After receiving the CCCO's complaint regarding Chicago, James Quigley, HEW assistant secretary, said the agency was trying to figure out the applicability of Title VI outside of the South. "I'm inclined to feel that title VI does not apply to complaints of de facto segregation, but might be applicable to some conditions in the north," Quigley said. "If we find that Negro children are in fact being treated differently from white children in Chicago, for example, title VI would give us the power to act."[53]

While federal officials were weighing their options in Chicago, the *Tribune* railed against the threat of withholding federal funds from the city's schools. Describing the CCCO's complaint as "the latest example of extremism in this movement," the *Tribune* predicted, "If the government should be silly enough to mount an offensive against Chicagoans by withholding money it has wrung out of them in taxes, the resentment predictably would be great and general." In language that drew on anti–civil rights propaganda funded by far-right conservatives and the state of Mississippi, the *Tribune's* editorial saw Title VI as "a hundred billion dollar blackjack . . . with which to club the American people into submission."[54]

School officials shared this anger and provided little assistance to the federal investigators. John Coons, who studied Chicago's schools in 1962 for U.S. Commission on Civil Rights, ran into administrative resistance while preparing a report for HEW regarding Chicago's compliance with the Civil Rights Act. Coons recalled having the sense that school officials and principals "were uneasy in their chairs when you talked to them."[55] Over the course of a three-month survey, Coons was granted only a ten-minute meeting with Superintendent Willis, which, Coons remarked, "consisted of a denunciation of my mission and myself."[56] Coons described Willis's "refusal to cooperate" as "final and total" and wrote to school board member Frank Whitson in an attempt to find someone from the schools to provide information to balance the civil rights complaints. "This situation would have some aspects of comedy were it not for my responsibility to report to the Federal Government," Coons said.[57] New York congressman Adam Clayton Powell told Francis Keppel, who oversaw HEW educational policy as U.S. commissioner of education, that Willis's lack of cooperation "would seem to me to constitute open defiance of the requirements of the civil rights act of 1964."[58] To put more pressure on Chicago, Powell arranged hearings as chair of the House Education and Labor Committee to investigate "de facto racial segregation" in Chicago's schools.

On September 30, 1965, Keppel wrote to Illinois superintendent of public instruction Ray Page indicating that Chicago's schools were in "probable noncompliance" with the Civil Rights Act and that the city's application for $30 million as part of Elementary and Secondary Education Act would be deferred under Title VI. Al Raby, a Chicago native and former teacher who emerged as CCCO's leader, called the decision "the first crack in school segregation in Chicago."[59] The *Defender* saw HEW's decision as a vindication of the black community and years of school segregation complaints: "Keppel's action freezing $30 million dollars in Federal aid for Chicago public schools establishes beyond the shadow of a doubt that the charges of de facto segregation were not figments of psychotic imagination."[60]

News of the federal fund withholding also topped the front page of the *Tribune* ("City School Aid Halted"), and the paper's coverage anticipated how HEW's intervention in Chicago would play out over the next week.[61] The *Tribune* quoted U.S. congressman Roman Pucinski, who represented a heavily Polish-American northwest Chicago district, calling the decision "arbitrary, capricious, unjustified, and a violation of the civil rights act itself."[62] Congressmen Daniel Rostenkowski and John Klucsynski also spoke out against HEW, as did Senator Everett Dirksen, who, as Senate minority leader, had helped craft the Civil Rights Act and its focus on enforcement in the South.[63] The *Tribune's* editors phrased their opposition to HEW as an open challenge to the state's leading politicians: "How humiliating it must be for Mayor Daley and Gov. Kerner, the leading Democrats of Illinois, to be kicked in the teeth by a petty burocrat *[sic]* of the Johnson Democratic administration! . . . The Tribune warned that [the Civil Rights Act] would become a dangerous new stick in federal hands. The stick is now being used to beat Chicago."[64]

Daley did not need the *Tribune's* editorial to convince him to fight to get the $30 million in federal funds restored to Chicago's schools. As mayor of Chicago and head of the Cook County Democratic organization, Daley was one of the most powerful and influential politicians in the country. At the local level, he had control of tens of thousands of city and county jobs; at the national level, Daley could deliver votes to Democratic presidential candidates and support from Chicago congressmen for presidential legislative priorities.[65] Daley had the ear of President Johnson, and when both men were in New York on October 3 for an immigration bill signing, he told the president about his anger and confusion over the funds withholding.[66] The next day at the White House, President Johnson conveyed Daley's anger to Keppel and made it clear that he wanted HEW to settle the issue as quickly as possible.[67] Ruby Martin, who later directed HEW's Office of Civil Rights, speculated that the first lady's efforts to bring more flowers to U.S. cities and highways figured in the president's decision. "There are some people who suspect that Lady Bird's Beautification Program was at stake," Martin recalled in a 1969 interview, "and that Mayor Daley controls eleven votes in Congress, and he threatened to pull all eleven of them back to Chicago or off the floor when Lady Bird's Beautification Bill came up."[68] On October 5, HEW undersecretary Wilbur Cohen flew to Chicago to negotiate a settlement with school board president Frank Whitson. Under the terms of the agreement, HEW released the funds and withdrew its investigators until the end of the year. In exchange, the school board only had to agree to investigate school attendance boundaries and reaffirm two policies regarding trade schools and apprenticeship programs.[69]

HEW's abrupt surrender in Chicago reverberated locally and nationally. "We are shocked at the shameless display of naked policy power exhibited by Mayor Daley," CCCO's Al Raby said. "Not a single segregated situation will be substantially altered by the terms of the agreement reached between HEW and Whitson. We are still saddled with the Willis system of separate, inferior education. A school board committee has been appointed to investigate school district gerrymandering. For the same school board which created the gerrymandering to investigate its own handiwork is absurd."[70] For others, securing the status quo in Chicago's schools was a positive outcome. Representative Pucinski, who also lobbied the White House to persuade HEW to restore the funds, described the decision as "an abject surrender by Keppel—a great victory for local government, a great victory for Chicago."[71] The negotiated settlement involved only "minor concessions," Pucinski said, "face-savers for the Office of Education. They don't mean a thing."[72] The *Tribune* called Willis "a man among midgets" and praised him as the "only official who has had the courage to stand up against the power play of the federal office of education."[73] Writing in the *Washington Post*, columnists Rowland Evans and Robert Novak said that after the "fiasco" in Chicago, "Willis is more than ever a white folk hero and will be harder than ever to get rid of."[74] *The New York Times* saw the Chicago fund case as "a singular instance of a northern city's cry of 'states rights'—more precisely, 'city's rights'—to defeat a Johnson Administration strategy."[75] For Adam Clayton Powell, Chicago "represented the first abject surrender to the principle that separate but equal is wrong in the South, but acceptable in the North— particularly if a city can muster enough Northern politicians and educators with a segregationist mentality to practice this shameful hypocrisy."[76]

For HEW, Chicago ended discussions of using Title VI to eliminate "de facto" segregation and significantly limited federal investigations of school segregation outside the South.[77] Keppel met with school officials from the fifty largest cities at the end of October 1965 to calm their fears about federal intervention in large cities.[78] "It is obvious that the question of civil rights in the big cities won't be answered to my satisfaction or that of people in my position, for years," Keppel remarked.[79] A January 1966 HEW memo to the White House outlined the logic for focusing on de jure segregation in the South:

> The primary reason for taking this approach is our lack of factual information about the various issues, situations, possibilities and probabilities in the North and West. We have had almost a year and a half of dealing with the South, but we have only been concerned with the North and West for about four or five months. The general consensus is that we should be more knowledgeable before we issue standards which we may live to regret, either because they are too narrow, too broad, or inadequate. The answer to queries about *why* we are not dealing with the North and West is that, while Title VI applies to the North and West as well as to the South and while we are investigating complaints of discrimination against Northern and Western schools, we simply have not had enough experience as yet in these areas to issue guidelines of general applicability.[80]

Ruby Martin described Chicago as a "tremendous setback" for HEW. After Chicago, she said, "We made a conscious decision—some people call it a political decision—not to take on any large school districts ... because our resources are limited. You can get involved in a large city for two years and come out of it bloodied, bruised, and scarred, and nothing [is] going to change the situation."[81] For school officials, politicians, and civil rights advocates in other northern cities who were following the case, the lesson from Chicago was that federal authorities did not have the resources or political will to combat school segregation in the North. HEW's surrender in Chicago encouraged school officials and politicians to maintain positions of resistance and noncompliance with regard to school desegregation, while it led black parents and students to doubt that any federal authority could successfully address their concerns.

"NO ONE LIKES TO BE PUSHED"

After thirteen years as the controversial superintendent of Chicago's public schools, Benjamin Willis resigned in 1966. Civil rights advocates greeted Willis's departure with relief and the hire of the new superintendent, Dr. James Redmond, with cautious optimism. HEW officials hoped that Redmond's appointment would lead to voluntary compliance on some of the issues raised in the prior year. Harold Howe, who replaced Francis Keppel as commissioner of education, was an old friend of Redmond's and struck a cautious tone compared with HEW's initial efforts in Chicago. After ensuring that "Mayor Daley approves of our plans," Howe sent Redmond a report that, he wrote, "outlines serious conditions in the Chicago schools which, in our view, may involve violations of Title VI of the Civil Rights Act. We believe that the constructive way to proceed is to seek your cooperation in moving rapidly to correct the conditions outlined in the report."[82] While this approach lacked any threat of withholding federal funds, Redmond was far more receptive than Willis to drafting a plan to increase school integration.

When Redmond submitted his report, "Increasing Desegregation of Faculties, Students, and Vocational Education Programs," to the board of education in late August 1967, it was quickly attacked as a "busing" plan. Days after the plan was made public, white parents from southwest- and northwest-side community groups slowed traffic with a hundred-car motorcade. The cars carried signs reading "Stop School Bussing" and "Does Supt. Redmond Teach Education or Integration?" and many contained children holding railroad flares out of open windows.[83] State senator Joseph Krasowski, who represented the white southwest side, criticized "busing" as an "ivory tower plan" that would "hinder good education." "I don't oppose school integration," he argued, "but the school board shouldn't stress integration more than education. . . . You can't foist this upon the people. No one likes to be pushed, and when they are they'll push back."[84]

These "busing" protests continued into 1968 as the school board considered implementing Redmond's proposals. Hundreds of white parents, many wearing buttons reading "Willis for Superintendent," pressed into a board of education meeting room with the goal of "getting our faces on camera for a

70 · SURRENDER IN CHICAGO

FIGURE 10. White demonstrators gather at the Chicago Board of Education to protest superintendent Dr. James Redmond's "busing" plan. Associated Press photo, January 1968.

change," as one demonstrator said. "Put Redmond on a Bus—Leave the Driving to Us," read one sign.[85] White parents staged another motorcade in January 1968, with signs reading, "Stop Integrating, Start Educating," "Down with Busing," and "Redmond, Resign Right Now." "I'm 100 per cent against busing," Harry Kuhr, chairman of the Taxpayers Council of the Northwest Side, told the *Tribune*. "Regardless of what kind of teachers you give these people, they are not going to learn."[86] As this reference to black students as unteachable suggests, antiblack racism fueled these "busing" protests. "The proposed busing of Negro students from crowded Austin area elementary

FIGURE 11. White parents protest Chicago superintendent Dr. James Redmond's plan to begin school desegregation. This mother's button reads, "Reading, Rittin, Racism. Out with Bus Plan." *ABC News,* January 10, 1968.

schools to Northwest Side schools has aroused racism to white heat," the *Defender* editorialized.[87]

Unedited ABC news footage of the protests shows white demonstrators struggling to articulate their opposition to school desegregation and their defense of "neighborhood schools" without explicitly expressing racist sentiments. "We picked our neighborhood for schools, for shopping," a mother explained to ABC's reporter. "Why should they take my five or six year old child and bus it eight miles way, when I've got a school a block away. It don't make sense. You're taking the rights away from the Americans. This is the only right we have left to fight for, our children." The next woman to speak expanded on this sentiment: "They got everything. What, Abraham Lincoln gave them freedom, so they want all of Chicago, 'cause it's Illinois? I have nothing against them, but they should stay in their own schools. . . . Let them stay where they belong." When another mother added, "Let them stay in their own territory," her fellow protestors redirected her: "No, no, bad answer." She reframed her remarks: "When I wanted to transfer my children to the school of my choosing, they told me, it's out of the district. So why are they coming to the district I moved to? Why don't they stay in their own district?" The protestors were sometimes less careful with their wording. When the ABC reporter asked a protestor, "Is this a matter of Negroes coming into your school?" she replied, "No, because I went to school with niggers, there was nothing wrong with it."[88]

These interviews are interesting because they make clear the logic that underscored the argument for "neighborhood schools." These white mothers understood that Chicago was among the most segregated cities in America and that so long as school district lines tracked with neighborhood boundaries, their schools would be untouched by racial integration. In 1966, just two years before these "antibusing" demonstrations, Martin Luther King Jr. and the Southern Christian Leadership Conference partnered with local civil rights activists to lead marches in Chicago to call attention to housing segregation and rally support for federal open-housing legislation. White neighborhoods in Chicago and the neighboring working-class suburb of Cicero responded with mob violence. King, who was hit with a rock thrown by one of the four thousand white southwest-side residents who blocked the marchers, told reporters he had "never seen as much hatred and hostility on the part of so many people."[89] If white "antibusing" activists had intimate knowledge of how segregation in Chicago was maintained, they also understood that in public contexts they were best served by framing their defense of white neighborhoods and schools in language that was not explicitly racist. They therefore emphasized "freedom of choice" and "neighborhood schools" to make their case that they had a right to white schools.

Like Parents and Taxpayers in New York, these Chicago demonstrators also argued that they had a right as taxpayers to avoid school desegregation. "We're middle-class working people," one mother stated. "We own homes, they're not big homes. . . . We pay $500 in taxes a year." Another white mother argued, "We are here because the Board of Education is our city's spokesman for what we want. . . . We expect the Board of Education not to determine what they're doing in the city of Chicago by what HEW or the federal government tells them to do. We are paying taxes, the tax money comes back to us. We should determine what our tax money is and is not used for."[90] Without explicitly referencing race, these protestors argued that white taxpayers were more important citizens and more worthy of the school board's attention than black Chicagoans/taxpayers.

As in New York, opposition to "busing" emerged in Chicago on a much larger scale than the proposed use of buses in school desegregation plans.

And as in New York, "antibusing" protests persuaded school officials to curtail what were already modest plans. In December 1967, Redmond proposed a plan to bus five thousand black and white students between the South Shore and Austin areas.[91] After white protests, this two-way plan was discarded in favor of a one-way plan involving just over one thousand black students. State senator Richard Newhouse noted the disproportionate attention "busing" received relative to the number of students set to be bused for school desegregation: "The great cloud of smoke rising from the school busing proposal has obscured the fire of the real issue. School busing is a supposed answer to federal charges that Chicago operates segregated and unequal schools. But the plan for busing—despite the furious debate over it—applies to only 1,035 children, fewer than one per cent of the black children in the city's schools."[92] Congressman Roman Pucinski interpreted these numbers differently. "Mr. Redmond's plan initially calls for busing only 1,035 pupils, but it says in his report that 75 per cent of the pupils in the city's schools may be bused in the not too distant future," Pucinski told a crowd of eight hundred people gathered at an "antibusing" meeting at Norwood Park Elementary School. "That means busing 450,000 children."[93]

Fears about "busing" continued to develop at a series of rallies and meetings with school officials in early 1968. The school board took the desires of white "antibusing" parents into account in rejecting Redmond's plan to bus 1,035 black students to white schools.[94] The *Defender* saw the failure of the plan as yet another example of how school officials prioritized white parents' demands: "By capitulating to a howling mob of racists and political mountebanks, the Chicago Board of Education shows that it has neither the courage of its convictions nor a sense of the direction in which the public schools should go. Negro parents here are choking with bitter resentment over the Chicago Board of Education's indefensible resolution. Even the Little Rock Board of Education had more gumption."[95]

The "busing" plan that the school board eventually implemented, in March 1968, called for one-way "busing" of only 573 black students. Of these eligible students, only 249 participated on the first day.[96] Redmond said he could understand why black parents in the west-side Austin neighborhood, who had lobbied to have students bused out of overcrowded schools, would have soured on the plan. "How would I feel—how would anyone feel—after all the weeks of oratory and threats?" Redmond said. "I am encouraged that there are this many."[97] With police escorts, the buses carried black students to eight white elementary schools, where the young students encountered reminders that to many in the neighborhood they were unwelcome. "They can't get into our neighborhoods, so they are trying to ruin them for us," one heckler shouted. Another yelled, "They ran me out of two neighborhoods already, and I'm not going to let them run me out of here."[98] At another school, two white mothers were arrested for throwing eggs at buses carrying black students.[99] *ABC News* underscored these sentiments by emphasizing that "busing" was a story about white parents and white neighborhoods. "These people behind me are white parents," ABC's reporter said, "and today for the first time their white children are going to school with Negro children. Many of the people feel that what they witnessed today is the start of what they are sure will be the destruction of their neighborhoods."[100] Still, the *Defender* described the start of "busing" for school desegregation as a "smooth beginning." One of the black mothers who stood outside the new school to encourage and protect the arriving black students expressed resolve in the face of resistance. "The first day my child came home crying," she said. "The second day it wasn't so bad at all."[101]

. . .

"How long should it take an obvious truth to become a bona fide, recognized, undeniable fact?" Black journalist Vernon Jarrett raised this question in 1979 in response to a new HEW statement on Chicago's schools. Drawing on school board meeting minutes and including over one hundred pages of supporting evidence, the statement charged that since 1938 Chicago's school board had "created, maintained, and exacerbated . . . unlawfully segregated schools systemwide."[102] This charge of intentional segregation validated the complaints made by civil rights advocates over the previous twenty years. The 1979 HEW statement again faced a resistant school board and lack of federal support, especially after the Reagan administration reorganized HEW into Human Services and shifted what little civil rights enforcement there was to the Justice Department. In 1983, U.S. district judge Milton Shadur approved a consent decree between the Chicago school board and the Justice Department that called for majority-white schools to have at least 30 percent minority enrollment and for increased use of magnet schools to encourage voluntary integration, but did little to improve educational opportunities at the city's remaining all-black or majority-minority schools.[103]

Chicago stands out in the history of "busing" for school desegregation as the paramount example of the inability of federal authorities to uproot school segregation outside the South. Despite overwhelming evidence that Chicago school officials were not innocent bystanders to the creation and maintenance of racially differentiated schools, the federal government lacked the political will and resources to require school desegregation in the city. Civil rights activists, parents, and students were organized, creative, and persistent in their protests, but Benjamin Willis and Mayor Daley, a recalcitrant school leader and a powerful political boss, ultimately thwarted their efforts. Willis, as founder and president of the Research Council for the Great Cities Program for School Improvement, which brought together the leaders of the fourteen largest city public school systems, was the nation's most influential school superintendent in this era.[104] His near absolute resistance to civil rights, in the face of public protests and federal investigations, surely influenced what school officials in cities like Cleveland, Detroit, Los Angeles, and San Francisco felt was necessary or required to satisfy federal civil rights standards.

Boston school officials were among those who took notice of HEW's retreat in Chicago. Two days after HEW withheld funds from Chicago, and before Mayor Daley successfully pressed for them to be restored, the *Boston Globe* published an article titled "And Boston Begins to Sweat." "As a stunned Chicago learned it may lose $34 million in Federal school funds," the article began, "a government team continued to investigate possible discriminatory practices in Hub schools."[105] After getting drummed out of Chicago, the federal investigators trod very lightly in Boston, allowing "antibusing" resistance to school desegregation to expand and flourish in the Cradle of Liberty.

THREE

Boston before the "Busing Crisis"

BLACK EDUCATION ACTIVISM AND
OFFICIAL RESISTANCE IN THE CRADLE
OF LIBERTY

Jim Crow—must go! The School Committee—must go! De facto—must go! Mrs. Hicks—must go!

— Boston civil rights demonstrators protesting against
educational discrimination, 1963

I believe in the neighborhood school, and I'm opposed to busing. And if that's being anti-Negro, then I guess I'll have to live with it.

—LOUISE DAY HICKS, Boston School Committee member, 1967

SIX MONTHS BEFORE New York's white mothers staged a high-profile demonstration against school desegregation, more than six thousand black and white protestors marched through Boston's Roxbury neighborhood to protest against school segregation. The Boston march concluded at Sherwin School, built in 1870, five years after the end of the Civil War.[1] Pointing to the dilapidated ninety-three-year-old building, Thomas Atkins, executive secretary of the Boston branch of the NAACP, told the crowd, "This is where Negro kids go to school in Boston! What are you going to do about it!"[2] After observing a moment of silence for the four young girls killed a week earlier in the bombing at Sixteenth Street Baptist Church in Birmingham, Alabama, the crowd joined Susan Batson, the teenage daughter of Boston civil rights leader Ruth Batson, in a chant that clearly outlined the marchers' demands. "Jim Crow," Batson shouted. "Must go!" the crowd replied. "The School Committee"—"Must go!" "De facto"—"Must go!" "Mrs. Hicks"—"Must go!"[3] Like black people across the country, black Bostonians wanted to end the system of legal segregation known as "Jim Crow," and like protestors in other cities and towns outside the South, they wanted to label and defeat de facto segregation. Atkins made reference to the Boston School Committee's refusal to use the term *de facto segregation* when he told the crowd, "The School Committee is unable to decipher a Latin phrase. So we are here today to tell them that there is segregation, in fact, in Boston today."[4] Susan Batson and the crowd coupled calls to end "Jim Crow" and "De facto," which resonated with other national and regional campaigns, with local references to the Boston School Committee, the local officials responsible for maintaining segregated schools in Boston, and the committee's chairwoman, Louise Day Hicks. When Boston's "busing crisis" exploded in the mid-1970s, the media's focus on the violence in South Boston and white resistance to desegregation obscured years of black civil rights activism in Boston and the specificity of the changes black activists, parents, and students sought to bring about. The thousands of people who marched to Roxbury's Sherwin School on a cold afternoon in September 1963 knew that to desegregate Boston's schools they would have to defeat school officials who had risen to power on the promise that they would never let this happen.

In Boston, pressure from civil rights protests encouraged state legislators to pass the Racial Imbalance Act in 1965, making Massachusetts the first state in the nation to announce that schools with more than 50 percent non-white enrollment would have to be desegregated.[5] Louise Day Hicks and the Boston School Committee (BSC) staunchly opposed the law's implementation in Boston, claiming that it would require forced "busing" of white students, even though the law included a provision, added at the behest of white parents, stating that "no child can be moved without parents' permission."[6] The Racial Imbalance Act played out in Boston like a local version of the Civil Rights Act, promising on paper but with little impact on the city's schools. Opposition to the Racial Imbalance Act and "busing" helped Hicks emerge as a national icon of white resistance to civil rights. As in New York and Chicago, once the school desegregation story in Boston was framed around "busing" and "white backlash" in the late 1960s, it was easy to forget that black Bostonians had fought for years to secure equal education or that powerful local officials underwrote school segregation in the city.[7]

BOSTON BEFORE "BUSING"

The campaign against school desegregation in Boston would not have developed without the work of Ruth Batson. Born and raised in Roxbury, Batson recalled being exposed to politics at an early age by her Jamaican parents, who supported Marcus Garvey. "Every Sunday there were meetings held in a hall that was called Toussaint L'Ouverture Hall," Batson remembered,

> And I would have to go with [my mother] to these meetings. And at these meetings I heard Africa for the Africans at home and abroad. And we heard racial issues constantly being discussed. And so as I grew up I was not swayed as much as some people I knew by this business of Boston being such a wonderful place to grow up, being such a great city with the cradle of liberty. I knew, even though I wouldn't have expressed it this way, that there were flaws in the cradle of liberty. I know I used to go home and tell my mother things that the teacher said or did and she would go up to school and say something to them but it was an unusual upbringing that I had.[8]

As a student and later a parent of three girls, Batson gained personal knowledge of how Boston's public schools shortchanged black youth. Baton began working formally on school and political issues in the 1950s. She become active in the local NAACP and the state Democratic primary committee, and though she was not elected, she became the first black person to run for the BSC in nearly fifty years.[9]

Batson and a group of parents affiliated with the NAACP started investigating Boston's schools with the aim of forcing city and state officials to acknowledge and remedy the condition of predominately black schools. "When we would go to white schools," Batson recalled, "we'd see these lovely classrooms, with a small number of children in each class. The teachers were permanent. We'd see wonderful materials. When we'd go to our schools we would see overcrowded classrooms, children sitting out in the corridors and so forth. And so then we decided that where there were a large number of white students, that's where the care went. That's where the books went. That's where the money went."[10] By 1960, over 80 percent of black elementary school students attended majority-black schools. Most of these predominantly black schools, like the Sherwin School, were overcrowded, and the buildings needed repairs. Across Boston's public schools, spending per pupil averaged $340 for white students compared to only $240 for black students.[11] These reports failed to persuade state or local officials, as both the Massachusetts Commission Against Discrimination (MCAD) and the BSC continued to insist that racial segregation was not a problem in Boston.

Batson and other black parents and activists continued to press their case in the summer of 1963. On June 11, 1963, three hundred black Bostonians demonstrated outside city hall, while Batson and other NAACP members met with the BSC. "We make this charge: that there is segregation in fact in our Boston public school system," Batson told the BSC. "The injustices present in our school system hurt our pride, rob us of our dignity, and produce results which are injurious not only to our future but to those of the city, state and nation."[12] In a hearing room crowded with press, the BSC did not respond positively to these charges. "We made our presentation and everything broke loose," Batson recalled. "We were insulted. We were told ... our kids were stupid and this was why they didn't learn. We were completely rejected that night."[13] Paul Parks, a black engineer who chaired the Boston NAACP's Education Committee, described the disastrous meeting with the BSC as a decisive moment for the city's civil rights activists. "Up until then, it was the quality of the schools and fairness when it came to resources that we were after—not desegregation," Parks recalled. "In the beginning, we didn't care that much about whether our kids were going to schools with their kids or not. We just wanted to make sure our schools got the same things as they did." Mel King, a community organizer who ran unsuccessfully for the BSC three times in the 1960s before being elected as a state representative in 1972, remembered that by June 1963 "the energy that was now coming out of the black community became focused on desegregation."[14]

A week after being rejected by the BSC, civil rights advocates organized a "Stay Out for Freedom" protest, with nearly three thousand black junior- and senior-high-school students staying away from public school.[15] Organizers preferred *stay out* to *boycott* because students were staying away from public school to attend community-organized "Freedom Schools."[16] "I feel that the Stay Out for Freedom Day was a success," Batson told the *Boston Globe*. "It demonstrated to the Boston community that the Negro community is concerned and that they want action."[17]

The Boston School Committee was particularly resistant to the charge that school segregation existed in Boston. The BSC, an elected five-person committee, wielded enormous influence over the city's schools. Democrat Louise Day Hicks was initially elected as a moderate in 1961 but quickly took up opposition to school desegregation as her defining issue. The gulf between civil rights advocates and the BSC was evident in a second meeting in August 1963. After Batson raised the issue of "de facto segregation," Hicks replied, "The committee has decided and voted by a majority not to discuss the question of de facto segregation."[18] The meeting, scheduled for an hour, ended after only a few minutes with the BSC unwilling to have anyone use the phrase *de facto segregation* during the hearing. Batson told the *Globe,* "We're not quibbling about a word. It is not the word. It is the fact that it exists. Our whole quarrel is with their refusing to admit that the situation exists."[19] June Shagaloff, who attended the meeting from the NAACP national office, said after the meeting, "The Boston School Committee can't afford to bury its head in the sand. They can't go on pretending there is no segregation in Boston schools."[20] Interviewed years later, Batson noted how the BSC members benefited from digging in their heels and resisting school desegregation. With school desegregation, Batson argued, "we found out that we had brought to them a wonderful political issue, and that this was an issue that was going to give their political careers stability for a long time to come."[21] As civil rights pressure continued through the fall of 1963, Hicks and the BSC only grew stronger in their opposition to school desegregation. When Hicks received the most votes in the November 1963 Boston School Committee election, she saw the election as a referendum on school desegregation. "The people of Boston have given their answer to the de facto segregation question," Hicks opined.[22]

Having failed to oust Hicks or elect someone to BSC who would support school desegregation, the black community organized a second "Stay Out for Freedom" on February 26, 1964. The "stay out" kept more than twenty thousand students (over 20 percent of the city's public school students) out of school and connected Boston to similar school boycotts that had taken place earlier in the month in New York and Chicago. The "stay out" got the attention of Massachusetts governor Endicott Peabody, who the next day assembled a committee led by state commissioner of education Owen Kiernan to examine discrimination in the state's schools. The Kiernan Commission released their report, "Because It Is Right—Educationally," in April 1965. It found that the majority of nonwhite children in the state attended predominantly nonwhite schools and that most white children attended schools that were either all white or had only a handful of minority students. "It is imperative that we begin to end this harmful system of separation," the committee asserted. "The means are at hand. Each day of delay is a day of damage to the children of our Commonwealth."[23] While the report did not find the BSC or other local school committees to blame for school segregation, the Kiernan Commission offered official support for the black community's critiques of Boston's schools.

Coupled with the Kiernan Commission's findings, black protests of school conditions encouraged Massachusetts's legislators to pass the Racial

Imbalance Act on August 18, 1965. The Racial Imbalance Act called for an annual racial census of public schools and for local school boards to take steps to ensure that no school's nonwhite enrollment exceeded 50 percent.[24] "Today we write another page in the history of Massachusetts' leadership in education with the signing of this bill guaranteeing truly equal educational opportunity to all our children," Governor John Volpe said as he signed the legislation. "Our signing of this bill affirms our commitment to strike at the causes of prejudice."[25] In theory, the Racial Imbalance Act could have closed the loophole in the Civil Rights Act of 1964 that excluded "racially imbalanced" northern schools from the definition of desegregation. In practice, it became a touchstone for both foes and supporters of school desegregation, with white parents and politicians railing against "busing" and black parents organizing mass tests of the city's open enrollment policy. With these positions clashing at the start of school in 1965, the *Globe* warned that "the Boston school crisis is threatening to become a local Viet Nam—limited but with broad consequences, difficult to solve and indefinite in length."[26]

Led by Hicks, the BSC repeatedly voiced its opposition to the state's Racial Imbalance Act and worked to limit meaningful school desegregation efforts. Of the dozens of suggestions made by the state committee that studied remedies to school segregation, Hicks seized on the proposed cross-"busing" of five thousand students to reduce racial imbalance.[27] "Mrs. Hicks' temerity is totally insulting," said Brandeis professor Lawrence Fuchs, who worked on Kiernan Commission. "She doesn't want to discuss the recommendation, she simply seized on the [bus] transfers as one issue."[28] Hicks's colleague Joseph Lee made the BSC's fixation on "busing" clear: "White children do not want to be transported into schools with a large proportion of backward pupils from unprospering Negro families who will slow down their education. White children do not want large numbers of backward pupils from unprospering Negro families shipped into their present mainly white schools either."[29] Hicks remained unconcerned with charges that opposition to school desegregation was racist. "I believe in the neighborhood school, and I'm opposed to busing," she said. "And if that's being anti-Negro, then I guess I'll have to live with it."[30]

In August 1965, days before Governor Volpe signed the Racial Imbalance Act, Hicks led the Boston School Committee in a 3–2 vote against "any further busing of children in any form for any reason under any conditions."[31] Paul Parks called the vote "the committee's first overt act of containment of Negro children."[32] The vote was primarily designed to signal BSC's opposition to "busing," since the Racial Imbalance Act, in deference to concerns of white parents, already included a provision against "forced busing" ("No school committee ... shall be required ... to transport any pupil to any school ... outside the school district established for his neighborhood, if the parent or guardian of such pupil files written objection thereto with such school committee").[33] Hicks viewed the overwhelming support she received in the school board primary election in September 1965 as a vindication of her position. "I feel the people of Boston have spoken," Hicks declared. "They have endorsed the policies of the school committee majority—my policies. Education, not transportation, is the answer to the question of imbalance in Boston schools."[34]

By focusing on "busing" rather than school desegregation, Hicks and the BSC seized on an issue that made it possible to oppose school integration without having to explicitly support segregated schools. And this "busing" frame resonated in national media. Under the heading "Boston's Busing Battle," a *Time* magazine article opened with a quote from Hicks: "I believe that little children should go to school in their own neighborhoods with the children with whom they play—it's as simple as that."[35] *Look* magazine described how "'busing' has become a brand-new, six-letter, dirty word" that "sends edgy white parents into the street or out to the suburbs."[36] Hicks's mayoral campaign in 1967, where she lost to Kevin White by only 12,000 votes, drew further coverage from national news media. In a cover story titled "Backlash in Boston—and Across the U.S.," *Newsweek* featured Hicks's mayoral campaign as a news peg for white resistance to civil rights in cities from Cincinnati to San Diego.[37] In an *ABC News* interview, Hicks responded to a question about whether her stand on "neighborhood schools" meant she was bigoted. "I have challenged civil rights leaders, or anyone who has ever made this statement that I am bigoted, to prove it," Hicks said. "No statement of mine has ever been anti-Negro.... In fact, I'll put my record of achievement for the Negro children of this city against the record of anyone in the city of Boston."[38] Similar to interviews with "antibusing" parents in New York and Chicago, this television reporter asked no follow-up questions on the school subject and allowed Hicks to define her resistance to school desegregation as not being about race.

Throughout the battles over "busing," the news media gave northern politicians and parents the freedom to define the issue of school desegregation in ways that let them off the hook. *ABC News'* segment on Hicks would have appeared very different if they had interviewed Hicks's black and white critics in Boston. Ellen Jackson, who founded a voluntary "busing" program for black students, described Hicks as a "racial bigot who used the race issue to further her political aims."[39] Reverend Jack Mendelsohn, an activist Unitarian Universalist minister, told his congregation, "Mrs. Hicks is a sick person. She must be. Only a sick person would deliberately build a political career by exploiting the primitive prejudices of the majority white community, and goading the deepening frustrations of the minority Negro community. Thus has she become a major force pushing this city toward a stark human tragedy of racial conflict."[40] More important than these criticisms and charges that Hicks was prejudiced, Judge Arthur Garrity's 1974 ruling in *Morgan v. Hennigan* found that Hicks and her fellow Boston School Committee members "took many actions in their official capacities with the purpose and intent to segregate the Boston public schools and that such actions caused current conditions of segregation in the Boston public schools."[41] News media gave Hicks national attention but failed to look into the local school conditions and policies that made her so controversial.

While television and magazines allowed Hicks to define the issue of school desegregation in ways that cast her in a favorable light, the news media also frequently treated Hicks and South Boston condescendingly. *Newsweek* described a South Boston neighborhood meeting as being like the lowbrow characters in the "Moon Mullins" comic strip.[42] Journalists downplayed Hicks's education, class status, and political power. While she was often associated with working-class South Boston, Hicks was a lawyer, and her father was a judge, which helped give her name recognition when she entered politics. And while national media frequently cast her as a symbol of white working-class resistance, as BSC chair her power over Boston's schools and the terms of the school desegregation debate was never merely symbolic. "It was Mrs. Hicks who kept talking against busing children when the NAACP hadn't even proposed busing," Robert Levey wrote in the *Globe* in 1965. "And it was she who gaveled the last meeting with Negro leaders to a close in something short of three minutes when the speaker mentioned the words, de facto segregation—just mentioned the words."[43] Thomas Atkins, who was elected to the Boston City Council in 1967 and served as Boston NAACP president in the mid-1970s, put it more bluntly: "Louise Day Hicks ran for years on the slogan, 'You know where I stand.' We knew where she stood. She was trying to stand on our neck."[44] Seeing Hicks as a symbol of "white backlash" downplayed the fact that she led a committee which for years had prioritized the preferences and expectations of white parents over the rights of black students. As the *Globe* noted when the BSC submitted a plan for token compliance with the Racial Imbalance Act, "Compliance with the attitude of white Bostonians is greater than compliance with the law."[45]

Surveying the impact of the Racial Imbalance Act after three years, *Globe* columnist Robert Levey wrote, "The course of the racial imbalance issue in Boston has been glowing on paper and laughable in practice. The state legislature drafted the first racial imbalance law in the nation, and Boston school officials came up with a do-nothing imbalance plan that eventually was accepted by the State Board of Education in a mood that was more conciliatory than courageous."[46] Neil Sullivan, who served as Massachusetts commissioner of education after leading successful desegregation efforts in Berkeley (California) and Prince George's County (Maryland), argued that the Boston School Committee "[has] used every devious means at their disposal to avoid integration of the schools. . . . [T]hey could integrate the schools in two months if they wished and use fewer buses than they now use in their massive busing program to avoid integration."[47]

The BSC's resistance to "busing" and token compliance with the Racial Imbalance Act meant that Boston's black students continued to attend overcrowded schools. Overcrowding led many black schools to run double sessions, where students were in class 25 percent fewer minutes per day.[48] School overcrowding, as well as concerns about aging school buildings, limited curricular options, high percentages of temporary teachers, and racism in textbooks and teacher-student interactions, led black parents to organize mass tests of the city's open enrollment policy. Boston had started an open enrollment policy in 1961 that allowed students to transfer to schools with open seats, but like southern "freedom of choice" plans, Boston's open enrollment policy had served primarily to allow school officials to avoid more substantial desegregation policies. The city's open enrollment policy also placed enormous demands on parents, who needed to research school openings and provide their own transportation. Nevertheless, some black parents successfully used open enrollment to seek better education opportunities for their children.

OPERATION EXODUS

In 1965, black parents led by Ellen Jackson organized a large-scale test of the open enrollment policy called Operation Exodus, to transport black students from Roxbury and North Dorchester to schools outside their neighborhoods with open seats and more resources. While it involved fewer than one thousand of the twenty thousand black students in Boston, Operation Exodus demonstrated the resolve of black parents and students to secure quality education. Like Ruth Batson, Jackson was raised in Roxbury. "I like Roxbury and I don't want to move," Jackson said. "I call it 'the gold mine.' But I want to see it fixed up; we pay taxes and we should get things."[49] In speeches to gather community support for Operation Exodus, Jackson called on other middle-class African Americans to not turn "their backs on the plight of their less fortunate brothers and sisters."[50] Jackson, like Batson, was a parent activist with five children enrolled or soon to be enrolled in Boston schools. Before founding Operation Exodus, Jackson had been a parent organizer with the Northern Student Movement, a civil rights group that organized tutoring programs in cities of the Northeast.[51] Speaking at the Roxbury YMCA in 1966, Jackson told the crowd,

> I come to you today, not as an expert on education, not as a professional woman, not as a civil rights worker. I come to you as a life-long resident of our community, a mother and a housewife. . . . Operation Exodus was founded and built and is now being run by parents like myself. By parents whose basic concern is for their children. It is run by fathers who work two jobs . . . but somehow manage to find time on weekends or evenings to organize a recreation program now serving 400 children in the neighborhood; and by mothers who open the Exodus office at 7 A.M., work shifts during the day, and close it at 5 P.M. to rush home and prepare dinner for their children; then return to the office two or three evenings every week to meet and talk with other parents and to seek ways of raising money.[52]

While this description of "parents whose basic concern is for their children" could also be applied to scores of "antibusing" mother activists, Jackson made it clear that Operation Exodus grew out of the specific efforts, experiences, and needs of black parents and students in Roxbury and prioritized black participation and leadership. Speaking about black power in West Newton, Jackson told her mostly white audience that Operation Exodus was a "self help organization whose staff is mostly black." For the whites in the group "to stay and work effectively with Exodus," Jackson continued, "they must be willing to follow the orders of their black colleagues. . . . [U]nlike the NAACP and the Urban League, we have never had any problem with white domination."[53] In addition to the "busing" program, Operation Exodus included tutorial and cultural arts programs for students, as well as a cultural revival program that brought national leaders such as Fannie Lou Hamer of the Mississippi Freedom Democratic Party, Charles Sims of the Deacons for

Defense and Justice, Stokely Carmichael of Student Nonviolent Coordinating Committee, and Nation of Islam leader Louis X to speak in Boston.[54]

Operation Exodus garnered attention from civil rights activists and news media outside Boston. Speaking before Exodus parents, James Farmer, national director of the Congress of Racial Equality (CORE), said, "Project Exodus has given us a great deal of hope and expectation across the country—the eyes of the nation are focused on Roxbury.... [T]he [Exodus] buses represent for us the freedom ride of 1965, and you are carrying the banner for civil rights in the North."[55] The *New York Times* and *Chicago Tribune* cast Operation Exodus in a less favorable light, describing the project as an "invasion" of white schools.[56]

NBC's *Frank McGee Report,* a weekend television news program, profiled Operation Exodus in 1967. McGee's introduction to the segment on Operation Exodus noted the parallel development of white opposition to "busing" and school integration:

> This is Operation Exodus. It takes many busloads of children out of Roxbury every school day. The passengers are all Negroes, nearly 900 boys and girls taken out of their neighborhoods to twenty-five predominately white schools spread out over the rest of Boston. Now that busing has become so intertwined with integration, it's taken on new meaning. To some people, especially Negro parents, busing is a hopeful idea, an alternative to crowded, inferior, segregated schools. To others, especially white parents, it is a dirty word that threatens someday to take their own children away, maybe to the same schools that Negroes are running away from.[57]

While this segment focused on Operation Exodus, it presented black community initiatives to address school segregation in Boston as equivalent to white resistance to desegregation. Like the point-counterpoint structure that framed the New York school desegregation story as a disagreement between Parents and Taxpayers' leader Rosemary Gunning and school boycott leader Reverend Milton Galamison, the *Frank McGee Report* cut between Ellen Jackson and Hicks or unidentified white parents who opposed "busing." The resulting sound bites were successful at highlighting points of disagreement:

> HICKS: I feel that busing has no advantage educationally for our little children. It will take them far from their neighborhoods and will bring them into very strange neighborhoods.
>
> WHITE MOTHER 1: If I had to bus my child, I'd keep her home.... I'll go to court, I'll fight it. I will not let her be bused out of South Boston or anywhere.

JACKSON: Unfortunately, the resistance to busing is not for educational purposes. It's based on race prejudice. What I mean by that is that most white parents refuse to bus their children because of the fact that they are prejudiced, period.

WHITE MOTHER 2: There's no racial prejudice here. We have colored all over South Boston.

JACKSON: Boston basically is a prejudiced city, strange as it may seem to many people. And it's not only apparent in the educational system, but it's apparent in housing, it's apparent in employment.[58]

While the segment presents Jackson as a serious political voice and she is given the last word, the point-counterpoint exchange is framed, as Hicks and her allies preferred, in terms of "busing" rather than desegregation or the educational rights of black children.

The exchange presents the differing opinions as equally valid, without regard for the official statistics on school segregation in Boston or the civil rights protests over the prior five years that had forced Boston's schools into the national spotlight. Jackson and her fellow black parents in Operation Exodus decided to bus students as a last resort, only after years of intransigence by the Boston School Committee. "I think I can safely say that the major goal of Operation Exodus has never been to integrate the public schools," Jackson said in 1966.

> Our goal has been to find for our children the best educational situations possible. A year ago, when the Boston School Committee announced three schools in North Dorchester would have to go on double sessions, our reaction was to get our children out of those schools so they would no longer be overcrowded. If we had been able to find adequate seating in schools near where we lived, we would gladly have done so. But because the School Committee has not built new schools in our community, there were no vacant seats nearby. We had to bus.[59]

In contrast to seeing Operation Exodus as the culmination of years of frustration and organizing by black Bostonians, NBC pegged it to the news hook of "busing." People like Ellen Jackson and Louise Day Hicks, NBC suggested, simply disagree over "busing." This lack of attention to how "busing" had emerged as an issue in Boston allowed the television producers and viewers to view the story as unexpected. "It may come as a surprise to most people to hear that Boston, the cradle of liberty, could be accused of prejudice," Frank McGee noted. This sense of surprise at racial prejudice and civil rights

FIGURES 12 AND 13. When NBC profiled Operation Exodus, led by Ellen Jackson, in 1967, the segment was framed in terms of "busing" rather than the educational rights of black children. Politician Louise Day Hicks popularized the term *busing* as a way to describe and oppose school desegregation efforts. *Frank McGee Report,* NBC, January 22, 1967.

in Boston (and the North more broadly) would continue throughout Boston's "busing crisis" in the mid-1970s.

Operation Exodus, which ran for four years, required tremendous work and fund-raising by black parents, who described being "exhausted, physically and mentally" by the program's demands.[60] "At the time we regarded our operation as a temporary measure to relieve the distressing conditions existing in our local schools," commented Jackson at a press conference announcing the end of the Exodus bus transfers in 1969. "We also hoped by our voluntary action to dramatize the School Committee's responsibility to bus children to less crowded schools elsewhere in the city."[61] In 1966, a year after Operation Exodus started, the Metropolitan Council for Educational Opportunity (METCO) "busing" program began. METCO, developed from a plan by MIT professor Leon Trilling, earned federal, state, and foundation grants to conduct a voluntary one-way "busing" program that brought black students from Boston to predominately white schools in the suburbs. Ruth Batson was an early METCO supporter and served as the program's director in the late 1960s. METCO expanded from 220 students in the first year to over two thousand students in the mid-1970s, but remained open to only a small percentage of Boston's black students. Suburban communities like Concord, Lincoln, and Lexington welcomed a small number of black students from Boston city schools through the METCO program but opposed affordable housing programs, two-way "busing" (that is, sending suburban students to Boston schools and vice versa), and other policies that would have threatened their white suburban privilege.[62] While the BSC opposed Operation Exodus and METCO, it still pointed to the students transferred by the programs as evidence that Boston school officials were taking steps to address school segregation.[63] "Although we have had little or no cooperation and no financial assistance whatsoever from any public source—least of all the Boston School Committee," Jackson stated, "that Committee has nonetheless blatantly pointed to the Exodus busing program to substantiate their claim that they have acted to correct racial imbalance in Boston Schools, thereby freeing state funds which were withheld until the Committee demonstrated compliance with the Racial Imbalance Law."[64]

. . .

Boston's school desegregation battles in the 1960s showed that school officials could openly defy state laws and secure local power and national attention in the process. When Hicks launched a drive to repeal the Racial Imbalance Act, she delivered a petition to state Attorney General Elliot Richardson surrounded by reporters and photographers, saying she was "filing the petition to bring the racial imbalance question before 'the highest court of public opinion, the people.'"[65] Hicks's opposition to school desegregation drove her political career for over a decade and led her to the U.S. House of Representatives. By framing this resistance to school desegregation around "busing," Hicks and other school officials further established "busing" as the totality of the school desegregation story. And by opposing school desegregation throughout the 1960s, Hicks and her fellow BSC members postponed dealing with the structural problems that emerged in the mid-1970s Boston "busing crisis."

While New York, Chicago, and Boston were the most important sites of conflict over "busing" for school desegregation in the 1960s, "busing" emerged as a hotly contested issue in several other cities in this decade. Like Boston's METCO program, at least seven other metropolitan areas had one-way city-to-suburb "busing" programs by the mid-1960s, including Hartford, Newark, New Haven, Rochester, Springfield, Washington, DC, and Waterbury. Most of these programs were primarily designed to provide academic enrichment to small numbers of black students and to address overcrowding in city schools, not to desegregate city and suburban schools.[66] In Milwaukee, civil rights advocates protested against "intact busing," a practice in which classrooms of black students were bused from overcrowded black schools to white schools, where they remained in separate, segregated classrooms. Activists carrying signs reading "Stop Bussing for Segregation" blocked school buses.[67] In Saint Louis, the Committee for Parents of Transported pupils staged similar protests in response to "intact busing." Two thousand black and white demonstrators crowded the streets of the city's downtown during rush hour in June 1963 to call for bused black students to be integrated into activities at the receiving white schools.[68] In the *Cleveland Call and Post,* columnist Al Sweeney reported that black students bused to relieve overcrowding encountered similar issues in Cleveland. "The bussed pupils were treated like lepers in the so-called receiving schools," Sweeney wrote. "The were not permitted to use the toilet facilities, they were denied recess, they [were] kept away from the play areas during their lunch period and their lunch periods were separate from those of the other youngsters in the school."[69]

By the end of the 1960s, every American who watched television news or read a newspaper would have seen dozens of stories regarding "busing" for school desegregation, even though the issue directly affected only a small fraction of America's students. This media attention and the strong emotions "busing" provoked made the issue appealing to politicians from across party and regional lines. These politicians reflected and fed their constituents' fears and cemented "busing" as the common-sense way to describe, debate, and oppose school desegregation.

FOUR

Standing against "Busing"

BIPARTISAN AND NATIONAL POLITICAL
OPPOSITION TO SCHOOL DESEGREGATION

If it was wrong in 1954 to assign a black child to a particular
school on the basis of race, it is just as wrong to do the same thing
to other children in 1972. This is "Jim Crowism" in reverse.

—U.S. REPRESENTATIVE NORMAN LENT, *1972*

SPEAKING IN NEW YORK'S Madison Square Garden in late October
1964, Republican presidential nominee Barry Goldwater told the crowd, "If
you ever hear me quoted as promising to make you free by forcibly busing
your children from your chosen neighborhood school to some other one just
to meet an arbitrary racial quota—look again because somebody is kidding
you!" To cheers and shouts of encouragement from the boisterous audience,
Goldwater continued, "I believe in our system of neighborhood schools, and
I want to see them preserved and improved. I don't want to see them destroyed
or be sacrificed by a futile exercise in sociology which will accomplish nothing—but lose much."[1] Goldwater's speech drew a twenty-eight-minute ovation from the crowd of over eighteen thousand, while another five thousand
people listened to the speech over loudspeakers outside the arena.[2]
Goldwater's message resonated in New York City, where "busing" had been
debated and feared for almost a decade and where thousands of white parents
had organized as Parents and Taxpayers (PAT) in resistance to the school
board's desegregation plans. Several signs in the audience read, "PAT Backs
Barry." *New York Amsterdam News* journalist and executive editor James
Booker covered the rally for the city's leading black newspaper and described
what it was like to be "one dark spot of high visibility in a prejudiced gutter
of screaming Goldwater supporters at Madison Square Garden." "As I slowly
began marching back up the steps [to the upper press row]," Booker said, "the
eyes began to stare at you throughout the crowd. The same kind I got from
Southern cops when I have covered racial incidents there." When Goldwater

hit "busing," Booker continued, "bedlam almost broke out . . . and Goldwater knew he had hit their soft spot."[3]

Goldwater's attack on "busing" in Madison Square Garden expanded on a speech he had made at a GOP fund-raiser at the Conrad Hilton Hotel in Chicago earlier that month. In the Chicago speech, penned by Goldwater speechwriter Henry Jaffa and Phoenix attorney (and future Supreme Court chief justice) William Rehnquist, Goldwater told the 2,500 supporters, "To me it is wrong to take some children out of some of the schools they normally would attend and bus them to others just to get a mixture of ethnic and racial groups that somebody thinks is desirable. This forced integration is just as wrong as forced segregation. It has been well said that the Constitution is colorblind. And so it is just as wrong to compel children to attend certain schools for the sake of so-called integration as for the sake of segregation."[4] While Goldwater was a vocal opponent of the 1964 Civil Rights Act, the Chicago and New York speeches, delivered in the last month of the campaign, were his most explicit statements on racial issues as a presidential candidate. With President Lyndon Johnson holding a significant lead in the campaign's final days, the Goldwater campaign paid to broadcast the video of the Madison Square Garden speech over a nationwide CBS television hookup, bringing Goldwater's "busing" critique to hundreds of thousands of viewers.[5]

Resistance to "busing" was one of the few issues on which Goldwater and Democrats found common ground. President John Kennedy, replying to a question in September 1963 about whether he thought "as a parent" it was "right to wrench children away from their neighborhood family area and cart them off to strange faraway schools to force racial balance," cautiously said, "In the final analysis [this] must be decided by the local school board. This is a local question. If you're asking me my opinion—faraway strange places and all the rest—I would not agree with it."[6] Speaking in Buffalo, New York, in September 1964 as a senatorial candidate, Robert F. Kennedy stated his opposition to "long-distance busing" and echoed his late brother's sentiments regarding local control: "My feeling is strongly in favor of local control over education. The school boards have had a difficult time dealing with this problem, and I think they deserve our gratitude."[7] James Donovan, president of the board of education in New York City, replied that Kennedy must "be talking about programs in other cities. In the program for New York there is no long-distance busing involved."[8] Hubert Humphrey, the Democratic vice presidential candidate who championed the Civil Rights Act, also spoke out against "long-distance" "busing" in September 1964. Replying to a question about the school boycott in New York against "busing," Humphrey said, "So that that the record will be straight, the Civil Rights Act of 1964 does not ask for busing of students; in fact, to the contrary. There is a proviso in the act saying that the act shall not be applied for the purpose of busing students from one district to another.... My own personal view is that we should improve the quality of our neighborhoods. I personally do not feel that we ought to be giving students long-distance rides at the expense of families and students."[9] While Democrats expressed their concerns in more measured tones than Goldwater or George Wallace, they were no more likely to publicly endorse "busing" for school desegregation. And Democratic legislators, joined by moderate Republicans like New York's Jacob Javits and Ohio's William McCulloch, played a more important role than Goldwater or Wallace in ensuring that the Civil Rights Act included an "antibusing" amendment to protect "racially imbalanced" school districts outside the South.

This bipartisan and interregional political opposition to "busing" and school desegregation expanded over the next decade. Democratic and Republican members of Congress from every region looked for legislative ways to limit or stop "busing." Opposition to "busing" created unusual political alliances that found Democrats who had previously supported civil rights legislation, like Edith Green (Oregon) and James O'Hara (Michigan), on the same side of the issue with conservative Republicans like John Ashbrook (Ohio) and Norman Lent (New York), as well as southern segregationists like John Stennis (Mississippi) and Jamie Whitten (Mississippi). At the state level, several governors voiced opposition to "busing." Most notably, Florida governor Claude Kirk protested court-ordered "busing" by suspending a local school board in Manatee County (Bradenton, Florida) and appointing himself school superintendent. For politicians who aspired to the national stage, "busing" offered a recognizable issue on which to take a stand, and in his school standoff Kirk appealed not only to Florida voters but also to television viewers in cities like Nashville, Saint Louis, and Seattle, many of whom wrote to convey their support.

While staking out "antibusing" positions did not always lead to political success (much of the proposed "antibusing" legislation failed to pass or was watered down by subcommittees, and Kirk lost the 1970 gubernatorial election to Reubin Askew, who supported "busing"), the widespread opposition to "busing" by elected officials sowed confusion and led many Americans to believe that school desegregation was moving much faster than it actually was. Politicians helped make "busing" appear to be a "massive" issue, even though only a small percentage of students were ever bused for school desegregation. Bipartisan and interregional opposition to "busing" also helped justify resistance to school desegregation across the country and established a common-sense view that, through "busing," the rights of parents and homeowners were being violated by activist judges and federal bureaucrats. Finally, in their carefully worded opposition to "busing," northern Democrats and moderate Republicans enforced the distinction between unconstitutional de jure segregation and innocent de facto segregation, even as courts revealed this distinction to be largely illusory. Like Humphrey, New York senator Jacob Javits repeatedly reminded his colleagues that the Civil Rights Act did not allow "busing" to correct "racial imbalance" and that de facto segregation was not against the law. "We have no right to deal with anything that does not break the law," he argued.[10] The chorus of politicians who opposed "busing" overwhelmed the voices of public officials, parents, and scholars who urged compliance with school desegregation law or made it clear that northern school segregation was not the result of natural market forces. Reflecting and feeding their constituents' fears of school desegregation, politicians helped make "busing" into a recognizable issue that was easily vilified.

ANTI-HEW PROVISIONS

The controversy over the Department of Health, Education, and Welfare's (HEW) brief withholding of federal funds from Chicago was still fresh in the minds of members of Congress when President Johnson introduced his Model Cities legislation in early 1966. Legislators introduced measures to prevent HEW from acting against "racial imbalance" in the North and to make it more difficult for the agency to withhold funds in the South. The goal of these anti-HEW measures was to keep federal authorities away from northern cities like Chicago and to ensure that HEW could not require "busing" for "racial balance" in any part of the country.

In the debates over the Model Cities legislation, Democratic congressman Abraham Multer of Brooklyn proposed an "antibusing" amendment that was included in the final Demonstration Cities and Metropolitan Development Act of 1966. Multer's amendment proposed that "nothing in this section shall authorize the Secretary [of Housing and Urban Development] to require . . . the adoption by any community of a program to achieve a racial balance or to eliminate racial imbalance within school districts within the metropolitanwide area."[11] A week earlier, Democratic congressman James O'Hara, who represented metropolitan Detroit, offered a successful amendment to the Elementary and Secondary Education Act specifying that HEW could not "require the assignment or transportation of students or teachers in order to overcome racial imbalance."[12] "I believe that is about as clear as we can make it," O'Hara told his colleagues. "Title VI of the Civil Rights Act deals with segregation and in no way deals with any so-called racial imbalance. It deals with racial discrimination and racial segregation. It gives no warrant or authority to deal with so-called racial imbalance."[13] In the ensuing discussion, Minnesota Republican Albert Quie asked O'Hara to clarify what the amendment would limit: "So what we would prohibit here, then, is they would be prohibited from busing from one school to another in order to achieve racial balance in another school which is a neighborhood school." "That is correct," O'Hara replied.[14] Bronx congressman Paul Fino worried that neither Multer's nor O'Hara's amendments were clear enough about limiting "busing," and proposed another amendment (ultimately unsuccessful) so "that there is no question in anyone's mind that it is strictly an antibusing amendment."[15] Fino also warned his colleague that the Model Cities legislation would provide "supplemental grants to school districts to eliminate neighborhood schools and create metropolitanwide school districts."[16]

These issues reemerged in June 1968, when Congress considered the annual HEW appropriations bill. In an attempt to prevent HEW from upsetting southern "freedom of choice" plans that nominally complied with *Brown* but resulted in little if any actual school desegregation, Mississippi congressman Jamie Whitten introduced an amendment that stated, "No part of the funds contained in this Act, may be used to force busing of students, abolishment of any school, or to force any student attending any elementary or secondary school to attend a particular school against the choice of his or her parents or parent." Whitten also proposed that the "force[d] busing of students" could not be used as a requirement to "obtain Federal funds otherwise available to any State, school district, or school." These amendments, Whitten argued, "would prohibit HEW from requiring busing indirectly, by abolishing schools or forcing students to change schools against the will of their parents."[17] After the House passed the HEW appropriations bill, the Senate added the phrase "in order to overcome racial imbalance" to the Whitten amendments. While this language weakened the Whitten amendments and ensured that HEW could still pursue cases of de jure segregation, it further cemented the distinction between de jure segregation and racial imbalance. The Senate's adoption of Whitten's proposed language also established a pattern for future HEW appropriations bills, where the Whitten amendments were regularly included.

The Senate also went beyond the Whitten amendments in calling for HEW to enforce its guidelines uniformly across the country. The Senate-approved HEW appropriations language called for HEW to "assign as many persons to the investigation and compliance activities of Title VI of the Civil Rights Act of 1964 ... in the other States as are assigned to the seventeen Southern and border States to assure that this law is administered and enforced on a national basis."[18] If the Senate's addition of "racial imbalance" weakened the Whitten amendments, Whitten saw the Senate's move toward national enforcement of HEW guidelines as a positive step that would increase resistance to school desegregation nationally. "Freedom of choice is one thing; but forcing attendance at a particular school against the wishes of the parent is something else," Whitten told his colleagues. "We all know the Federal Government, including the Attorney General, the Department of Education and the Federal courts are not going to carry out the Senate directive in the rest of the country. ... Federal judges are going to learn that the American people are tired of being run over by the Department of Education and the Federal courts, and the people can stop it."[19]

Whitten's fellow Mississippian, Senator John Stennis, made the call for a uniform national policy on school desegregation the centerpiece of his effort to slow school desegregation in 1969 and 1970. In the summer of 1969, Stennis sent Senate Appropriations Committee investigators to talk with school administrators and gather statistics on school segregation in cities in the North and West. Stennis also tasked a staffer with researching the legislative history of Title IV of the 1964 Civil Rights Act, focusing on the "racial imbalance" language.[20] Stennis railed against the hypocrisy of his northern colleagues in the 1964 Civil Rights Act debate, and he reprised many of these points in a series of speeches at the end of 1969, in which he highlighted how the federal government ignored segregation in northern schools. "Let me state what has happened outside the South, very briefly, about this busing," Stennis said. "Look to New York ... what have they done about busing? I say to New York, 'You can integrate those schools in Harlem, if you really want to.' The Federal Government can do it, or the State government can do it. Just put enough manpower and womanpower in there to do it, haul those children out to the areas where the white schools are, and bring a like number of the white students in, and you will have them integrated." Stennis used this hypothetical "busing" plan to desegregate New York's schools to set up his next point. "But what has New York done about it? Have they tried? No. They passed a law this year—on May 2, 1969—a State law which prohibited busing of children on account of racial imbalance. . . . They absolutely prohibited busing." Moments later, Stennis turned his attention from the nation's biggest city to the second largest. "What happened in Chicago, in the great State of Illinois?" Stennis asked. "Three or four years ago, someone in HEW sent them some kind of communication about integrating their schools. . . . But here came a message back from Mayor Daly [sic]. As I remember, he came to Washington about it. . . . Anyway, they swept it under the rug somewhere, I do not know where, and that is the last that has been heard of that case."[21] Stennis made these points over and over again on the floor of the Senate before introducing an amendment in February 1970 calling for a nationally uniform policy on school desegregation.

With his litany of northern school segregation statistics and his call for a single national policy, Stennis believed, like Whitten and other southern politicians, that increased federal investigations and enforcement of school desegregation in the North would lead more white parents to protest, which would thwart school desegregation nationally. "Mothers who live outside the South . . . will be knowing a whole lot more about this in 1972 than they know now," Stennis predicated.[22] The Stennis amendment received unexpected support from Connecticut Democratic senator Abraham Ribicoff, who challenged his liberal colleagues to move proactively to address school segregation in the North. "The North is guilty of monumental hypocrisy in its treatment of the black man," Ribicoff argued. "Without question, northern communities have been as systematic and as consistent as southern communities in denying the black man and his children the opportunities that exist for white people. . . . If Senator John Stennis of Mississippi wants to make honest men of northern liberals, I think we should help him. But first we must be honest with ourselves."[23] Ribicoff's passionate speech and his surprising alliance with Stennis made the debate over the Stennis amendment into front-page news across the country.[24]

The Senate approved the Stennis amendment on February 18, 1970, but the House-Senate conference committee watered it down before approving the education bill a month later. The legislators limited the national uniformity aspect of the Stennis amendment to de jure segregation, again leaving de facto segregation and "racial imbalance" untouched.[25] While legislators weakened the Stennis amendment, the debate and the media coverage it received promoted confusion about the pace and necessity of school desegregation. A Gallup poll conducted shortly after the Senate passed the Stennis amendment found that three of four Americans believed school integration was proceeding "too fast."[26] More broadly, the widespread congressional support for "antibusing" legislation made school desegregation seem to be a question of popular opinion rather than constitutional rights, which emboldened more parents and politicians to resist "busing."

GOVERNOR CLAUDE KIRK'S POLITICS OF CONFRONTATION

Like members of Congress, many governors staked out positions against "busing." In 1969, New York Republican governor Nelson Rockefeller signed the nation's first statewide "antibusing" legislation, which his more conservative party colleagues expected him to veto.[27] In California, Governor Ronald Reagan criticized Judge Alfred Gitelson's initial 1970 ruling in the *Crawford v. Los Angeles Board of Education* case as "utterly ridiculous" and warned that "busing" would "shatter the concept of the neighborhood school."[28] Reagan's legal staff supported the Los Angeles School Board's appeal of the *Crawford* ruling, which stayed the case for five years. In Georgia, Governor Lester Maddox encouraged white students to steal the tires from buses to prevent integration.[29] In a televised speech to the state school board convention in February 1970, Louisiana's John McKeithen told delegates, "I will not allow my children to be bused." The next day his office reported receiving 1,500 calls and telegrams supporting his position.[30] Like Maddox and McKeithen, Florida's Claude Kirk was governor of a state that faced a court-ordered desegregation deadline of February 1, 1970. In a year when politicians were competing to prove their "antibusing" bona fides, no one received more media attention for their stand against "busing" than Kirk.

Claude Kirk, Florida's first Republican governor since Reconstruction, became the focus of national attention in spring 1970, when, in defiance of a court order, he suspended the entire Manatee County School Board and appointed himself school superintendent. "Not since George Wallace's 'stand in the schoolhouse door' in 1963," the *New York Times* noted, "had a Southern Governor used his office in open defiance of the law."[31] Kirk argued that a single judicial standard on school desegregation should be applied consistently both within and outside the South, an argument that southern segregationists used against federal policies they felt were unduly critical of the South, ignoring so-called de facto segregation in other regions. Kirk's defiance echoed complaints from other southern leaders, but unlike most legal and legislative arguments, Kirk's organized his "antibusing" opposition to garner the maximum media attention. For example, he delivered a speech condemning "busing" from a maternity ward following the birth of his second child, "surrounded by blushing nurses, gurgling babies and television cameras."[32] These stunts vexed the Nixon administration, which moved cautiously to enforce school desegregation orders in the South, while also trying to broaden the Republican Party's electoral appeal to white Southerners. The administration's carefully worded opposition to "busing" drew a sharp distinction between de jure (legal) segregation and de facto segregation, understood to be a product of market forces and private decisions that government had no legal responsibility to address. In practice, the Nixon administration oversaw desegregation gains among southern school districts that maintained dual systems, but did not use the power of the federal government to tackle the deeply entrenched segregation that resulted from state and federal housing policies and school zoning policies in the South or other regions. Kirk's ongoing "busing" battle in Florida was close at hand when Nixon issued his first major statement on school "busing" in March 1970, endorsing the "neighborhood school," criticizing "massive busing," and arguing that "the law [on de jure school segregation] should be applied equally, North and South, East and West."[33] Like Nixon's appeal to citizens and viewers, "North and South, East and West," Kirk's protests and the television coverage he garnered helped propel "busing" for school desegregation into an issue that resonated nationally.

From his first days as governor, Kirk sought and received national attention. He averaged ten out-of-state appearances each month in 1967 and continued to travel extensively during his term.[34] Kirk's national ambitions were supported by William Safire, a New York–based public relations executive who served as Kirk's special political consultant (Safire also worked as a speechwriter for Nixon and Agnew). Journalist David Halberstam, in one of several profiles of Kirk in national magazines and newspapers, described Safire's role: "For $90,000 a year, he promotes Florida as well as Kirk, producing a salable substance on the national market and in the action-hungry televised politics of the 1960s."[35] Much of this national travel and promotion was in the service of Kirk's ill-fated campaign for the vice presidential nomination in the 1968 election. Kirk billed himself as a southern governor who could successfully prevent George Wallace's third-party campaign from hurting the Republicans in the presidential election.[36] While this vice presidential gambit backfired—Kirk's endorsement of New York governor Nelson Rockefeller put him at odds with the Nixon administration and much of the Republican Party for the rest of his career—Kirk established himself as one of the most media-savvy politicians to emerge from a transitional moment in southern politics. While Kirk's challenge to the integration order recalled earlier protests by southern governors like Orval Faubus, Ross Barnett, or George Wallace, Kirk insisted that he was a new breed of southern politician. He declined to attend a 1967 southern governors meeting in Montgomery, Alabama, calling it "divisive and unwise."[37] "I'm not one of these red-necked governors like Lester Maddox. I'm the only good guy in the South," Kirk told the *Saturday Evening Post*.[38] Kirk also wrote a letter to the editor of the *New York Times* in which he disagreed with an editorial that described him (alongside Strom Thurmond and others) as "hardshell conservatives" who were "notably unsympathetic to the Negro drive for increased political participation."[39] "There really is a new South," Kirk argued. "We have not solved all our problems, but at least we are willing to try. One-party government with its old racist appeal is finished, whether it knows it or not."[40] Halberstam described Kirk's "New South" approach as a "politics of confrontation— seeming action and seeming motion, issues seeming to be resolved. . . . [T]he Governor seems to be standing up to *them;* or it. That there is often little substance in the issue, that the problems will be the same tomorrow does not matter, for something dramatic has happened, and the Governor is credited with an unusual action."[41] Kirk's "politics of confrontation" was particularly well suited to television news, which favored flamboyant individuals and fresh developments over staid politicians and complex continuing stories. For his part, Kirk grasped the power of television and worked to make himself comfortable in front of television cameras, repeating his press statements separately for each of the four local television teams that covered the state capitol in Tallahassee.[42] Kirk's "busing" protest put his "politics of confrontation" on national display.

School segregation in Florida long preceded Claude Kirk's election in 1966. Ten years after the U.S. Supreme Court's *Brown v. Board of Education* (1954) ruling against "separate but equal" schools, less than 3 percent of Florida's black students attended integrated schools. In Manatee County, which became the focus of the "busing" standoff, only 170 of 3,900 black students attended integrated schools in 1965.[43] Like many southern school districts, the Manatee County School Board implemented only token desegregation throughout the 1960s, with their attorneys fending off regular legal challenges from the NAACP. Manatee County ran out of legal options after *Green v. County School Board of New Kent County* (1968), where the U.S. Supreme Court found "freedom of choice" plans like those in Manatee to be insufficient tools for desegregation, and *Alexander v. Holmes* (1969), which denied further delays in southern desegregation and replaced "all deliberate speed" with a new standard that the "obligation of every school district is to terminate dual school systems at once and to operate now and hereafter only unitary schools."[44] The Supreme Court, overturning the Fifth Circuit Court and refusing a requested delay from the Justice Department, set the "at once" deadline for Florida and five other southern states as February 1, 1970.[45]

Kirk joined southern politicians like Strom Thurmond, Lester Maddox, and George Wallace in attacking this desegregation deadline, but he received most of the media attention. Kirk traveled to Washington, DC, twice in late January 1970, each time appearing at the Supreme Court and on ABC and CBS newscasts. In their reports on Kirk's first visit, where he hand-delivered a request for a delay in the desegregation order, both stations quoted the governor's statement that it would be "financially and physically impossible" for Florida to meet the deadline.[46] ABC's Stephen Geer noted that Kirk came to the Supreme Court to "dramatize his extraordinary action."[47] Kirk returned to the Supreme Court four days later, to ask the court to declare that all school systems be held to the same school desegregation standards. "The February 1 deadline will cause forced busing, which is unconstitutional, which is against the Civil Rights Act, which would cause fiscal irresponsibility, and therefore I will stand against forced busing now and in the future," Kirk told the reporters and camera crews gathered outside the high court.[48] Kirk promised to go to jail to stop "busing" if necessary. "I would feel I am going to jail for a philosophical cause," he argued, "just as our prisoners in Vietnam are in jail for a philosophical cause."[49] CBS news anchor Walter

Cronkite described Kirk's plea for a uniform national policy as part of a "new southern school strategy."[50] Indeed, Kirk was not alone in calling for the North and South to be treated alike with respect to school desegregation policy. On the same day as Kirk made his second appearance at the Supreme Court, the attorneys general of Louisiana, Mississippi, and Alabama announced plans to intervene as friends of the court in the Pasadena, California, school desegregation case, with the stated goal of making sure that the same desegregation rules applied to Pasadena as to the southern states.[51] The following month, U.S. senator John Stennis of Mississippi introduced an amendment to a federal education bill calling for common desegregation policies in both North and South. Stennis's motivation, historian Joseph Crespino argues, "was the hope that accelerated desegregation in the North would spark a broader, national backlash against school desegregation."[52] While he did not comment publicly on the Stennis amendment, Kirk's call for a uniform policy regarding desegregation also worked to make "busing" an issue that resonated nationally, before "busing" orders affected most cities. The important difference was that, as a governor, Kirk was closer to the front lines of the "busing" battle and in a better position to plead that he and his state were the victims of unfair judicial orders and federal policies. And unlike President Nixon, who sought to avoid flare-ups on the "busing" issue, Kirk was well positioned to benefit from such controversies. As Nixon told his advisers in February 1970, "There is no mileage in doing the right thing here, there's only mileage for demagogues. There's mileage for anybody who wants to be Governor, no mileage for somebody who has to be President. . . . Kirk down in Florida . . . can emphasize the negative . . . maybe it's okay for a candidate, not a President."[53] Television news cameras were eager to broadcast Kirk's regular acts of defiance, in the process establishing "busing" as a national issue and Kirk as a key voice in this debate.

CLAUDE KIRK'S TELEVISED STAND IN THE SCHOOLHOUSE DOOR

While the Supreme Court declined to answer Kirk's appeals for delay, federal judge Ben Krentzman extended the deadline for all but one of the Florida school districts under court order to September 1, 1970. The remaining school district, Manatee County, was given until April 1, 1970 to desegregate. Kirk issued an executive order announcing that the Manatee School Board and

FIGURE 14. Florida governor Claude Kirk addresses media during his takeover of the Manatee County school administration building. Associated Press photo, April 9, 1970.

superintendent would face suspension if they complied with the order, and he made good on this promise when he took over the school district in early April and directed students to ignore the integration plan.[54]

The school takeover propelled Kirk back onto the nightly news broadcasts and the front pages of national newspapers. "Probably not since George Wallace made his stand in the school house doorway in Alabama in 1963," ABC anchor Frank Reynolds noted, "has a state governor placed himself in such direct conflict with the federal government."[55] The following report showed Kirk speaking to reporters from the superintendent's office, which he and his staff had occupied. "We're involved here in forced busing," Kirk said. "Now that's the clearest-cut, most violent circumstance in the nation's and world's history." CBS broadcast a different part of the news conference, with Kirk arguing that "[Judge Krentzman] is in defiance of my constitutional rights as an individual and governor."[56] Television news reports framed Kirk's school takeover as a conflict between Kirk and federal authority or between Kirk and "busing," rather than an instance of opposition to school integration as such. Referring to Kirk's outsize role in the case, Judge Krentzman commented, "I have to keep reminding myself that Manatee schools are a party to this case."[57] Unlike the earlier southern school protests to which Kirk was frequently compared, there were no specific black students, like Elizabeth Eckford and the Little Rock Nine, Vivian Malone Jones and James Hood at the University of Alabama, or James Meredith at the University of Mississippi, whose rights seemed to be at stake in these reports. Manatee therefore received extended media coverage as a new southern integration crisis without Kirk being framed as a racist demagogue.

Kirk's successful management of television news coverage was most clearly on display as the school showdown stretched into its fourth day and federal marshals tried unsuccessfully to remove Kirk's men from the school building, while Kirk answered reporters' questions from the maternity ward of a Tallahassee hospital where his wife had recently given birth. ABC broadcast a tense exchange between Kirk and reporter Gregory Jackson. "Confrontation has been turned 180 degrees," Kirk contended. "The Federal government is the violator and I am the man who asks for law. I am the man who asks for his day in court. I am the man who pleads for hearing of my grievance." In response to Jackson's question, "Then why don't you follow the federal law which ordered desegregation?" Kirk raised his voice and pointed his finger at Jackson: "Oh, you're a fool. This is the number one compliance state in the nation. . . . You can tell your broadcasters in New York that as soon as they comply as much as Florida has, as the number one state in the nation in compliance, that's the whole difference."[58] Kirk's contrast of Florida and New York reiterated his call for a uniform national policy on desegregation and the widespread feeling among southern politicians that New York and the North got a free pass on de facto segregation from federal officials. Less obviously, Kirk's pointed reference to "your broadcasters in New York" echoed Spiro Agnew's attack on television news' geographical bias: "Of the men who produce and direct the network news, the nation knows practically nothing. . . . We do know that to a man these commentators and producers live and work in the geographical and intellectual confines of Washington, D.C., or New York City, the latter of which James Reston terms the most unrepresentative community in the entire United States."[59] Here again, Kirk positioned himself as defending Florida from a barrage of unjust external powers.

If Kirk successfully turned this verbal exchange to his advantage, he also benefited from the less than optimal filming conditions offered by the mater-

FIGURE 15. Florida Governor Claude Kirk affirms his opposition to "busing" to media outside hospital maternity ward in Tallahassee where his wife had just given birth. Associated Press photo, April 9, 1970.

nity ward. The footage broadcast on both ABC and CBS is cramped and a bit chaotic. The ABC cameraperson struggles to keep track of Kirk, producing a medium shot that floats to Kirk's right and left and focuses for several seconds on his right arm and hand at his side. CBS's footage, shot behind Kirk's left shoulder, is even less clear, with Kirk in profile and the side of his face barely visible. What is clear in both clips is that media personnel surrounded Kirk in an untraditional and unfamiliar filming environment. While this footage lacked the "good" images television news producers usually preferred (e.g., clearly framed subjects, steady cameras, and appropriate lighting), Kirk had by this point established a national profile that made the scene newsworthy. The chaotic filming conditions and close proximity (off camera) of his wife and newborn daughter also helped Kirk, who was six feet two inches tall and weighed over two hundred pounds, seem less like a physically imposing bully than like someone whose personal and familial space was being violated by the news personnel. The subtext that "busing" opponents frequently invoked parents' rights to defend their children could not have been lost on Kirk or television viewers. With this televised maternity ward confrontation, Kirk made visible what millions of Americans felt was at stake in the battle over "busing."

THE SILENT MAJORITY WATCHES KIRK

While it is difficult to gauge how people judged Kirk's protests, the governor's office received (and archived) over 1,500 letters and telegrams, which offer insight into how citizens and viewers made sense of Kirk's defiance. Over 95 percent of the mail Kirk received regarding "busing" in these months was positive, with most of the negative letters coming from his Florida constituents.[60] What is striking in this correspondence is how many people outside the South supported Kirk's protests and how many explicitly identified themselves as members of the "silent majority." "I saw on the news tonight the stand you took on the schools," a telegram from Cleveland said. "Please stand firm on it I am 100% behind you." A writer in Youngstown noted, "Many of us, here up North, wish to commend you, for your stand on 'bussing' students," while "A Concerned Senior Citizen" from Syracuse suggested, "There are many Northerners opposed to busing but you do not hear about them." A mother from Detroit expressed concern that Kirk's call for a uniform policy would hurt the North: "I speak for everyone of us white middle income suburban parents . . . we are completely in sympathy with you. . . . But for heaven's sake, don't attack us, help us to work together to protect our children. Certainly if hundreds of millions of white parents stick together we are a greater force than some supreme court judges." A mother from Seattle thanked Kirk "for speaking out and supporting the sometimes too silent majority who oppose the forced integration policy in our public schools," and a letter signed "Silent Majority" from South Bend predicted, "If you need funds, make a request, and I'm sure the Silent Majority will come thru."[61] Kirk's "busing" protests would not have reached as large a national audience—from Syracuse to Seattle and South Bend to San Antonio—without television news. Television news made a local integration dispute in Bradenton, Florida, meaningful for people across the country and helped establish "busing" as a national issue. Ultimately, Kirk was more successful at rallying support and fueling the emotions of these national "busing" opponents than he was at stopping "busing" in Florida.

Faced with a contempt of court ruling from Judge Krentzman, the threat of a $10,000 per day fine, continuing pressure from the Nixon administration to stop his protest, and the lack of further legal options, Kirk ended his standoff and removed his personnel from the school board building on April 12. In a statewide television address, Kirk downplayed the conflict: "Basically, Florida and the Department of Justice are in agreement. We believe we must obey and carry out our Constitutional mandate. We agree the solutions to our problems must lie in the duly constituted courts."[62] Despite Kirk's extended protest, "busing" started days later in Manatee County without violence and with limited absenteeism.[63] Jack Davidson, the reinstated school superintendent, described the start of integration as "really going very smoothly. . . . The people still don't like forced busing. I don't like it either, but the great majority of our people agree that the place to settle the question is in the courts, not the streets."[64]

Kirk initiated the "busing" standoff because he was sincerely opposed to the court order and, most historians and Kirk's contemporaries agree, because he thought it would help him in a difficult reelection campaign later in the year. Kirk's lieutenant governor, Ray Osborne, recalled that Kirk "wanted to stand in the schoolhouse door and have a confrontation. No one could turn him around on that. . . . He was trying to hit the home run which would bring him back."[65] Reubin Askew, who defeated Kirk in the 1970 gubernatorial election and was one of the few politicians to urge compliance with "busing" orders, remarked, "I don't think Governor Kirk was a racist, I think he just exploited the issue as many politicians did. In fact, it was almost the normal thing to exploit the issue. . . . He was exploiting it because he thought it would really put him in a good position."[66] In interviews decades after the controversy, Kirk remained convinced that his stand was sound. "I was right and I was proven right," Kirk told his biographer, Edmund Kallina Jr. "The thesis of the Manatee school affair was that forced busing was not conducive to education. What was not fair or honest was to put a child in a bus and take him one hour from one inadequate education to another inadequate education."[67] If anything, Kirk argued in the late 1990s, he was ahead of his time on the "busing" issue: "[Floridians] didn't understand forced busing at the time. It hadn't hit enough families. It is still a cancer today."[68] While his protest might have been mistimed in Florida, the broad televisual

FIGURE 16. Former Florida governor Claude Kirk speaks at a rally of Parents Against Forced Busing at Al Lang Field in Saint Petersburg, Florida. Associated Press photo, August 28, 1971.

reach of Kirk's protests brought his campaign against "busing" to millions of families in cities and suburbs in every region. Kirk appeared at rallies across the country as a spokesman for Parents Against Forced Busing, a Florida-based group that worked to create a national coalition of "antibusing" organizations. While Kirk's school standoff did not bring him the political success he sought, he became a hero to "antibusing" parents.

• • •

Among those who were inspired by Kirk and invited him to speak was Pontiac's Irene McCabe, who led a 620-mile "mothers' march" from Michigan to Washington, DC. The specific length of the march was selected to recall House Joint Resolution 620 (H.J. Res. 620), the "antibusing" amendment sponsored by Norman Lent. As a state senator representing Nassau County, Long Island, Lent had introduced a similar "antibusing" bill that passed the House and Senate in New York and was signed into law by Governor Nelson Rockefeller in 1969, before being found unconstitutional by a federal court the following year.[69] The Lent-Kunzeman "neighborhood schools" bill generated national interest among integration opponents and became a model for similar "freedom of choice" school legislation in several southern states, including Georgia, South Carolina, Tennessee, Louisiana, and Alabama.[70] New York's "antibusing" bill also influenced U.S. senator John Stennis of Mississippi, who in 1970 introduced an amendment calling for a uniform national school desegregation policy, with the hope of sparking more national opposition to "busing" and desegregation.[71] As Lent campaigned for H.J. Res. 620 in 1972, the *Long Island Press* noted that the support for "antibusing" legislation among northern congressional representatives had made a "prophet" out of Stennis.[72] The H.J. Res. 620 amendment read, "No public school student shall, because of his race, creed, or color, be assigned to or required to attend a particular school" and "Congress shall have the power to enforce this article by appropriate legislation."[73] "I stole the language from the Federal Civil Rights Law of 1964," Lent boasted, which "has liberals in Washington in a state of apoplectic disarray."[74]

Like supporters of southern "freedom of choice" plans, Lent's amendment identified and sought to exploit the fact that Title IV, section 401b, of the federal Civil Rights Law of 1964 drew a sharp distinction between de jure and de facto segregation: "'Desegregation' means the assignment of students to public schools and within such schools without regard to their race, color, religion, or national origin, but 'desegregation' shall not mean the assignment of students to public schools in order to overcome racial imbalance." While Yale University Law School professor Alexander Bickel contended that H.J. Res. 620 "would justly be read as repudiating *Brown v. Board of Education*" and Reverend Theodore Hesburgh, chairman of the Commission on Civil Rights and president of Notre Dame University, criticized it as a "fundamentally antiblack amendment," Lent contended that "House Joint Resolution 620 is intended to restore the rule of the *Brown* cases to our Constitution, our laws and our institutions and to reverse *Swann* and other departures from the *Brown* mandate of color-blindness."[75] "If it was wrong in 1954 to assign a black child to a particular school on the basis of race, it is just as wrong to do the same thing to other children in 1972," Lent argued. "This is 'Jim Crowism' in reverse."[76] (Lent's references to *Brown* anticipated later appeals to constitutional color blindness, such as Supreme Court justice Clarence Thomas's concurring opinion in *Parents Involved v. Seattle* (2007): "What was wrong in 1954 cannot be right today.")[77] Lent's appeals to *Brown* and color blindness elided the fact that the school districts "threatened" with court-ordered "busing" had been found guilty of unconstitutional discrimination. Among nearly forty "antibusing" constitutional amendments proposed in 1971 and 1972,

FIGURE 17. Former Florida governor Claude Kirk joins Irene McCabe at a National Action Group Rally in Pontiac's Hawthorne Park. Associated Press photo, September 26, 1971.

H.J. Res. 620 received the most attention because of Lent's status as a northern "busing" opponent and because Lent's amendment received grassroots support, most visibly from McCabe and Pontiac's marching mothers.

As the 1972 presidential campaign started to heat up, "antibusing" sentiment in Florida and H.J. Res. 620 figured prominently in how President Nixon's administration approached the issue of school desegregation. The path Nixon charted on "busing" overlapped at different times with politicians from across the political spectrum. Like the southern politicians he and his party courted, Nixon sought to throttle the desegregation enforcement power of HEW and the Justice Department. Like moderates from both parties, he wanted to manage the "busing" issue and avoid violent incidents. And like many liberal Democrats, he drew a sharp distinction between de jure and de facto segregation and believed that the 1964 Civil Rights Act and subsequent legislation explicitly prevented "busing" to correct "racial imbalance." Despite these similarities, Nixon differed from other politicians in a crucial respect: he was president during a pivotal six-year period that ultimately decided whether "busing" for school desegregation would work nationally or not.

FIVE

Richard Nixon's "Antibusing" Presidency

It seems to me that there are two extreme groups. There are those who want instant integration and those who want segregation forever. I believe we need to have a middle course between these two extremes. That is the course on which we are embarked. I think it is correct.

—PRESIDENT RICHARD NIXON, *1969*

PRESIDENT RICHARD NIXON MADE his most important statement on "busing" in a televised presidential address in March 1972. The speech came shortly after Florida's Democratic presidential primary, in which the "busing" issue propelled George Wallace to a landslide victory and 74 percent of Floridians signaled their opposition to "busing" in a ballot straw poll. Nixon called on Congress to enact a moratorium on new "busing" orders and pass new legislation that would "establish reasonable national standards" rather than the "unequal treatment among regions, states and local school districts" ordered by the courts.[1] While the compromise bill Congress eventually passed was weaker than Nixon's proposal, White House adviser John Ehrlichman later described the televised speech as a political victory: "Whether Congress passed the busing moratorium was not as important as that the American people understood that Richard Nixon opposed busing as much as they did."[2] Nixon's televised speech prompted the NAACP Legal Defense and Education Fund to publish "It's Not the Distance, 'It's the Niggers,'" a report that fact-checked Nixon's claims about "busing."[3] The speech also intensified tensions between the White House and the civil rights lawyers in the Justice Department who worked on school desegregation cases, seven of whom resigned in protest. In a letter published in the *Washington Post*, one of the lawyers wrote, "As I sit here watching President Nixon make his statement on school busing I am sickened. Sickened because it is the job of the President to unite and lead the nation to the future, not buckle under the weight of politi-

FIGURE 18. President Richard Nixon calls for a moratorium on new "busing" orders in a nationally televised address. CBS, March 16, 1972.

cal pressure and retreat to a dark and miserable past."⁴ Nixon's administration had announced only two days earlier that the speech would be a televised address and did not release the customary advance copy to the media. All the networks carried the address, but with limited time for commentators to analyze the text of the speech, Nixon was able to present his views on "busing" with almost no critical commentary. Senator and Democratic presidential candidate Hubert Humphrey called the speech a "TV commercial" for "antibusing" views, and Roy Wilkins, executive director of the NAACP, criticized Nixon for using his televised address to speak "as a committed advocate of one side of a major national controversy" and wrote to ABC, CBS, and NBC requesting equal time to reply.⁵

President Nixon's televised speech on "busing" was consistent with his administration's broader media strategy. Nixon favored presidential addresses over news conferences, because it allowed him to speak directly to what strategist Kevin Phillips called "the great, ordinary, Lawrence Welkish mass of Americans from Maine to Hawaii."⁶ By the time he resigned in 1974, Nixon had made more live prime-time television addresses than Presidents Eisenhower, Kennedy, and Johnson combined. The Nixon administration also developed the infrastructure of modern political media strategy, creating the Office of Communications, establishing a manager of communications position, and carefully monitoring news media coverage of the president and relevant foreign and domestic political issues.[7] Lyndon (Mort) Allin, who worked on Nixon's daily news summaries, explained that television news coverage figured prominently in this news monitoring. "The real emphasis as far as the basic summary itself would be on television, because that's where, you know, 70% of the public gets most of their information," Allin explained in 1974. "The President didn't see television and most of the staff people didn't see more than one network if even one network. There were meetings then, people were with their families or dinner, so you always gave a complete report on television no matter what the story was, how insignificant, you'd at least give it a line or two."[8] Nixon's team kept careful tabs on news coverage as a warning to broadcasters and reporters, and regularly attacked the news media for coverage that the administration felt was not favorable to the president. Following Nixon's November 1969 speech on Vietnam, where he asked for the "great silent majority" of Americans to support the continuation of the war, Vice President Spiro Agnew delivered a speech attacking the television news industry to the Midwest regional Republican Party conference in Des Moines, Iowa. "When the President completed his address," Agnew argued, "his words and policies were subjected to instant analysis and querulous criticism. The audience of 70 million Americans gathered to hear the President of the United States was inherited by a small band of network commentators and self-appointed analysts, the majority of whom expressed in one way or another their hostility to what he had to say. It was obvious that their minds were made up in advance."[9] Agnew and other members of the administration continued to monitor and complain about news coverage through Nixon's time in office, and administration veterans Pat Buchanan and Kevin Phillips brought this criticism of the news media to *TV Guide*'s "News Watch" column in the mid-1970s.[10] The Nixon administration sparred constantly with the news media and, prior to Watergate at least, won more battles than it lost.[11]

As Nixon's critics understood, the president was in a unique position to shape the debate over "busing," and through television addresses, policy statements, and press releases, the Nixon administration used this power to normalize resistance to federal court school desegregation orders. Nixon aide Bryce Harlow described the White House's posture on school desegregation as a "calculated waffle," and many of the Nixon administration's statements on "busing" were designed to send different messages to different audiences. To southern politicians and parents, Nixon signaled that he would move more slowly on school desegregation than the Johnson administration had. To politicians and parents in the North and West, Nixon promised that he would limit government oversight to unconstitutional de jure segregation, most commonly associated with the South. Nixon's "political compass told him to stay away from the whole subject of race," John Ehrlichman, Nixon's domestic affairs adviser, remembered. "And if he could not stay out of it, the best political position was on the side of the white parents whose children were about to get on those hated buses."[12] Nixon's speeches and statements on school desegregation and "busing" were crafted so that politicians and parents from Charlotte to Los Angeles would view the Nixon White House as being on their side.

While the Nixon administration skillfully used media to communicate nationally their opposition to "busing," Nixon's politics on "busing" were not just symbolic. Unlike George Wallace, Claude Kirk, Louise Day Hicks, or the hundreds of other state and local politicians who spoke out against "busing," Nixon, as president, had control over governmental bureaucracy with the authority and power to force school districts to desegregate. Nixon warned his appointees and the lawyers and officials who worked in the Justice Department and the Department of Health, Education, and Welfare (HEW) that they could either support the administration's evolving school desegregation policies or lose their jobs. After slow, fitful progress during the Johnson administration in getting more school districts to comply with school desegregation requirements, the Nixon administration ordered Justice and HEW to go no farther than required by the courts and to avoid upsetting local parents and politicians. Like HEW's 1965 retreat in Chicago, where the agency withheld $30 million in federal funds for "probable noncompliance" with Title VI of the Civil Rights Act and then restored the funds five days later under pressure from Mayor Daley and President Johnson, the Nixon administration's reining in of Justice and HEW emboldened opponents of school desegregation.

The Nixon administration's limitations on Justice and HEW were part of a strategic choice to shift the job of enforcing school desegregation to the courts. The goal was that the courts, rather than the White House, would attract the attention and anger of parents and politicians when school desegregation could no longer be delayed. Nixon and his aides regularly criticized court decisions with which they disagreed, contributing to the public perception that "forced busing" and "massive busing" were the result of overzealous judges. At the same time, Nixon appointed 231 federal judges (then a record), including four Supreme Court justices (Warren Burger, Harry Blackmun, Lewis Powell, and William Rehnquist). Through these appointments and public criticism of court orders, Nixon worked to bend the judiciary to his views on school desegregation and "busing." These efforts were ultimately successful. In *Milliken v. Bradley* (1974), Potter Stewart joined the four Supreme Court justices appointed by Nixon in a 5–4 ruling that overturned a lower court and blocked a metropolitan desegregation plan that would have involved Detroit and its suburbs. *Milliken* placed a nearly impossible burden of proof on those seeking school desegregation across city and suburban lines by requiring evidence of deliberate segregation involving multiple school districts. *Milliken* meant that most suburbs were untouched by school desegregation, while city schools grew more segregated by race and class. Considering how he leveraged the presidency's unique political power and media platform, Nixon played the most important role in limiting "busing" for school desegregation.

A "MIDDLE COURSE" ON DESEGREGATION

The foundations of the Nixon administration's approach to school desegregation were laid on the campaign trail in the 1968 presidential election. In the summer of 1968, Nixon met in Atlanta with southern political leaders, including U.S. senators Strom Thurmond of South Carolina and John Tower of Texas. Nixon's promise to move slowly on school desegregation played an important role in securing Thurmond's and Tower's support, and these southern leaders helped make Nixon the Republican nominee. Alabama governor George Wallace, running as an independent, made "busing" an unavoidable subject in the election and forced Nixon to take a position. Recalling his presidential statements on school desegregation, in September 1968 Nixon drew a distinction between de jure segregation and so-called de facto segregation or "racial imbalance." "In the first there is a deliberate policy of keeping the races from mixing in the schools," Nixon argued. "But 'racial imbalance' is used to describe a situation were the schools are open to all races, but where—usually because of residence—it turns out that once race or another predominates in a given school."[13] Candidate Nixon also outlined his opposition to HEW's threat to force compliance by withholding funds: "What I am against is using the threat of withdrawing federal funds to force a local school board to balance its schools racially by busing children all over a city for instance. If the local school board thinks busing is best, that's up to them. But federal money, or the threat of its withdrawal, should not be used to force them. On the other hand in the case of a deliberate policy of segregation, the Executive is obliged by Congress and the courts to withdraw federal funds. Of course, I would execute that law in order to end overt segregation."[14] This promise to restrain HEW was the practical step required to slow school desegregation, as he had promised Thurmond and Tower. As a candidate, Nixon explained that if elected he would not go beyond the requirements of existing civil rights legislation: "I oppose any action by the Office of Education that goes beyond a mandate of Congress; a case in point is the busing of students to achieve racial balance in the schools. The law clearly states that 'desegregation shall not mean the assignment of students to public schools in order to overcome racial balance.'"[15] By quoting the "racial imbalance" loophole from 1964 Civil Rights Act (Title IV, section 401b), included in the legislation to convince northern senators and representatives that their states would be safe from the law's enforcement, Nixon indicated that he understood the broad contours of the "busing" debate and how to chart a course of minimal compliance in both the South and the North.

Nixon had been in office only eight days when his administration took its first controversial action on school desegregation. On January 29, 1969, new HEW secretary Robert Finch gave a sixty-day extension to five school districts in North Carolina, South Carolina, and Mississippi facing a cutoff of federal funds for failing to produce acceptable desegregation plans. While Finch said he faced pressure from southern congressmen to grant the school districts indefinite extensions, civil rights advocates saw the sixty-day extension as the first sign that the Nixon administration would move more slowly on school desegregation than had the Johnson administration. "The districts in question do not need another 60 days since they have been dodging compliance with the law for more than 14 years," said Roy Wilkins, NAACP executive director.[16] "Mr. Finch forgets that it will be fifteen years this coming May 17 that segregated schools were ruled unconstitutional by the Supreme Court," argued former Morehouse College president Benjamin Mays. "Left to most of the Southern districts, they would never desegregate.... They are encouraged now to drag their feet some more and they will."[17] Senator Thurmond, in contrast, said he was "encouraged" by the decision.[18]

Both Nixon and Finch received thousands of letters in the administration's first months demanding that Nixon not move too fast on school desegregation. "Dear Mr. President: The South elected you in 1968. The South will defeat you in 1972 if you don't fulfill campaign promises," wrote a man from Lakeland, Florida. A woman from Elysian Fields, Texas, wrote, "The South feels that we had a commitment from you guaranteeing true freedom of choice in attending schools. You were elected by conservatives and middle of the roaders. I, myself, was influenced by Senator Strom Thurmond."[19] A flurry of mail arrived in advance of the deadline for compliance with desegregation, which the Johnson administration had set as September 1969.

Finch continued to attract attention with a March interview in *U.S. News and World Report* where he said that Johnson administration guidelines would be changed to make them "more responsive and realistic in terms of what is happening in education" and "nationally applicable."[20] Alluding to "racial imbalance," Finch said, "I'm convinced that we just can't work with raw percentages and say, 'You've got to have the same percentages of blacks and whites in every school.' You can go into parts of Chicago and Harlem and Pasadena, Calif., into Washington, D.C. and you find all-black situations. It's totally artificial to insist on busing schoolchildren if it may be detrimental to the level of education."[21] While these statements started to sketch out the Nixon administration's position on school desegregation, school officials, parents, and politicians eagerly awaited an official policy statement.

Finch and Attorney General John Mitchell released the administration's first official statement on school desegregation on July 3, 1969. Within the Nixon administration, Finch was considered to be in the liberal camp with advisers like Daniel Patrick Moynihan, while Mitchell was in the conservative camp with Harry Dent, who helped craft Nixon's Southern Strategy to bring white southern voters into the Republican Party. These political differences resulted in a statement that columnists Rowland Evans and Robert Novak described as "filled with ambiguities and contradictions."[22] Most notably, the Finch-Mitchell statement indicated that school districts should move toward full compliance by the end of the 1969–70 school year, but also indicated the administration would not enforce any "arbitrary dates" and that "in some districts there may be sound reasons for some limited delay."[23] The Finch-Mitchell statement also signaled that the administration would limit HEW fund cutoffs and would seek "full compliance with the law in a manner than provides the most progress and the least disruption and friction."[24] Roy Wilkins said the statement was "almost enough to make you vomit," while Michigan senator Philip Hart responded to the policy statement by saying, "I have never made the charge that President Nixon made a deal with the South to win the nomination, but events are beginning to speak for themselves."[25] Strom Thurmond again approved of the "improvement over past policy" language, which "recognizes that flexibility and reason—not blind adherence to rigid social doctrine—must be a part of desegregation procedures."[26] Ruby Martin, HEW operations director in the Johnson administration, said the Nixon administration had opened the "floodgates" and predicted that southern school districts would seek to renegotiate or hold out for more time.[27]

The practical reality of the Finch-Mitchell statement became clear in fall 1969, when Nixon advised Finch to petition the Fifth Circuit Court of Appeals to grant an extension to thirty-three Mississippi school districts facing a desegregation deadline.[28] The case marked the first time, Harry Dent noted, "the Department of Justice was seated at the table with the South rather than with the NAACP."[29] In response, the NAACP Legal Defense Fund appealed to the Supreme Court and ran a full-page advertisement in *The New York Times* with the headline, "On August 25, 1969 the United States Government Broke Its Promise to the Children of Mississippi."[30] At his White House news conference, President Nixon defended the action as a moderate "middle course" on desegregation. "It seems to me that there are two extreme groups," Nixon said. "There are those who want instant integration and those who want segregation forever. I believe we need to have a middle course between these two extremes. That is the course on which we are embarked. I think it is correct."[31] Jerris Leonard, chief of the Justice Department's Civil Rights Division, also defended this policy, arguing, "If the Court were to order instant integration nothing would change. Somebody would have to enforce that order. There just are not enough bodies and people [in the Civil Rights Division] to enforce that kind of a decision."[32] Vice President Spiro Agnew told the Southern Governors Conference, "I am against busing," and said, "The Administration's goal is to achieve integration without exacerbating community tensions."[33] White House press secretary Ronald Ziegler confirmed that Agnew represented the administration's position, but was careful to frame the opposition to "busing" in terms of "racial balance": "The President is not for imposing busing as a way to achieve racial balance."[34]

In addition to characterizing the demand for school integration in Mississippi—which had maintained unconstitutionally segregated schools for fifteen years after *Brown*—as "instant integration," Nixon and his aides characterized the lawyers, parents, and activists trying to enforce *Brown* as "extreme" segregationists. Nixon's framing of the issue echoed President Dwight Eisenhower, under whom Nixon had served as vice president from 1952 to 1960. Eisenhower answered a question in 1956 regarding mob violence against school integration in three southern towns by comparing "extremists" who "are so filled with prejudice that they even resort to violence" with those "on the other side . . . who want to have the whole matter settled today."[35] Speaking to the frustration of civil rights activists with Nixon's "middle course," Coretta Scott King said, "There is no middle ground between integration and segregation."[36] The *Washington Post* editorialized that "the 'extremists' to whom Mr. Nixon referred must necessarily be taken to include Father Hesburgh and the Civil Rights Commission, the majority of attorneys working in the Civil Rights Division of Attorney General Mitchell's Justice Department, the Senate Republican Minority Leader, Hugh Scott, and the U.S. Commissioner of Education [James Allen] whom Mr. Nixon appointed and whose office worked out the plan his administration junked."[37]

The Nixon administration's call for a delay on desegregation plans in Mississippi drew complaints from sixty-five of the seventy-four attorneys in the Justice Department's Civil Rights Division. Two leaders of the dissident lawyers, Gary Greenberg and John Nixon (no relation to the president), protested more vehemently and were asked to resign by Civil Rights Division head Jerris Leonard.[38] Greenberg said he "would not and could not defend the Government's position," while John Nixon said the Justice Department "is pursuing a policy of selective enforcement of the civil rights statues for political reasons—and I don't want any part of it."[39] These forced resignations sent a clear message to the lawyers and officials in the Justice Department and HEW that they must stay in line with the Nixon administration's school desegregation policies, and several more civil rights supporters were fired, were forced to resign, or resigned in protest over the next three years.

The Supreme Court ruled on the Mississippi case on October 29 in *Alexander v. Holmes County.* In a unanimous two-page decision, the court declared that "the obligation of every school district is to terminate dual school systems at once and to operate now and hereafter only unitary schools."[40] The call for desegregation "at once" replaced the *Brown* standard of "all deliberate speed" and was a rebuke to the Nixon administration's call for additional delays. Columnist Anthony Lewis said the terse decision "read as if the issue were really beyond discussion, as if no informed person could expect the Court to allow more delay on school desegregation at this late date."[41] Publicly, President Nixon said the administration would abide by the Supreme Court's ruling and asked the country to do the same "in full respect for the law."[42] Privately, he was defiant, telling aides, "Let's see how they enforce it."[43] Asked if the president considered the Supreme Court, led by his appointee Warren Burger, to be an "extreme group" for demanding "instant integration," press secretary Ron Ziegler replied, "[President Nixon] hasn't addressed himself in those terms to the Supreme Court."[44]

While *Alexander v. Holmes County* ran counter to the Nixon administration's school desegregation policies, Nixon benefited from the perception that the court rather than the administration was demanding desegregation. Strom Thurmond thanked Nixon for having "stood with the South."[45] "The President is looking good down in Dixie because the Supreme Court shot him down with the state of Mississippi," John Ehrlichman told his White House colleagues.[46] "The Supreme Court is being blamed," Harry Dent wrote to Nixon the day after the decision. "The reaction we are getting from Southerners today . . . is that time is working in our favor at this moment if we can keep Administration officials from saying the 'wrong' thing on the decision."[47]

The official Dent had in mind was HEW chief Leon Panetta, who wanted the department to play a larger role in investigating and enforcing school desegregation not only in Mississippi but across the country. By the end of 1969, Panetta was suggesting in speeches and interviews that the government should look more critically at so-called de facto segregation in the North and West. "It has become clear to me that the old bugaboo of keeping federal hands off northern school systems because they are only de facto segregated, instead of de jure segregated as the result of some official act, is a fraud," Panetta argued. "There are few if any pure de facto situations. Lift the rock of de facto and something ugly and discriminatory crawls out from under it."[48] The conservative newspaper *Human Events* took note of Panetta's comments, as did Nixon and others in the administration. "If [Panetta] gets his way," *Human Events* predicted, "educational fund cut-offs, compulsory busing and all the other paraphernalia that is being used to attack deliberate segregation in the South will be employed to assail unplanned segregation in the North."[49] Nixon would not tolerate a "rights zealot" in his administration or the perception that the White House planned to confront school segregation nationally, and Panetta was fired in February 1970.[50] "In these race matters, one strong action is better than a lot of words," Nixon told his aide John

Ehrlichman, "Firing Panetta is worth dozens of speeches and statements about integrating the schools."[51] Speaking to the Women's National Press Club after his ouster, Panetta said, "Some of the ambiguity shown previously by the White House was sharpened to become a statement of personal preference for neighborhood schools and against busing. The message was pretty clear: I am on your side if desegregation is difficult."[52]

These attempts to rein in HEW and the Justice Department could not slow state and federal court cases that found unconstitutional discrimination in school districts in Los Angeles and Charlotte. In Los Angeles, Judge Alfred Gitelson found that the Los Angeles Unified School District "Board has, since at least May of 1963, by and through its actual affirmative policies, customs, usages and practices, doings and omissions, segregated, de jure, its students." Gitelson continued, "The court finds that [the] Board's separate but allegedly equal schools were not equal in fact, either as to plant or facilities or teachers and curriculum, and that Board has not made available to all its students equal educational opportunity."[53] In Charlotte, Judge James McMillan found that "the Charlotte-Mecklenburg schools are not yet desegregated." McMillan's rulings doubted the sincerity of "neighborhood school" supporters, noting, "When racial segregation was required by law, nobody evoked the neighborhood school theory to *permit* black children to attend white schools close to where they lived. The values of the theory somehow were not recognized before 1965. . . . The neighborhood school theory has no standing to override the Constitution." McMillan also ruled that buses could play a role in desegregating Charlotte's schools: "Busses for many years were used to operate segregated schools. There is no reason except emotion (and I confess to having felt my own share of emotion on this subject in all the years before I studied the facts) why school busses can not be used by the Board to provide the flexibility and economy necessary to desegregate the schools."[54]

"Antibusing" movements were already established in both cities, and parents were quick to express their displeasure to the president. Nixon received more than five thousand letters and telegrams from Charlotte and its suburbs in the first two weeks of February 1970. One father implored the White House to "come to the rescue of the silent majority who may not be silent much longer. The silent majority has been pushed about as far as it will tolerate."[55] Speaking for the Nixon administration in February 1970, Finch described the Charlotte and Los Angeles decisions as "totally unrealistic" and "moving in the wrong direction."[56] Within the White House, Nixon told aids that "busing" "can't be carried out" because "people won't stand for it."[57] An NAACP attorney from the Charlotte case lamented the "cruel irony that when an able and conscientious Southern federal judge has the courage to apply the Constitution to his home town, federal officials encourage defiance."[58]

With the Charlotte and Los Angeles cases, federal and state courts threw open the question of what it would mean to desegregate large urban school districts and what role "busing" could play in the process. "As soon as possible," Chief Justice Warren Burger wrote in a case involving the unitary status of schools in Memphis, "we ought to resolve some of the basic practical problems when they are appropriately presented including whether, as a constitutional matter, any particular racial balance must be achieved in the schools; to what extent school districts and zones may or must be altered as a constitutional matter; and to what extent transportation may or must be provided to achieve the ends sought by prior holdings of the Court."[59] Jerris Leonard said that when the Supreme Court declined to rule on the "busing" aspect of the Memphis case, "we were in a position where we probably weren't going to get the issue on the calendar this year. The President realized, as did a lot of the rest of us, that the pressure was building. We had to make decisions."[60]

Nixon's response to the federal court desegregation orders and growing public furor over "busing" was to craft a statement on desegregation. "I could do a speech about the failure of integration—most of the country would agree—but then you'd have the Court coming out against us and we would have a Constitutional crisis," Nixon told his speechwriter William Safire. "You have to remember somewhere down the road I may have to carry out this law. I can't throw down the gauntlet to the Court. I have to move the Court now, before the decision, by mobilizing public opinion."[61] As the statement went through multiple drafts, speechwriter Raymond Price stressed that the "whole subject is a mine-field of code words, subtleties and sensitivities." Price expressed concern that Nixon would be influenced by "the Southern Strategists or Court-Confrontationists" in the administration who "might make seemingly minor changes that would have devastating impact in print."[62] The *Washington Post* reported that in addition to studying several legal briefs on school desegregation, Nixon met with more than fifty private citizens, including black *Washington Post* columnist William Raspberry, several of the president's black appointees, and a half dozen black ministers suggested by the Reverend Billy Graham.[63] Bryce Harlow, a White House counselor, recalled that Nixon thought carefully about how to present his views to parents, politicians, and judges. "On no other document in the years

I was there did the President deliberate more than on this one. When it was finished, it said just exactly what he wanted it to say."[64]

President Nixon's March 24, 1970, statement on school desegregation forecast how the battle over "busing" would play out in the months and years to come. After stating his personal belief that *Brown* "was right in both constitutional and human terms" and noting that as a private citizen he supported the Civil Rights Act of 1964, Nixon outlined what the law did and did not require in terms of school desegregation, and how his administration would approach these legal requirements. Referring to Chief Justice Burger's recent statement that the court had not yet resolved the questions of "racial balance" and "busing," Nixon quoted from the Civil Rights Act and the 1966 amendments to the Elementary and Secondary Education Act to demonstrate that both prohibited "transportation of students" to achieve "racial balance." "I am advised that these provisions cannot constitutionally be applied to de jure segregation," Nixon said. "However, not all segregation as it exists today is de jure. I have consistently expressed my opposition to any compulsory busing of pupils beyond normal geographic school zones for the purpose of achieving racial balance." While noting that "lawyers and judges have honest disagreements about what the law requires," Nixon described Judge Gitelson's Los Angeles ruling as "probably the most extreme judicial decree so far." Nixon detailed what it would cost to desegregate a huge school district like Los Angeles and stated, "Considering the always heavy demands for more school operating funds, I believe it is preferable, when we have to make the choice, to use limited financial resources for the improvement of education—for better teaching facilities, better methods, and advanced educational materials—and for the upgrading of the disadvantaged areas in the community rather than buying buses, tires, and gasoline to transport young children miles away from their neighborhood schools."[65] To this end, Nixon called for $1.5 billion to be dedicated to improve education in "racially impacted" areas.

Black congressman Augustus Hawkins, who represented Los Angeles, was upset with Nixon's reference to the court case in his city. "The court found the Los Angeles School Board guilty of officially segregating school children contrary to law," Hawkins said, "and Nixon completely concealed the fact with vague generalities about the cost of bussing and why racial quotas are bad." Hawkins also found Nixon's preference for education aid to be inconsistent: "The President's desegregation message says let's spend more on compensatory education but a few weeks ago . . . he said such programs inherited from his Democratic predecessor were not paying off."[66] New York congresswoman and 1972 Democratic presidential candidate Shirley Chisholm viewed Nixon's statement in terms of his administration's "Southern Strategy." "Nixon's 'desegregation' policies are designed to make sure that the federal government does not interfere in the racist policies of any local school district," Chisholm argued. "Nixon's statement this week was veiled in a dense fog of vague, fine sounding phrases. But it was also larded with code words like 'neighborhood school' and references to school busing that made it easy for southern segregationists to understand what it means. Nixon is paying off another installment of his 1968 debt to Dixie, and trying to store up credit for 1972."[67]

The most important aspects of Nixon's statement were the distinctions he drew between de jure and de facto segregation and the commonalities he highlighted between North and South. "There is a fundamental distinction between so-called de jure and de facto segregation," Nixon argued. "De jure segregation arises by law or by the deliberate act of school officials and is unconstitutional; de facto segregation results from residential housing patterns and does not violate the Constitution." At several points, Nixon carefully decoupled de jure and de facto from their usual regional associations. "De facto segregation, which exists in many areas both North and South, is undesirable but is not generally held to violate the Constitution. Thus, residential housing patterns may result in the continued existence of some all-Negro schools even in a system which fully meets constitutional standards." Nixon predicted that these housing patterns would limit school desegregation in many cities across the nation:

> With housing patterns what they are in many places in the Nation, the sheer numbers of pupils and the distances between schools make full and prompt school integration in every such community impractical—even if there were a sufficient desire on the part of the community to achieve it. In Los Angeles, 78 percent of all Negro pupils attend schools that are 95 percent or more black. In Chicago the figure is 85 percent—the same as in Mobile, Alabama. Many smaller cities have the same patterns. Nationwide, 61 percent of all Negro students attend schools which are 95 percent or more black.[68]

Nixon returned to this theme again in stating his administration's principles of enforcement. "De facto racial separation, resulting genuinely from housing patterns, exists in the South as well as the North; in neither area should this condition by itself be cause for Federal enforcement actions," Nixon said. "De jure segregation brought about by deliberate school-board gerrymandering exists in the North as the South; in both areas this must be remedied. In all respects, the law should be applied equally, North and South, East and West."[69] These references to regional similarities resonated with the amendment introduced by Mississippi senator John Stennis in February 1970 calling for uniform national school desegregation policy. Like the Stennis amendment, which the Nixon administration supported, Nixon's regional comparisons pointed toward minimum national requirements and away from robust efforts to uproot school segregation across the country.[70]

Nixon's sharp distinction between illegal de jure segregation and acceptable de facto segregation offered a road map for those, in the South and the North, who wanted to avoid school desegregation. At the time of Nixon's statement, courts outside the South had found evidence of intentional discrimination in school districts in New Rochelle (New York), New York City, Englewood (New Jersey), Los Angeles, and Pasadena. Pontiac, Boston, Denver, Detroit, and San Francisco would join this list before Nixon left office in 1974. It is likely that this list would have been much longer if civil rights organizations had the money and resources necessary to bring more lawsuits or if the government had conducted more vigorous investigations. In the Supreme Court's majority opinion in *Keyes v. School District No. 1, Denver* (1973), where the court found that the Denver School Board "intentionally created and maintained the segregated character of the core city schools," Justice William Brennan wrote, "If one goes back far enough, it is probable that all racial segregation, wherever occurring and whether or not confined to the schools, has at some time been supported or maintained by government action."[71] Rather than emphasizing that unconstitutional segregation was common in both the North and the South, Nixon's statement focused on de facto segregation as bridging the traditional regional divide. In stressing that de facto segregation would not be cause for federal investigation or enforcement, Nixon presented de facto as a safe haven from the inconveniences of school desegregation. While Nixon's public statement presented de jure and de facto as clearly defined and distinct, within the administration he recognized that the lines were easily blurred. Nixon instructed HEW officials and Justice Department lawyers, "When in doubt call segregation *de facto,* not *de jure.*"[72]

Looking back on the Nixon presidency, John Ehrlichman said that Nixon "thought himself to be, in his own words, 'one of the greatest desegregators' of schools in the country. . . . But he wanted it done his way, with conciliation and understanding and not in a fashion that would abrade the political sensibilities of southerners and conservatives."[73] This belief rested largely on the call for overdue enforcement of *Brown.* In the process of drafting the statement, speechwriter Raymond Price argued that Nixon should reaffirm his "'personal belief' that *Brown* was 'profoundly right.'" "We owe it to the White South to make this clear. Nothing would be more cruel . . . than to raise another set of false hopes among the last-ditch resisters."[74] For Nixon, who had served as vice president when the Supreme Court handed down the *Brown* ruling in 1954, putting the White House on the right side of the decision in 1970 was no doubt important. Over the course of eight thousand carefully chosen words, Nixon made it clear that the government intended to enforce the minimum requirements of *Brown* but would go no farther.

SWANN V. CHARLOTTE-MECKLENBURG BOARD OF EDUCATION

The president's statement on school desegregation had a direct impact on *Swann v. Charlotte-Mecklenburg Board of Education,* which reached the Supreme Court in October 1970. In preparing the government amicus brief for the case, solicitor general Erwin Griswold advised his lawyers to heed Nixon's words. "Several [paraphrased] passages from the President's speeches were built into the brief," Griswold recalled, to ensure "that the brief was consistent with the President's stated position." The amicus brief followed Nixon in arguing that the Constitution did not require "racial balance" and that school districts did not need to integrate "every all-white, all-Negro, or predominately Negro school," if it was not feasible to do so.[75] In addition to shaping the government's position in *Swann,* John Ehrlichman said that the Nixon administration "made a constant effort to keep in touch with [Chief Justice] Burger." "On several occasions," Ehrlichman recalled, "Nixon, [Attorney General] Mitchell and I openly discussed with the Chief Justice the pros and cons of issues before the Court." These conversations included a December 1970 meeting, four months before the court released its opinion in the *Swann* case. "The President pointed out to the Chief Justice the enormous importance of the 'school cases' before the Court," Ehrlichman said. "They discussed the issues of forced integration of the schools, the relative merits of 'tracking' and desegregation in Northern schools and the President's intention to 'set the course' for the country."[76] (When *CBS News* asked Burger about this in 1982, he knocked the camera off the shoulder of a television cameraman.)[77]

The Supreme Court issued its *Swann* ruling on April 20, 1971, upholding Judge McMillan's ruling and finding that "busing" was an acceptable "remedial technique" to achieve comprehensive desegregation. The press interpreted the unanimous decision, authored by Burger, as a rebuke of Nixon. Reporting on *CBS Evening News,* Daniel Schorr described the *Swann* decision as "a stunning blow from the Burger Court to the Nixon administration ... for this decision strikes at the heart of President Nixon's policy favoring the neighborhood school and opposing 'busing.' ... [T]he effects of this decision are almost incalculable."[78] On *NBC Evening News,* David Brinkley described the court's ruling as "somewhat different from the views of the Nixon administration, [which] has opposed massive busing and supported neighborhood schools."[79] The *New York Times'* front-page headline read, "Supreme Court, 9–0, Backs Busing to Combat South's Dual Schools, Rejecting Administration Stand."[80] The *Washington Post* described the decision as "brushing aside the Nixon administration's position against mass busing," while the *Los Angeles Times* wrote that the justices "upheld cross-town busing" and "rejected the high priority given neighborhood schools by the Nixon Administration."[81] Speaking for the White House, press secretary Ronald Ziegler said, "The Supreme Court has acted and its decision is now the law of the land. It is up to the people to obey it."[82]

While *Swann* seemed to be a setback for Nixon's policies on school desegregation and "busing," the administration interpreted the ruling differently. Solicitor general Griswold felt that the administration's view, which he had presented to the justices, "was the view which was taken by the Court in [its] unanimous decision."[83] "The important thing is that we are not faced with this *de facto* question and not faced with racial balance," Attorney General Mitchell told Nixon.[84] The Nixon administration had reason to be encouraged by the ruling. While the court upheld Judge McMillan's ruling, the justices held that a strict racial balance was not a constitutional right: "The constitutional command to desegregate schools does not mean that every school in every community must always reflect the racial composition of the school system as a whole."[85] More importantly for the "busing" debate, while the Supreme Court found bus transportation an acceptable "remedial technique," the court also endorsed the Fourth Circuit's "reasonableness" standard, and ruled that "an objection to transportation of students may have validity when the time or distance of travel is so great as to either risk the health of the children or significantly impinge on the educational process."[86] The Supreme Court's *Swann* ruling was therefore more of a victory for the Nixon administration than the press suggested.

"Busing" continued to be an unsettled political issue in the months after *Swann*. By the end of 1971, there were more than forty lower court decisions made in line with *Swann*. Outside the South, judges found evidence of unconstitutional school segregation in cities like Denver, Pasadena, and Pontiac and ordered school boards to implement plans to integrate schools by changing attendance zones, altering school siting policies, and most commonly, by transporting students in school buses. While court-ordered "busing" for school desegregation affected only a small percentage of public school students, politicians and parents railed continually against "busing," arguing that the rights of parents and homeowners were being violated by activist judges and federal bureaucrats.[87]

In light of these court decisions and escalating "antibusing" protests, in the late summer of 1971, Nixon called on Attorney General Mitchell and new HEW secretary Elliot Richardson to hold "busing" "to the minimum required by law." The timing of this move came in response to a school case in Austin, Texas, where HEW prepared a plan, its first since the *Swann* ruling, calling for extensive "busing" to desegregate Austin's schools. The federal judge rejected HEW's plan in favor of a plan drafted by the Austin School Board that would have left several schools segregated. The Nixon administration decided the best political course was to appeal the judge's ruling because it fell short of *Swann* but disavow the HEW plan so as not to appear to be "pro-busing."[88] Nixon issued a statement reading,

> I would like to restate my position as it relates to busing. I am against busing as that term is commonly used in school desegregation cases. I have consistently opposed busing of our Nation's schoolchildren to achieve racial balance, and I am opposed to the busing of children simply for the sake of busing. Further, while the executive branch will continue to enforce the orders of the court, including court-ordered busing, I have instructed the Attorney General and the Secretary of Health, Education and Welfare that they are to work with individual school districts to hold busing to the minimum required by law.[89]

Press secretary Ziegler made it clear that the president expected officials and lawyers in HEW and Justice to fall in line. "Those who are not responsive to the President's policy will find themselves in other assignments, quite possibly assignments not in the Federal government," Ziegler told reporters. "The President expects his policy to be followed and it will be followed."[90]

The importance of Texas in the 1972 election figured prominently in Nixon's appraisal of the Austin case. Influential Texas senator John Tower and several Republican state officials expressed their displeasure and the anger of their constituents to administration officials. "Busing" "is by far the top issue in Texas," commented George Willeford, state chairman of the Texas Republican Party. "If these things don't shape up, it will be very difficult for President Nixon to carry Texas."[91] Willeford continued, "The buck stops at Nixon. People look to this as Mr. Nixon's busing, regardless of the Supreme Court or what, and I think he has to assume responsibility for his administration. I think people are anxious to see that his actions correlate with his words."[92] Dallas County Republican Party chairman Tom Crouch said his constituents were not interested in another carefully worded statement from the president. "The people don't want to be reasoned with on busing," Crouch said. "The PTA and neighborhood meetings have been uncontrollable. My phone has been ringing off the wall. In my neighborhood the local guy thinks the county chairman talks to the President every day. They want me to express to the President my displeasure. It's easily the biggest crisis in my political career. It's been the biggest outburst of anti-administration sentiment I can remember. Mr. Nixon couldn't have carried Dallas County the weekend they decided to appeal the Austin decision."[93]

The administration's moves in Austin and Nixon's call for "busing" to be held "to the minimum required by law" promoted confusion and frustration among those making a good faith effort to craft school desegregation plans. Columbia, South Carolina, school board member Hayes Mizell said, "I think I can speak for almost every member of the board, that it puts an additional burden on us because it makes it appear that we are doing something different from what the President wants, and what is national policy."[94] Hal Sieber of the Greensboro, North Carolina, Chamber of Commerce remarked, "Whenever Nixon made a statement in opposition to busing, there was an immediate feeling of strength by those who were opposed. It meant that we had a lot more work to do to sell integration and busing. It really was devastating."[95] Syndicated columnists Evans and Novak contended, "The President has now gone so far in the no-busing direction that he has alienated school boards even in the South."[96] Gladys McNairy, president of Pittsburgh Board of Education, felt that Nixon's comments also emboldened resistance to desegregation in the North: "When he says, in effect, don't bother about busing, you can imagine the effect on people in the North who subtly support segregation. They've been waiting for something like this."[97] The U.S. Commission on Civil Rights commented, "What the nation needed was a call to duty. Unfortunately, the President's statement almost certainly will have the opposite effect . . . of undermining the desegregation effort."[98]

New York Times columnist Tom Wicker presented his critique of the Austin situation in terms of the president's unique ability to dominate media coverage of "busing." Wicker noted that in the days leading up to Nixon's statement, dozens of school administrators, academics, and other witnesses testified regarding school desegregation to Senator Walter Mondale's Select Senate Committee on Equal Educational Opportunity but received little media attention. "President Nixon's bitter antibusing statement was circulated to millions last week by newspapers, radio, and television," Wicker wrote. "But it went almost unnoticed that the very next day the school superintendent of Harrisburg refuted the Nixon position point by point, in an account of the actual experience of that city. This is a classic demonstration of the extent to which the American press—print and electronic—merely reacts to the statements of important officials rather than trying to make independent judgments on the facts. Mr. Nixon's distortions were trumpeted in headlines, because he is President; the facts put forward by Dr. David H. Porter were ignored, because he was not 'newsworthy' enough."[99] Wicker, like Nixon's critics and political rivals, understood that the president's policy statements became lead stories in newspapers and magazines and that the administration could request and receive frequent television and radio broadcast time to bring his views directly to the American public. While the administration insisted that the press treated Nixon unfairly, his team was savvy about turning the media to their advantage. As the presidential campaign heated up in March 1972, Nixon turned to television to reiterate his opposition to "busing."

"A QUESTION WHICH DIVIDES MANY AMERICANS"

When "busing" emerged as the key issue in the Florida Democratic primary, President Nixon decided it was time to restate his views on the subject. Nixon did not initially plan to present his statement on television. Following the logic of the detailed eight-thousand-word statement he presented two years earlier, press secretary Ziegler said Nixon would again send his message to Congress rather than speaking on television "because of the complexity of the problem."[100] The results of the Florida primary changed Nixon's mind. George Wallace won Florida with 42 percent of the vote, and 74 percent of Floridians signaled their opposition to "busing" in a ballot straw poll. The next day Nixon announced he would speak directly to the American people on television and radio about his views on "busing." "I knew the message from Florida would get to Washington pretty quick," Wallace remarked.[101]

The president's "busing" speech on March 16, 1972, began by noting, "My own position is well known. I am opposed to busing for the purpose of achieving racial balance in our schools. I have spoken out against busing scores of times over many years." Nixon asserted that "North, East, West, and South—States, cities, and local school districts have been torn apart in debate over this issue" and that "the great majority of Americans, white and black, feel strongly that the busing of schoolchildren away from their own neighborhoods for the purpose of achieving racial balance is wrong." Both claims resonated with two recent "busing" stories in television and print news: "antibusing" activist Irene McCabe had led a group of "marching mothers" on a 620-mile protest march from Pontiac to Washington, DC, while the National Black Political Convention in Gary, Indiana, advanced an agenda that favored community-controlled schools over "busing" for school desegregation. Pointing to this national and multiracial opposition to "busing," Nixon argued, "What we need now is not just speaking out against more busing. We need action to stop it." Nixon discussed the idea of a constitutional amendment to block "busing" but concluded that "it takes too long." (Congress had considered dozens of "antibusing" constitutional amendments, and legislators were then fighting over House Joint Resolution 620, an amendment sponsored by New York congressman Norman Lent). To stop "busing" more quickly, Nixon proposed imposing "a moratorium on new busing" orders until July 1, 1973, and providing $2.5 billion "in the next year mainly towards improving the education of children from poor families."[102]

Within the administration, the speech was considered a great success. Speechwriter Ray Price said he was "greatly relieved" and that the "emphasis on both anti-bussing and pro-desegregation was good and well balanced."[103] Clark MacGregor, counsel to the president on congressional relations, described the speech as "the President's best presentation in the field of

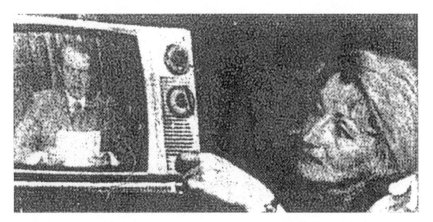

FIGURE 19. Irene McCabe watches President Nixon's speech on "busing" in a motel en route to Washington, DC. Associated Press, March 17, 1972.

domestic affairs. Very straight forward in style and understandable in content. The Congressional response will be good."[104] Beyond the substance of the speech, Mark Goode, Nixon's media consultant, noted that Nixon's "face looked good—Eyes well defined."[105] Nixon aide Pat Buchanan felt that the speech would win the president significant points against the Democrats in the election. "If there was ever a matter on which we ought to draw a line in the sand between us and the Democrats for the nation to see—it is on busing," Buchanan argued. "Equal time for such a television address is no factor because the Democrats wouldn't know what to do with the time on this issue if they got it."[106]

As Buchanan suggested, the Nixon administration had outflanked its critics and opposing politicians with the televised speech. CBS estimated that sixty million Americans viewed the speech on one of the three networks (80 percent of all television viewers that evening), with millions more listening on the radio.[107] Only the president could request and receive this level of primetime broadcast exposure. None of the Democratic presidential candidates, except for Wallace, had a coherent position on "busing," and even if they did they could not access the national airwaves for free. Nixon's televised "busing" speech caught television news anchors off guard. Since the Nixon administration had announced two days earlier that the statement would be a televised speech and did not release an advance copy of the president's remarks to the networks, there was little for television news anchors to say in response. As a result, Nixon made his case against "busing" for twelve minutes to over sixty million Americans with almost no immediate criticism.

This led NAACP executive director Roy Wilkins to write to ABC, CBS, and NBC to request equal time for a reply, and senator and Democratic presidential candidate Hubert Humphrey to describe the speech as a "TV commercial" for "antibusing" views.[108] "It was an extraordinary moment in American history," wrote journalist Robert Semple Jr. "For 10 minutes before a nationwide television audience . . . President Richard M. Nixon asked that nearly two decades of legal tradition be countermanded and that Congress wrest from the courts the basic responsibility for deciding how equal educational opportunity for millions of minority American school children is to be achieved.[109]

South Dakota senator George McGovern, who finished sixth in the Florida Democratic primary but went on to win his party's nomination, was speaking at the University of Illinois-Urbana Champaign the night of Nixon's "busing" speech.[110] He brought a small television set on stage, with a microphone to project the sound over the loudspeaker system, so that the crowd could hear the president's views. When Nixon finished, McGovern told the crowd, "What we have just witnessed is a collapse of moral and political leadership by the President: a total surrender to Wallaceism and the demagoguery it represents."[111] Boston civil rights activist Mel King agreed, saying that Nixon was "attempting to out-Wallace Wallace."[112] The *Chicago Defender* extended the Wallace comparison, editorializing, "[Nixon] and George Wallace are bedfellows who should have enough guts to don in full public glare the KKK white sheets as emblematic of their unholy commitments to racism."[113] The *Baltimore Afro-American* argued that Nixon was more dangerous than Wallace: "[Nixon] places himself squarely in the schoolhouse door with racist Alabama Gov. George Wallace, but his is an even more sinister threat because he has the Justice Department . . . to enforce his whims—or to prevent the federal courts from enforcing busing orders."[114]

Beyond the racial undertones of Nixon's "busing" speech, other critics questioned the legality of the proposed moratorium on "busing" orders and the evidence supporting the president's call for additional funds for compensatory education. "The moratorium clearly contradicts the current substantive requirements of the fourteenth amendment," argued former Supreme Court justice Arthur Goldberg. "At least for those students situated in a school system where busing is required as an element of relief from unconstitutional segregation, the moratorium would inevitably postpone, and thus deny, their present equal protection rights."[115] Alexander Bickel, a Yale Law professor who had earlier advised Nixon on desegregation issues, said that if the Supreme Court allowed Congress to prevent it from administering "what it regards as the essential remedy, [the Court] will have accepted a more far reaching limitation on judicial power . . . than ever before in its history."[116] Several columnists pointed out that, counter to the president's references to "massive busing," an HEW-commissioned study of twenty-nine school districts by the Lambda Corporation (a computer modeling company using statisticians from MIT) in 1971 found that "almost complete elimination of segregation in the schools seems possible without exceeding practical limits for students' travel time or economically reasonable limits on the number of students bused."[117] HEW commissioned the Lambda Corporation to conduct a second study of forty-four cities, which found similar results.[118] The analytically rigorous Lambda reports modeled different scenarios for desegregating large and small cities, but the Nixon administration and HEW ignored these studies.

Several critics also noted that additional compensatory education funds to low-income schools were already provided by Title I of the Elementary and Secondary Education Act of 1965 and that it was not clear the funds were achieving the kind of results Nixon suggested. Professor Herbert Kiesling, author of a study HEW secretary Richardson described as "the most careful and analytical piece of evidence we have" supporting the administration's call for compensatory education funds, said the administration cherry-picked evidence from his research. "On balance, I don't think that there's any real evidence about what happens in core cities," Kiesling said. The evidence "is probably as much in support of prudent busing or some kind of socio-economic mix as against it."[119] In December 1971, the Rand Corporation, which published Kiesling's research and other studies on the subject, found that "virtually without exception, all of the large surveys of the large national compensatory education programs have shown no beneficial results on average. . . . Two or three smaller surveys tend to show modest and positive effects on compensatory programs in the short run."[120]

Nixon's "busing" speech was, of course, less about the empirical evidence supporting different policies and more about tapping into the wave of "antibusing" sentiment cresting in Florida and elsewhere. U.S. secretary of labor James Hodgson told the White House that he felt Nixon succeeded on this count. "[The President] wisely put emphasis on tone and feeling . . . not on the detail," Hodgson said. "He has a great ability to become very calm, reasoned and compassionate on issues which are the most controversial. That is

FIGURE 20. President Nixon meets with congressmen the day after his televised "busing" speech. At table, from left: Senate minority leader Hugh Scott of Pennsylvania, House majority leader Carl Albert of Oklahoma, President Nixon, Senate majority leader Mike Mansfield of Montana, and House minority leader Gerald Ford of Michigan. Associated Press, March 17, 1972.

an excellent touch!"[121] "With a TV soliloquy, the President gets to converse with the folks in good old-fashioned plain talk, avoiding all the background, legal argument, and educational policy that just happens to be [the] crux of the issue," *Boston Globe* columnist Thomas Oliphant suggested. "While burning political issues cry out for careful if lengthy treatment by public figures, they also make for great political speeches, and that's why Richard Nixon went on the tube last night."[122]

As with Nixon's earlier statements on school desegregation, the March 1972 "busing" speech prompted another wave of protests among the frontline Justice Department lawyers tasked with carrying out the president's policies. Attorney Arthur Chotin wrote to the *Washington Post* days after Nixon's speech to describe being "sickened" by the televised speech. "What happens now?" Chotin asked. "What happens to the work of thousands of people who believed in true equal opportunity for all, not the kind proposed by the President (equal opportunity in theory only)? What happens to the memories of people like Michael Schwerner, James Cheney, Andrew Goodman, Vernon Dahmer, Lemuel Penn, Medgar Evers, Viola Liuzzo, Martin Luther King Jr. and all the others who gave their lives in the fight for equal opportunity not just in education but in many other areas? Were they all murdered in cold blood so that the President might throw us back into a darker age?"[123] The next month more than one hundred of Chotin's fellow attorneys in the Justice Department's Civil Rights Division signed letters protesting efforts by Nixon and Congress to restrict "busing" for school desegregation (the black attorneys signed one letter and coordinated with the white attorneys, who signed a separate letter).[124] Praising the lawyers' protest, the *Washington Post* asked, "Can the administration argue that roughly two-thirds of the Civil Rights Division are incompetent or wrongheaded or unqualified to judge?"[125] In their letter, the ten black attorneys described the "busing" issue as a "sham." "As ardent students of the civil rights struggle," the lawyers wrote, we "have concluded that the recent fervor in the area of busing is nothing more than a thinly veiled attempt to sacrifice the rights of minority children to racist pressure groups and political expedience. . . . What we have been witnessing, when stripped of its shroud of innocence, is an attempted roll-back, a camouflaged effort to resurrect the concept of 'separate but equal,' and a deliberate effort to make the advancement of desegregation circular, beginning and ending with *Plessy v. Ferguson.*"[126] The lawyers charged that Nixon's policy of "benign neglect" on the issue of race had transformed into "malignant hypocrisy." Seven civil rights lawyers resigned in protest of Nixon's proposed ban on "busing."[127]

In addition to these lawyers, forty black federal appointees wrote a letter expressing their disagreement to the president.[128] Specifically, the officials criticized Justice Department interventions in cases in Denver, Detroit, Nashville, and Richmond, arguing that the actions "have already had a chilling effect on black people and others, inasmuch as it is made to appear that the resources of the federal government, under your leadership, are coming down on the side of those who stand in opposition to the constitutional rights of minority schoolchildren."[129] When asked how the black members of Nixon's staff would react to his "busing" stand, Harry Dent joked, "Oh, we got a boat for them that's leaving for Nigeria."[130]

Instead of Nixon's proposed "busing" moratorium or a constitutional amendment, Congress eventually reached a temporary compromise on "busing" in 1972. While the moratorium did not become law, Nixon's televised and widely viewed "busing" speech cemented his stature as the nation's most influential critic of school desegregation. Over the course of President Nixon's first term, through speeches, policy statements, and his administration's rigorous management of lawyers and officials in the Justice Department and HEW, Nixon did more than any other person to limit "busing" for school desegregation.

. . .

Richard Nixon's biggest victory in the "busing" battle came two weeks before he resigned from office amid the Watergate scandal. In *Milliken v. Bradley*, the Supreme Court overturned district and appeals court rulings that required a metropolitan desegregation solution, which would have consolidated the Detroit school district with fifty-three neighborhood and suburban districts. The decision, a 5–4 vote with the four Nixon appointees in the majority, meant that desegregation plans could not extend into suburban school districts unless multiple districts had deliberately engaged in segregated polices. This was a virtually impossible burden of proof for civil rights advocates to meet, and it meant that, except in school districts that were already consolidated, school desegregation remedies would be confined to cities and exclude suburbs. The majority opinion returned repeatedly to the point that "racial balance" was not a constitutional requirement. Chief Justice Burger wrote, "It seems clear that the District Court and the Court of Appeals shifted the primary focus from a Detroit remedy to the metropolitan area only because of their conclusion that total desegregation of Detroit would not produce the racial balance which they perceived as desirable." This was impermissible, the court argued, because *Swann* held that "desegregation, in the sense of dismantling a dual school system, does not require any particular racial balance" in each "school, grade or classroom." In his concurring opinion, Justice Potter Stewart, who joined the Nixon appointees in the majority, wrote that the "predominately Negro school population in Detroit" was "caused by unknown and perhaps unknowable factors such as in-migration, birth rates, economic changes, or cumulative acts of private racial fears."[131]

Supreme Court justice Thurgood Marshall strongly disagreed with the court's ruling. In his dissenting opinion, Marshall argued that "school district lines are both flexible and permeable for a wide variety of purposes, and there is no reason why they must now stand in the way of meaningful desegregation relief." Marshall emphasized that the lower courts had found the state of Michigan to have committed acts of de jure school segregation and that the metropolitan remedy was designed to correct these acts, not pursue "racial balance," as the majority suggested. "Desegregation is not and was never expected to be an easy task," Marshall said in his conclusion.

Racial attitudes ingrained in our Nation's childhood and adolescence are not quickly thrown aside in its middle years. But just as the inconvenience of some cannot be allowed to stand in the way of the rights of others, so public opposition, no matter how strident, cannot be permitted to divert this Court from the enforcement of the constitutional principles at issue in this case. Today's holding, I fear, is more a reflection of a perceived public mood that we have gone far enough in enforcing the Constitution's guarantee of equal justice than it is the product of neutral principle of law. In the short run, it may seem to be the easier course to allow our great metropolitan areas to be divided up each into two cities—one white, the other black—but it is a course, I predict, our people will ultimately regret.[132]

Nixon, engulfed in July 1974 by Watergate, did not comment publicly on *Milliken*. Speaking for the White House, Vice President Gerald Ford described the decision as a "victory for reason" and "a great step forward to finding another answer to quality education."[133] If Thurgood Marshall was right and the court's *Milliken* ruling reflected the "perceived public mood" more than the law, President Nixon deserved much of the credit or the blame. The court's interpretation of school desegregation law in *Milliken* strongly resembled the case President Nixon had made against "busing" to parents, politicians, federal officials, and judges over the prior six years. In the end, the *Milliken* ruling helped President Nixon make good on his promise to protect "neighborhood schools" and limit "busing."

SIX

"Miserable Women on Television"

IRENE MCCABE, TELEVISION
NEWS, AND GRASSROOTS
"ANTIBUSING" POLITICS

The slender mother of three alternatively goaded, rallied, calmed and steadied her followers through a long morning of active protest against pupil busing. Thousands of admirers—all of them white, most of them women, and all of them angry—followed Mrs. McCabe by protesting at the schools, chaining themselves to fences, blocking buses and defying arrest.

> —"WIRY MRS. IRENE MCCABE SPARKS
> ANTIBUSING GROUP," Holland Evening Sentinel,
> September 8, 1971

Hopefully people will look along the way at six miserable women on television and write their congressman in favor of the [antibusing] amendment.

> —IRENE MCCABE, quoted in "Mothers Begin
> Walk to Back Antibusing," Cumberland News,
> March 16, 1972

AFTER WALKING 620 MILES, Irene McCabe and her fellow marching mothers arrived in Washington, DC, with sore feet and, thanks to television cameras from ABC, CBS, and NBC, a nation of people watching. The mothers' march from Pontiac, Michigan, to Washington, DC, marked the end of eight months of intense protests against court-ordered "busing" for school desegregation initiated by McCabe and the "antibusing" National Action Group (NAG). The gendered connotations of the acronym were intentional, as suggested by a sign on the van that accompanied the group on their mothers' march to Washington: "If at first you don't succeed, NAG, NAG, NAG."[1] NAG's protests started locally in Pontiac but quickly drew media attention from television news networks, propelling McCabe into the national spotlight

FIGURE 21. Irene McCabe speaking at National Action Group Rally in Hawthorne Park, Pontiac, Michigan. Associated Press, September 19, 1971.

and making her a symbol of resistance to civil rights. While McCabe did not have any formal media training, she proved skillful at making NAG's protests into television-friendly events. "She got up on those platforms and you'd think she was born on the stump," NAG's lawyer, L. Brooks Patterson, noted after McCabe's death in 2004.[2]

Focusing on a series of widely televised NAG "antibusing" protests in the early 1970s, this chapter examines how McCabe cultivated a multifaceted television persona, combining political acumen and sexuality; how she articulated private and public identities of motherhood that both troubled and exemplified television's boundaries between private and public spheres; and how her self-inflicted suffering during the mothers' march lent the event a dramatic narrative quality that echoed other television genres. All of this unfolded against the backdrop of President Richard Nixon's administration attacking television news broadcasters for their liberal bias, which made McCabe more appealing to news producers as a representative of white opposition to civil rights.

McCabe is part of a long history of women from across the political spectrum who have rooted political claims in their identities as mothers or housewives.[3] African American women—like Ellen Jackson and Ruth Batson in Boston (discussed in chapter 3) and the Woodlawn Organization's "truth squad" mothers in Chicago (discussed in chapter 2)—worked as parent-activists to combat school segregation and to secure a better education for their children. McCabe's "antibusing" politics resonated with the "15,000 white mothers" who marched against "busing" in New York in 1964 (discussed in chapter 1). While motherhood figured prominently on both sides of the fight over school desegregation, McCabe and other white "antibusing" mothers benefited from political and cultural frameworks that privileged white families and mothers.[4] White mothers who complained about the government taking away their children through "busing" profited from decades of federal, state, and local policies that had created and maintained segregated neighborhoods and schools. Aggrieved mothers became the public face of "antibusing" politics, but their concerns about their children depended on defending white schools and neighborhoods. While thousands of mothers across the nation raised their voices against "busing," none received the same level of national television attention as McCabe.

More than simply enacting a white backlash to civil rights, McCabe learned from other protest movements, creating television-ready scenes that garnered attention and framed her cause in a favorable light. In particular, McCabe made use of several media strategies that African American civil rights activists had used just years earlier. If television news had played an important role in framing African American civil rights protests for a national audience in the 1950s and 1960s, by the 1970s news programs offered frequent and sympathetic coverage to "busing" opponents—what the *Chicago Defender* described as an "anti-democratic and anti-black movement."[5] As historian Nathan Irvin Huggins noted in 1978, "Media exposure [for minority movements] has cut both ways. The cameras recorded the White Backlash as eagerly as Black Power.... They broadcast the sentiments of the white Pontiac, Michigan, housewife protesting 'forced busing' as earnestly as they had the achievement of Mrs. Rosa Parks in the Montgomery bus boycott."[6] As Huggins suggests, McCabe successfully leveraged the characteristics of television news—its emphasis on newsworthy events and crisis, its selective use of historical context, its nominal political neutrality, and its emphasis on and production of drama and narrative—to make her case against "busing."

Born and raised in Pontiac, McCabe claimed to have never traveled south of Detroit before she started to protest "busing" at the age of thirty-six.[7] Like many other women who became grassroots activists, McCabe, a married mother of three, emphasized her lived experience as a mother and housewife as the reason she became involved in politics. McCabe regularly described her and her fellow marchers as "ordinary housewives and mothers," and she explained to a *Washington Post* reporter, "I'm an amateur. When I address people at rallies, if they can relate to me it's just because they know I'm the same type of person they are, that I am a housewife . . . just mainstream, grass-roots America."[8]

Most housewives, of course, were not interviewed in major newspapers and did not regularly appear on the nightly television news, but it would be a mistake to see these claims of ordinariness as empty rhetoric. McCabe's televisual appeal drew on her ability to visibly lead and capably speak for "antibusing" parents, while also being able to persuasively present herself as a representative member of this group. McCabe's authority to appear on television and speak on "busing" depended on her ability to identify as both an "ordinary" housewife and the president of a grassroots political group.[9] Like many in the crowd, television cameras looked to McCabe as a representative voice of white parents concerned about the federal government's role in their private family lives, but at the same time television also tracked McCabe as a public political figure who led a six-week mothers' march to Washington, DC, while her family was home in Pontiac.

These dual identities are clearly displayed in news coverage of the "antibusing" march McCabe led in Pontiac on September 6, 1971. Pontiac had been propelled into the news a week earlier when members of the Ku Klux Klan dynamited ten empty school buses that were parked in the bus depot.[10] The bus bombings prompted federal district court judge Damon Keith, who issued the "busing" order, to warn, "This case will not be settled in the streets of Pontiac."[11] With tensions high in Pontiac, McCabe led several hundred residents on a two-mile protest march from downtown Pontiac to Madison Junior High School in the northeast section of the city. CBS and ABC covered the march, which presented television news camera operators and viewers with easily identifiable images that differed sharply from the KKK's vigilante violence: orderly marchers with women and children foregrounded, dozens of U.S. flags, and clearly worded placards expressing support for the "busing" boycott (e.g., "Bury the Bus, Keep Freedom Alive" and "Our Kids Like Neighborhood Schools"). After wide shots of the crowd walking toward the camera (CBS estimated six thousand marchers, ABC four thousand), both stations cut to footage of McCabe addressing the large crowd from an elevated platform at the junior high school. These visuals quickly established that this was a mass gathering and that McCabe was recognized as a leader on this issue. CBS offered viewers a medium close-up of McCabe encouraging defiance of the "busing" order. "How many are going to keep their children home?" McCabe asked to cheers from the crowd. "Home, home, not a bus, nowhere but home *[crowd cheers]*. Don't weaken, don't get discouraged, don't let their threats frighten you, because they wouldn't hold up in court. And so what if they do, we'll go together *[crowd cheers and man, off-camera, yells, 'They can't put us all in jail']*. If we don't stand up now to this threat, we have no country left for our children. It's not busing; it's not integration; it's communism, and we will not have it *[crowd cheering]*."[12] McCabe's final phrase, "We will not have it," is nearly inaudible over her supporters' cheering. These audible displays of support coupled with crowd reaction shots gave viewers their first glimpse of McCabe's authority in local "antibusing" politics. ABC's coverage of the march offered another angle on McCabe's influence. After introducing her as "most prominent among the antibusing forces . . . Pontiac housewife, and leader of the National Action Group," ABC's caption listed her simply as "housewife." This caption fit the clip ABC selected, which featured an earlier part of McCabe's speech than the segment CBS aired. "When the buses roll from Le Baron Elementary," McCabe declared, "my daughter will not be on that bus, she will not be in a parochial school, she will be home *[crowd cheers]*."[13] As these clips suggest, McCabe's authority stemmed from her ability to address the crowd as both a "housewife" and, as the CBS caption read, "National Action Group President." Both of these roles would continue to be prominent parts of McCabe's television persona in the weeks and months ahead.

ABC's coverage of the Labor Day march is also notable because it showed the media attention that McCabe and the march generated. Whereas CBS's camera offered a view of McCabe's face as seen from the crowd, ABC's cameraperson was positioned on the dais to McCabe's right. The resulting medium shot placed McCabe in the center of the frame with members of the crowd and a large U.S. flag in front of her and a clutch of other media personnel around her on the platform. This vantage point reveals at least three microphones, a still photographer, and a video cameraman. While the rele-

IRENE McCABE
HOUSEWIFE

FIGURE 22. Irene McCabe speaks to a crowd at an "antibusing" rally in Pontiac. This camera angle gives viewers a sense of the media's focus on McCabe. *ABC Evening News,* September 6, 1971.

vance of McCabe and the "antibusing" march is implied by her inclusion in both the CBS and ABC broadcasts, the ABC clip also makes visible the substantial media interest in her.

This framing is quite different from the ways television news covered women's political activism in this era. McCabe stepped into the national spotlight in 1971, one year after the Women's Strike for Equality and other protests garnered extensive news coverage of the second-wave feminist movement.[14] The three broadcast networks portrayed these protests as absurd spectacles that were visually, but not politically, interesting to male viewers.[15] While McCabe was conventionally feminine and not afraid to use her body to draw attention, both ABC and CBS framed her in conventional shots that presented her as a newsworthy political actor.

Nightly news broadcasts featured segments on Pontiac for four days following the Labor Day march, reporting on the school boycott led by the McCabe and the National Action Group. These reports further established Pontiac as the major national site of tension over "busing" and McCabe, featured prominently in each segment, as the most important leader of the "antibusing" campaign. An ABC segment on September 7, the first day of the

NAG-organized school boycott, showed McCabe leading boycott supporters to the Pontiac Board of Education building where she rolled a toy school bus carrying two guinea pigs into the office of schools superintendent Dana Whitmer.[16] Outside the building, McCabe taunted Mayor Robert Jackson, yelling, "Come on Mayor Jackson, you're driving the bus. Come on, chicken."[17] Two days later, when McCabe asked protestors to stop gathering at the school bus depot and move elsewhere, all three news networks were on hand. Both CBS and NBC broadcast a heated exchange between McCabe and an unidentified marcher who was unhappy with McCabe's change of tactics. "You're the one who told us to come out here and walk," the woman yelled at McCabe. "We've walked till our legs are falling off, and you're telling us to give it up?" "Change your tactics now, stay one step ahead of them," McCabe advised.[18] The woman also questioned McCabe's willingness to stand with the protesters, shouting, "Martin Luther King marched with his people. He marched with his people; he went to jail with them."[19]

Citing King might seem like an odd way to criticize an "antibusing" leader, but McCabe drew freely on the language and protest tactics of the civil rights, black power, and antiwar movements. "Martin Luther King walked all over and he got a lot of things done," McCabe announced at a NAG "antibusing" rally. "This is our civil rights movement."[20] McCabe later told the *Washington Post* that she learned to make demands from "the black militants." "They've won many things, they've won their demands.... We've been losers because we haven't played the game by the rules that they've already set down.... I'm playing the game by their rules."[21] While McCabe did not elaborate on these rules, NAG's protests under her leadership dovetailed neatly with the conventions of television news coverage. NAG's protests generally occurred on weekdays during daytime hours so they could be filmed for later prime-time broadcast; they were well-organized public events; they were focused on a specific issue; and McCabe served as the group's clear leader and spokeswoman. To keep the "antibusing" protests in the media spotlight for as long as possible, moreover, McCabe organized different types of protests to give reporters new events to cover that built on the existing NAG storyline. "Publicity, attention—every day," she told the *National Observer,* "that's what we've got to have."[22] When a NAG picket line shut down a General Motors auto body factory, for example, it did not prompt GM to lobby for "antibusing" legislation (NAG's stated goal), but it did draw coverage from all three networks. CBS reported that NAG "tried something new today," while NBC reported that the group had adopted a "new tactic."[23]

CBS even noted the end of the school boycott, with anchor Walter Cronkite reading a quote from McCabe.[24] As a result of this repeated media exposure, McCabe received several speaking invitations that led her to "antibusing" meetings in Memphis, Dallas, and Columbus, Georgia.[25]

This recurring news coverage was important for McCabe because it allowed NAG's "antibusing" message to reach a large national audience at a time when the group could only claim a few thousand members in and around Pontiac and nearby Detroit. An NBC report on NAG's push for a new school boycott across Michigan on October 25, 1971, is particularly telling in this regard. As reporter Steve Delaney's introduction to the segment details, NAG's call for a statewide boycott was unsuccessful: "This was supposed to be school boycott day all over Michigan, but the drive by white parents to keep students home was effective only in Pontiac."[26] Still, the three-minute segment featured footage of McCabe and NAG supporters marching at the board of education building and relayed their call for more police in schools to prevent interracial violence. While McCabe and NAG lacked the statewide influence to move other Michigan parents to boycott, they found television news stations to be eager audiences for their protests.

In their pursuit of television visibility, McCabe and NAG benefited from the work of conservative politicians and media commentators who were beginning to hone their claims of liberal media bias. Vice President Spiro Agnew, for example, regularly criticized the media, singling out what he saw as the undue influence and liberal bias of television news. In a 1969 speech in Des Moines written by Pat Buchanan, Agnew argued that network newscasters "decide what 40 to 50 million Americans will learn of the day's events in the nation and in the world. We cannot measure this power and influence by the traditional democratic standards, for these men can create national issues overnight.... For millions of Americans the network reporter who covers a continuing issue—like the ABM [antiballistic missile] or civil rights— becomes, in effect, the presiding judge in a national trial by jury." Taking aim at civil rights, black power, and antiwar activists, Agnew also emphasized that television could shape protest tactics. "How many marches and demonstrations would we have," Agnew asked, "if the marchers did not know that the ever-faithful TV cameras would be there to record their antics for the next news show?"[27] Agnew's attack on television news prompted thousands of citizens to write similarly critical letters to the mailrooms at ABC, CBS, and NBC.[28] *NBC News* president Reuven Frank argued that "the Agnew speech shook every broadcasting professional," while the CBS Washington news director and bureau manager described the speech as sending "shock waves through the mass media."[29] More broadly, several newsmen shared the sentiment that the news media had given too much attention to minority protests. "In TV news departments we appear to know a lot about the black minority," NBC producer Shad Northshield commented. "It's the silent majority we must explore. We haven't done it. We didn't know it was *there!*" *CBS Morning News* anchor Joseph Benti concurred: "We spend so much time on angry blacks, angry youth. But what about that vast forgotten army out there? How many hardworking law-abiding whites are mad as hell because *their* story isn't being told?"[30] An NBC producer remarked simply, "The audience is becoming bored with Negro stories."[31] McCabe's "antibusing" protests were thus welcomed by television networks eager to broadcast more about the white working-class and middle-class citizens President Nixon called the "silent majority."

When Agnew complained that network news "can elevate men from obscurity to national prominence within a week," he was referring to Black Power activist Stokely Carmichael, but television news could also propel conservative grassroots activists like Irene McCabe to national prominence.[32] This television coverage prompted a critical editorial in the *Christian Science Monitor,* which argued that "giving national prime time and front-page headlines to a group of bellicose ladies has put the emphasis in the wrong place." Describing the history of school segregation in Pontiac, the editorial noted that the "busing" order should have been "no sudden surprise" and argued that "for the press and public to try to peg a history of bigotry and tension . . . on bussing is an injustice to the majority who are trying to do their best at the moment to accommodate needed social change."[33] This coverage of McCabe and NAG is emblematic of how television news presented "busing" disputes in different cities. While news stories occasionally included school board members, civil rights advocates, or parents who supported "busing," these voices made up only a fraction of the coverage. With their talking points broadcast repeatedly, "antibusing" activists controlled the terms of the debate.

In addition to benefiting from television news' preference for contemporary events, McCabe was candid about using her physical appearance and sexuality to draw more attention to herself and the "antibusing" cause. "I do these silly things to get attention. We women have to do our share of stirring up people power," she told journalist Maryanne Conheim. "Antibusing crusading can't all be so dour and long-faced."[34] McCabe frequently appeared in a tight-fitting T-shirt with the slogan "Bus Judges, Not Children" or with a

FIGURE 23. Irene McCabe in a National Action Group t-shirt at an "antibusing" meeting in Memphis, Tennessee. Associated Press photo, September 23, 1971.

bumper sticker across the front of her sweater. This brand of display worked well on television, more so than in newspapers, because television cameras presented viewers not just with attractive images of McCabe but also with footage of her leading marchers and confronting male politicians and education officials. Television news coverage of McCabe, while obviously edited, did not editorialize about or visually linger over McCabe's appearance. In contrast, newspaper reporters constantly searched for words to create a picture of McCabe for their readers. One journalist described McCabe as looking "like the pretty wife in television commercials," while other reporters described her variously as a "green-eyed frosted blonde with a voluptuous figure," an "uninhibited, shapely blonde who favors tight tee shirts, false eyelashes and heavy blue eye liner," a "slender, peppery housewife," and as performing with the "coolness of a veteran stripper."[35] Television viewers might have used these same terms to describe McCabe, but the terms were not inscribed into the television news segments in which she appears. Television news enabled McCabe, within the constraints of a male-dominated commercial medium, to speak for herself and present the physical image she desired. While scholars of this era of television news have shown how the assumed news spectator was constructed as male, television news must have also brought images of McCabe to female viewers across the country, many of whom shared her politics and others who did not.[36] Women played a significant role in leading "antibusing" protests across the country, and many of these women likely saw McCabe on television and drew inspiration from the skill she displayed as a grassroots activist on camera.[37] Rather than "men talking to men," as Harvey Molotoch described the news business in 1978, McCabe offers the interesting case of a woman, framed by men, talking to other women.[38]

PONTIAC BEYOND THE TV FRAME

The story in Pontiac was ostensibly about school desegregation, but none of the television networks referred to *Davis v. School District of City of Pontiac* (1970), the court case that led to the "busing" order. In *Davis,* Judge Keith wrote:

> This Court finds that the Pontiac Board of Education intentionally utilized the power at their disposal to locate new schools and arrange boundaries in such a way as to perpetuate the pattern of segregation within the City and thereby, deliberately, in contradiction of their announced policies of achieving a racial mixture in the schools, prevented integration. When the power to act is available, failure to take the necessary steps so as to negate or alleviate a situation which is harmful is as wrong as is the taking of affirmative steps to advance that situation. Sins of omission can be as serious as sins of commission. Where a Board of Education has contributed and played a major role in the development and growth of a segregated situation, the Board is guilty of de jure segregation. The fact that such came slowly and surreptitiously rather than by legislative pronouncement makes the situation no less evil.[39]

Keith's *Davis* ruling made Pontiac one of the first cities outside the South to be placed under court order to desegregate. The notion that the school desegregation controversy had moved north fueled much of the news coverage of

Pontiac, but Judge Keith's ruling made it clear that school segregation in Pontiac was not a new occurrence but had developed over several decades. Just as important, the *Davis* decision cast a critical light on so-called de facto segregation. Rather than seeing school segregation as a product of market forces and private decisions that government had no legal responsibility or authority to address, Judge Keith found that Pontiac school officials had taken specific actions regarding school siting, zoning, and student assignment that had contributed to the growth of a segregated school system and were unconstitutional. The *Davis* ruling was one of a number of successful cases brought by the NAACP and its Legal Defense Fund in the early 1970s regarding school desegregation outside the South, including cases in other Michigan cities—Benton Harbor, Kalamazoo, and Detroit—as well as *Keyes v. School District No. 1* (1973), the U.S. Supreme Court's decision that found evidence of unconstitutional segregation in Denver. The optimism prompted by these cases was severely constrained when the U.S. Supreme Court overturned federal district judge Stephen Roth's decision in *Milliken v. Bradley* (1974), ruling that desegregation plans could not extend into suburban school districts unless multiple districts had deliberately engaged in segregated policies. The Nixon administration, moreover, encouraged the Justice Department to focus its resources on de jure segregation in the South rather than de facto segregation.

The *Davis* ruling confirmed the existence of school segregation in Pontiac, a fact that was obvious to anyone who cared to look. A 1968 report from the Michigan Civil Rights Commission described Pontiac as "clearly segregated, with non-whites confined to a slowly expanding ghetto in the southern part of the city," which whites commonly referred to as "colored town."[40] "Although Pontiac adopted a 'Fair Housing Ordinance' last year," the commission's report continued,

> conditions remain as they have been for the past two or three decades.... Pontiac is a city divided by racial and ethnic prejudices and fears. Negro and Spanish American citizens are excluded from full participation in employment, housing, education, and social services. They are often denied equal protection under the laws and equal access to jobs and law enforcement agencies. The physical isolation which has resulted between white and nonwhite citizens has led to a communications gap of staggering proportions. Civil and governmental leaders have little concern for, or understanding of minority group problems. Negroes and Spanish Americans grow more and more distrustful of a community they feel is trying to contain them.[41]

Pontiac NAACP chairman Elbert Hatchett, who attended public schools in the city, knew well the dynamics of Pontiac's racial segregation and recalled that this knowledge had proved invaluable when he served as the plaintiff's attorney in the *Davis* case. "We knew the Pontiac school system backwards and forwards, and we knew that it was a system that had race as one of the considerations in the manner in which they undertook to educate the populace in the city of Pontiac," Hatchett recalled. "And we knew that the schools that were in the white affluent areas were given the benefit of much better facilities, much better equipment, much better everything than the counterparts in the predominantly black areas."[42] Like Hatchett, Pontiac teacher Jo Ann Walker understood the differences between the city's majority black and white schools and elaborated on these disparities in her testimony before the Senate Select Committee on Equal Educational Opportunity, describing the difference in resources and educational environment in these schools as "like going from hell to heaven." Whereas failing furnaces caused students in black schools to wear winter coats inside on cold days and teachers lacked pencils and chalk, at Le Baron, where the only black students were in special education classes, Walker noted that "there was a stockroom full of paper and pencils, everything you needed to do the job." Le Baron Elementary, Walker told the Senate committee, "is the school where Mrs. McCabe's daughter would go if she were not boycotting."[43] In his testimony to the same committee, Hatchett fielded a question from Senator Walter Mondale of Minnesota, the committee chairman, who asked, "Was your case *[Davis]* really so hard to prove as the Government often claims northern cases to be?" "The [school] board came to the court and forthrightly admitted . . . that the school system was segregated," Hatchett replied. "The only thing we were left with was to argue the cause. . . . So it was not quite as difficult as many of the northern cases."[44] The history of school segregation in Pontiac that preceded the *Davis* case and court-ordered desegregation was crucial to making sense of NAG's "antibusing" protests, but little of this context reached television viewers. Television news reporters were drawn to the Pontiac protests as a new northern angle on the school integration story, but did little to explain the series of events that had led to the "busing" conflicts.

More than simply providing balance to their "busing" coverage, had television news reporters spent more time talking to black residents in Pontiac, they would have found conflicted feelings regarding "busing" as a means of achieving education equality. Sadie Davis, whose son Donald Davis Jr. was the named plaintiff in the *Davis* case, told the *Detroit Free Press* that she "does not necessarily" support "busing," but that "I support total integration of the schools, and, in Pontiac, busing is the only way you can integrate."[45] Sadie's husband, Donald Davis Sr., made it clear that he was concerned about the limited curricular options and materials at the majority-black Franklin School. "I don't blame white parents for not wanting their children to go to Franklin," he said. "I didn't want mine to go there either. Maybe now they'll try to upgrade the education there."[46] Charles Tucker Jr., a black businessman and member of the city commission, also noted the importance of equal resources: "All I want is that every person gets equal services from the community's tax dollars. Blacks really aren't all that interested in living in areas because they're white areas. . . . It's hard to accept the fact that we must have integration in order to provide the same kind of services for people living on the (predominantly black) south end as they have had on the (predominantly white) north end. But I guess at this time, we must."[47] Television newscasts regularly sought out a black politician or parent as a representative voice to balance their focus on white "antibusing" protesters, but such voices received limited airtime and, more importantly, could not possibly represent the range of African American viewpoints regarding "busing." Many black parents opposed "busing" in favor of more control of schools in black communities, while others offered cautious and qualified support for busing while raising concerns about the quality of schools, the distance of bus rides, and the safety of black children bused to white neighborhoods. Rather than adapting their coverage to present the multiple and often conflicting black opinions on "busing," network newscasts structured their busing segments in ways that presented individual black politicians, activists, or parents as representative of black opinion.

The range of opinions on "busing" among white Pontiac residents was also more varied than television news coverage of McCabe and NAG would suggest. Shirley Frantz, president of the Alcott Parent-Teacher Association in northwest Pontiac, confessed that she "was afraid to go to the black end of town" but changed her opinion on "busing" after an exchange visit to the majority-black Bagley School, where her ten-year-old son was assigned. "All you ever heard was that Bagley was the worst school in Pontiac," she said. "But the principal helped to change my mind. He made me feel right at home and I know he'll take good care of [my son]. If more mothers had gone, they'd have felt better, too."[48] Several letters to the editor in the *Detroit Free Press* criticized McCabe and the white protesters. One letter argued that while "Irene McCabe may feel she is spouting good old fashioned WASP Christian ethic," she will one day need to answer charges of "inciting to riot through demagoguery" and "racism."[49] Michael Elli wrote, "I, and I suspect others like me, are becoming increasingly disgusted with the continuing antics of the white mobs in Pontiac. I sincerely wish that Irene McCabe would take her red-neck friends and go back to Alabama, where they belong, and make Michigan a better place to live in."[50] While this writer either did not know or wanted to ignore the fact that McCabe was born and raised in Pontiac and found abundant support among longtime Michigan residents, letters like these suggest that Pontiac's white residents were not as unified in their opposition to "busing" as television news coverage suggested.

Television news, of course, rarely offered this type of historical depth or detailed surveys of public opinion. William Grant, education editor for the *Detroit Free Press,* suggested that this was particularly true for school desegregation. "School desegregation is one of the issues which the media are least suited to cover," Grant argued.

> The media are best able to report on events which unfold within a short time span—a day, a week, a few weeks at most. Those things which develop over much longer periods of time are likely to be covered by many different reporters. It is difficult for newspaper stories, and even more difficult for broadcast reports, of a long-running event to capture the origins and history of the issue. . . . Desegregation involves understanding law, education, and social science. There are few lawyers, educators, or social scientists who have managed that broad understanding. It is not surprising that few journalists do either.[51]

If school desegregation was difficult for local reporters to cover, these challenges were even more acute for national television reporters, who arrived in cities like Pontiac with few local sources and little knowledge of the issues surrounding desegregation in that specific community. In the absence of the local knowledge or contacts required for informed background reports, television reporters and their camera operators were drawn to events and speakers that would make the issue easily legible to a national audience. McCabe and other activists understood that a highly vocal and visible "antibusing" minority could garner most of the media's attention. Television news personnel did not need to share the politics of grassroots activists to be drawn to "antibusing" leaders and protests and to deem these people and events worthy of regular news coverage.

Among the important strategies McCabe learned from media-savvy civil rights groups was to organize protests as television-friendly events. Her most successful and widely reported event was a 620-mile "mothers' march" from Pontiac to Washington, DC, to support a constitutional amendment prohibiting "busing." The specific length of the march was selected to recall the "antibusing" amendment, House Joint Resolution 620, sponsored by New York congressman Norman Lent. McCabe and five other Pontiac mothers set off on the six-week trek on March 15, 1972, and both print and television reporters noted the event's historical echoes. "How and why," one article asked, "did the trim housewife emerge as a national figure emulating the tactics of the civil rights marchers of the '60s?"[52] At the Pontiac send-off for McCabe and the marching mothers, ABC's Jim Kincaid noted, "Irene McCabe and her National Action Group have taken a page from other demonstrations in the past. It won't be the first walk to Washington, but it may be one of the longest."[53] In addition to the clear reference to the 1963 March on Washington for Jobs and Freedom, the marchers also made a side trip to Massillon, Ohio, the starting point of Coxey's Army, a group of unemployed workers who marched on Washington in 1894.[54] A 1967 Mothers' March on Washington by welfare rights activists, which did not receive extensive media attention, may also have factored into McCabe's planning.[55] As these historical precedents suggest, McCabe's "mothers' march" was designed to be easily recognized as a newsworthy event.

Television and newspaper coverage enabled McCabe and her fellow marchers to claim motherhood as both a private and public identity. Like other "antibusing" activists, McCabe framed her opposition in terms of her duty as a parent to protect the private spheres of home and family. "I object to the long arm of the federal government reaching into my home and controlling the children I gave birth to," she told a reporter in West Virginia.[56] At another stop on the march, McCabe remarked, "I would have been an unfit mother if I didn't try to do something about [my children being bused]."[57] To fulfill her responsibilities as a mother, McCabe argued, she needed to become a "marching mother." McCabe required media coverage to assume this public identity of motherhood, and in turn the "mothers' march" cast familiar conventions of women as homemakers and consumers of television in a different light. In their six-week march to Washington, McCabe and the other women traveled hundreds of miles from their children and husbands in Pontiac, and hundreds of miles from the domestic spaces that were central to television conventions for representing family life.[58] McCabe and the Pontiac mothers temporarily left their homes, families, and televisions and emerged via television news broadcasts and newspaper accounts as "marching mothers." These "mad mamas," as one newspaper called them, leveraged their public identities as mothers to became television performers rather than domestic consumers of television.[59]

Early in the march, McCabe told a newspaper reporter, "This is not my favorite thing—walking, but hopefully people will look along the way at six miserable women on television and write their congressman in favor of the [antibusing] amendment."[60] As McCabe's reference to "six miserable women" suggests, the physical pain endured by the marchers was a recurring theme in print coverage of the march. Two weeks into the walk, one marcher had her calves wrapped in bandages, and McCabe noted, "I'm wearing sun glasses to hide the tears."[61] After particularly hilly terrain in West Virginia, McCabe told a waiting reporter, "When you consider what we've been through, it's amazing. You think your chest is going to pop open, your heart explodes and then there's another vicious, vicious hill to climb."[62] A photo of McCabe icing her feet accompanied a story on the marching mothers' arrival in Maryland.[63] Just a day before reaching Washington, McCabe stopped for medical treatment on her feet. "I simply could not bear the pain any longer," she said. "It has been this way for almost two weeks. Every step, I don't know for how many days, has just been agony."[64] The marching mothers' misery became as much a part of the story as their opposition to "busing," and here again, coverage of the march built on and challenged television conventions. The mothers' suffering gave the march a narrative emotional quality similar to television soap operas or medical dramas, and like these genres, news accounts encouraged viewers and readers to follow along with the narrative and suffer vicariously with the mothers. The marchers encouraged this view of them suffering on behalf of others. As a sign on the group's support van declared, "Irene McCabe Is Walking to Washington DC, So Your Children Can Walk to School." At the same time, the marchers' visible suffering buttressed their authority as mothers in the public political sphere. A photo taken after the marchers reached the nation's capital, for example, shows McCabe meeting with U.S. senators William Brock of Tennessee and Robert Griffin of Michigan, who had cosponsored an "antibusing" constitutional amendment.[65] McCabe is seated on a couch in Griffin's office, with one shoe off and her leg elevated on an ottoman. Unlike the trope of women sitting on

FIGURE 24. CBS anchor Walter Cronkite announces Irene McCabe's arrival in Washington, DC. *CBS Evening News,* April 27, 1972.

sofas watching soaps and suffering vicariously, McCabe and the marchers undertook physical challenges in support of legislation and, thanks to their public suffering, earned an audience with powerful politicians.

The Associated Press and United Press International wire services distributed dozens of stories on the march, which appeared in newspapers across the country, and this print media coverage served as advance promotion for the culminating rally when the mothers reached Washington at the end of April 1972. The news reports inspired a group of eight mothers from Richmond, Virginia, to walk one hundred miles to join the Pontiac marchers. "Irene McCabe is a national heroine," said one of the Richmond mothers. "It was a spur of the moment thing, but I figured if she could walk 620 miles from Pontiac, Mich., to Washington then I could do it from Virginia."[66]

Television cameras from ABC, CBS, and NBC followed McCabe and the other mothers as they arrived in Washington. The coverage on each station picked up the themes that had circulated in print coverage over the prior six weeks, emphasizing that the marchers were attempting to bring national political attention to the "busing" issue, that they had endured physical pain during their long walk to Washington, and most importantly, that they

FIGURE 25. The "marching mothers" received media attention throughout their six-week trek from Pontiac to Washington, DC. Associated Press, April 27, 1972.

FIGURE 26. CBS's shot of the mothers' feet (McCabe is at right) echoed the newspapers' stories about the physical pain the mothers endured during the march. *CBS Evening News,* April 27, 1972.

undertook the march as mothers. The marchers' first stop at the steps of the Capitol, where they met with then Michigan congressman Gerald Ford, Tennessee senator William Brock, Massachusetts congresswoman and "anti-busing" leader Louise Day Hicks, and several other prominent politicians, reminded viewers of the political purpose of the mothers' march. As the mothers walked the final blocks to the "antibusing" rally on the grounds of the Washington Monument, the television reports segued to focus on how the mothers, especially McCabe, had gamely suffered in support of their cause. Each station mentioned the mothers' feet and their soreness after miles of walking. CBS cut to a medium shot of three of the mothers' feet, while reporter Tony Sargent said, "Mrs. McCabe and the others all had foot and leg problems along the way, some requiring doctors' care."[67] These scenes made the mothers' suffering, described in dozens of newspapers stories filed during the march, visible to a national television audience.

Not coincidentally, McCabe's speech at the rally picked up this theme, connecting the physical pain of the march and the pain of childbirth to the building of an "antibusing" coalition. McCabe limped visibly as she approached the podium, outfitted with several microphones. "I can't believe we walked the whole way," she told the crowd. "I personally have suffered a great deal of pain on this walk. It was far more physically grueling than I ever could have imagined. The only time I have ever been in such pain has been in labor. Whenever you're in labor, you finally give birth to something beautiful. We've labored long and we've been through a great deal of pain, but it's worth it, because we have given birth to the rekindling of the government of the people, by the people, and for the people. Look, you're here!"[68] McCabe claimed the authority to speak based on her status as a mother and her related ability to present a common-sense view on a complex political issue.[69] While McCabe's rhetoric drew on familiar themes of motherhood and populism, television gave her rallying cries a crucial visual component and broadcast her message on a scale inaccessible to the vast majority of grassroots female activists.

In another example of how television news reports framed McCabe differently from the way they framed feminist activists, none of the broadcasts discussed her in relation to her husband or children, despite her regular invocation of her identity as a mother and housewife and despite newspaper accounts of marital tensions while McCabe and the other mothers were away from Pontiac. The *Chicago Tribune,* for example, noted, "Not too many months ago, Charles McCabe wanted to divorce his wife Irene, the ardent antibus leader and organizer of NAG. Today he's staying home with the children while she walks to Washington to place her cause before Congress." The march forced Charles McCabe and the other "unpublicized husbands and families," the *Tribune* suggested, to "change their conception of women."[70] In leaving their husbands and children for six weeks, McCabe and the other marching mothers clearly stepped outside the bounds of traditional motherhood, but they prompted little of the gender anxiety that accompanied network news treatment of second-wave feminism.[71] While McCabe did not publicly identify as a feminist or an antifeminist, her support for "antibusing" politics, her visible affirmation of femininity, and her embrace of the terms *mother* and *housewife* likely led television reporters and commentators not to see McCabe as a threat to gender norms. At the same time, these assumptions enabled McCabe to engage in political action that surely would have brought censure to other women.

At the end of McCabe's speech, each network followed her cue ("Look, you're here!") and cut to the crowd. In those shots, those gathered, almost all white and mostly women, hold clearly worded placards reading, "Stop Forced Busing," "Pass H.J. Res 620," and "Welcome Irene." Behind the crowd, the Washington Monument is visible, ringed by U.S. flags. It is an impressive but misleading sight. While McCabe and the march promoters promised ten thousand people, the *Washington Post* estimated that only five hundred to eight hundred people attended the "antibusing" rally.[72] CBS's Tony Sargent noted drily, "Despite Mrs. McCabe's dramatic march, today's turnout was far smaller than expected."[73] L. Brooks Patterson, NAG's attorney, expressed his disappointment at the low turnout. "This hillside should have been covered with all your neighbors and friends," he told the crowd. "They scream the loudest when their children are bused, and they should be here to protest."[74] In Michigan, many questioned whether the rally accurately represented public opposition to "busing." While the Michigan House of Representatives passed a resolution (by a 61–28 vote) honoring McCabe, calling her "the symbol of tens of millions of people who are opposed to forced busing," the Detroit Urban League was unconvinced. "With the small rally turnout Mrs. McCabe received in Washington, how can the House assume or even support the notion that Mrs. McCabe represents such a large segment of the American population?" asked Detroit Urban League executive director Francis Kornegay.[75] For her part, McCabe expressed frustration with the turnout to the *Washington Post*: "If I can give up a year of my life (to fight busing) why can't they turn out for day?"[76] McCabe's disappointment was no

FIGURE 27. Irene McCabe addresses a smaller than expected crowd at the end of the mothers' march to Washington, DC. Associated Press, April 27, 1972.

FIGURE 28. While the turnout for the mothers' march on Washington disappointed Irene McCabe, the event reached millions of television viewers. These supporters hold signs endorsing McCabe and House Joint Resolution 620, an "antibusing" constitutional amendment. *ABC Evening News,* April 27, 1972.

doubt sincere, but it underestimated the march's success as a media event. The march reportedly cost $7,500 and was paid for by fund-raising in Pontiac and along the parade route.[77] Despite this small budget, it generated daily newspaper reports and television news coverage of the marchers' departure from Pontiac and their arrival in Washington. Here again, news media, especially television, helped McCabe dramatically scale up her "antibusing" message. Television news brought McCabe's rally, which despite a month of advance publicity failed to draw one thousand people, to a national audience of millions of television viewers. By any account, this was an extraordinary return on the time and money McCabe and NAG invested in the march.

The mothers' march reveals both the limitations and promises of television as a tool for political organizing. Television news asks that citizens view certain people, places, and events as newsworthy but does not necessarily lead to particular political outcomes.[78] Television brought McCabe's message to millions but moved mere hundreds to join the rally in the nation's capital. Television's importance to "antibusing" politics, however, was more significant and more diffuse that this low turnout suggests. Television news was never interested in McCabe in and of herself; rather, she drew the attention of television cameras as the leader of a group that organized television-ready protests focused on a specific issue. When the "busing" battle died down in Pontiac, television shifted from McCabe to "antibusing" protests in other cities. Television coverage did not drive massive numbers of people to NAG's rally in Washington or bring McCabe lasting political power, but it did help thwart "busing" for school desegregation. In Louisville, Boston, Cleveland, and several other cities, "antibusing" activists leveraged the characteristics of television news to argue that their rights as parents and homeowners were being violated by activist judges and federal bureaucrats. Likewise, politicians such as Florida governor Claude Kirk, Alabama governor and presidential candidate George Wallace, and President Richard Nixon voiced their opposition to "busing" in carefully planned events and speeches that played well on television.[79] Support for "busing," by contrast, was less organized and less vocal, and when "probusing" events were organized, like the forty-thousand-person march in support of desegregation in Boston in 1975, they received far less television coverage than "antibusing" protests.[80] As the "antibusing" activists who received the most media attention in this era, McCabe and her fellow marching mothers are the most visible example of how grassroots groups and politicians used television to frame the issue of "busing" for school desegregation.

While "busing" continued to be a major political issue throughout the 1970s, the mothers' march on Washington was the pinnacle of McCabe's political career. In Pontiac, tensions emerged within NAG over the media's focus on McCabe and over her leadership style. When asked what the march had accomplished, marcher Lorene Fligger noted, "Well, in my case, I walked to Washington." Another mother, Ardith Heineman, who quit NAG shortly after the march, said, "Irene's style of doing things is to tell you to do it. If you ask questions she whirls on you and tells you not to straddle the fence."[81] By February 1973, the Associated Press reported, "The National Action Group (NAG), once the most vocal and best publicized antibusing group in the nation, has fallen into a state of near chaos."[82] As NAG meetings became increasingly contentious and McCabe faced challenges from rival NAG factions, she stepped down, lamenting, "Too many people are interested in fighting me and not fighting busing."[83] After leaving NAG, McCabe campaigned unsuccessfully for a position on the county board of supervisors and floated the idea of challenging Michigan senator Philip Hart for his seat.[84] Unlike Boston's Louise Day Hicks or Los Angeles's Bobbi Fiedler, both elected to the U.S. House of Representatives largely on the strength of their "antibusing" credentials, McCabe's campaign did not lead to success in electoral politics.[85] She expressed frustration that the politicians and political advisers who had once eagerly met with her ignored her once she was out of the national spotlight. After L. Brooks Patterson, the former NAG legal adviser, was elected county prosecutor, McCabe noted, "I was once his voice of the average person. He doesn't need me now. He's elected. A guy from Hazel Park [a Detroit suburb] told me a long time ago, 'they're gonna use you, honey.' He was right."[86] McCabe also questioned the sincerity of John Ehrlichman, President Nixon's chief domestic affairs adviser, who had indicated when she met with him after the mothers' march that Nixon would support a constitutional amendment opposing "busing." "Perhaps he used us as a ploy to quiet down the antibusing protesting voices," she told a reporter.[87] "I'll never lift a hand to support another political hack," she later declared.[88] Reporters sought out McCabe's opinion on court decisions and "busing" protests for several years after the march, but by the late 1970s McCabe led her life away from television cameras, selling real estate in Clarkston, Michigan, ten miles northwest of Pontiac.

Just over a year after the mothers' march, the *New York Times* ran a follow-up story on McCabe. The report, "Busing Foe Fades from Limelight," began by noting, "Irene McCabe, who once waged an antibusing campaign that won national attention, is a sadder but wiser housewife again."[89] The story is a curious coda to McCabe's highly publicized campaign, focusing largely on the prosaic aspects of her life in Pontiac: her hobbies, her children's dentist appointments, and the change in "her hair color from streaked to platinum blonde." Removed from the public spotlight, the story suggests, McCabe was just a housewife. What the story misses is how McCabe's identities as housewife, mother, and grassroots activist were always closely intertwined, how these identities were articulated in both private and public spheres, how these identities functioned at both local and national scales, and how McCabe's engagements with television news made her the face of "antibusing" politics in the early 1970s.

. . .

After Pontiac faded from the national media spotlight, another television program took up the subject of the city's school desegregation. "As We See It" (1975–77) was researched, written, and coproduced by teenagers in sixteen cities that experienced "busing" for school desegregation, including Pontiac, Boston, Miami, San Francisco, and Memphis. Developed by Chicago PBS station WTTW with funding from the Department of Health, Education, and Welfare, the series used documentary techniques, narrative dialogues, skits, satires, and film segments to examine students' firsthand experiences of "busing," as well as the protests and controversies surrounding these desegregation efforts. The series' pilot episode, "Graduation Flashbacks," was set at the high-school graduation exercises for the first class to go through court-ordered "busing" in Pontiac. While valedictorian Joe Urla speaks, the camera focuses on a series of students in the audience, and we hear and see their memories of school desegregation. Tony Simuel, a black student in Pontiac who worked on the series, recalled that the episode was trying to show "each student's perspective on how they viewed their experience in the school." Simuel's graduation flashback notes how the school required hall passes after desegregation, commenting, "If you were me the guy was going to stop you every time in the hall."[90] The six different viewpoints—from white, black, and Puerto Rican young women and men—do not agree with the valedictorian or with each other. "As We See It" complicates the national news media's picture of "busing," because it resists easy talking points and focuses instead on perspectives rooted in the specific history of school desegregation in Pontiac.[91]

When Judge Keith's desegregation order went into effect in 1971, Tony Simuel attended Madison Junior High School, the school McCabe's daughter and several other children of NAG activists were scheduled to attend. "These kids from other neighborhoods were thrown in, and we were eleven years old, we didn't care," Simuel remembered. "It was a little scary at first, but that honestly did not last long at all. . . . The students got along fine if the parents would have just left us alone."[92] Some students surely had less positive experiences of school desegregation, but one of the problems with the news media's fixation on Irene McCabe is that it made it nearly impossible to hear what black students felt about "busing" for school desegregation in Pontiac or elsewhere.

SEVEN

"It's Not the Bus, It's Us"

THE COMPLEXITY OF BLACK OPINIONS
ON "BUSING"

What people who oppose busing object to, is not the little yellow school buses, but rather to the little black bodies that are on the bus.

—GEORGIA STATE LEGISLATOR JULIAN BOND, *1972*

We don't want Crestwood High to be a Junior High School, we want justice. We don't want your [year-round school] plan, we want justice. We don't want your four super high schools or your racist integration plans—we want justice. We want Crestwood High to remain a high school period.

— *Student from Crestwood High School (Chesapeake, Virginia) explaining opposition to the school board's desegregation plan, 1971*

"I THINK A BLACK MOTHER should be heard," called out Inez Andry as she strode confidently to the microphone. Speaking before the San Francisco Board of Education in the crowded Nourse Auditorium and before a local television audience via San Francisco's KPIX-TV, Andry interrupted the agenda of white mothers from Mothers Support Neighborhood Schools speaking against "busing." "We don't believe in busing either," Andry told the board, to applause from the crowd. "Not for the same reason," Andry continued. "We want our schools in our neighborhood. We don't want to go to no other neighborhood. But we want education, the kind we need in our neighborhood.... We want to see all kinds of books. Black books. We want to be recognized. We don't want integration, we'll get that. We want education. And integration will not educate our black children. Black books, more black principals, some more black people on the school board, a black woman up there too." After describing the school board's integration plan as a "game of craps," Andry told the board, "I don't know how to speak like these other ladies, because I didn't have that kind of education, and I don't want my kids to get that kind." "You don't need it," one of the young black men who flanked Andry responded. As a member of the Hayes Valley Schools Committee, Andry said, "two years we negotiated, we pleaded, we begged, I cried . . . and other people did it with me, but now is not the time for that, now is the time for fighting. . . . You want to keep your pretty little San Francisco pretty? Well you have to come with it. Because I want to live here and nobody's not running me out. And I'm going to fight for what I want here. And I'm not going to fight alone, because I got many back of me. And if I die fighting, I'll be dying for what I believe in." The applause from the mostly white audience was more tepid as Andry concluded her speech. "If we can't have these schools of our own and a board of education to go along with us, maybe it's time to have our own board of education."[1]

In just over seven minutes, Andry articulated a series of concerns and demands that reflected the sentiments of many black parents across the country. Like Andry, many black parents wanted to see more black school board members, black principals, black teachers, and black history and culture included in the curriculum. Various currents of black thought—Black Nationalism, Pan-Africanism, and grassroots educational traditions—fueled these calls for black community control of schools, and in each case, racial integration was not the horizon of educational equality or black freedom. While Andry had clearly formed opinions on the issue, "busing" did not fuel her political activity.

Andry therefore disrupted the February 1968 school board meeting not only by demanding an opportunity to speak but also by expanding beyond the "busing" frame preferred by media, school officials, and politicians. KPIX reporter Ben Williams opened the hour-long special by describing how the board was holding a special meeting to hear from citizens on the "feverishly controversial problem of school busing." Before Andry took the microphone, school board president Edward Kemmitt apologized to Mothers Support Neighborhood Schools for deviating from the "antibusing" agenda. "I do feel badly on this. I had worked with these people. I recognized their problem. I had several phone conversations with these people. I was assured that this was going to be the agenda. . . . I personally do not like this . . . but if this is the way it's going to go, I guess it's the way it's going to go."[2] KPIX reporter Rollin Post described Andry as making the proceedings more "complicated and exciting" and concluded by connecting the heated school board meeting in

San Francisco to the battle over "busing" in Boston: "I think we also learned tonight how someone like Mrs. Hicks in Boston could rise to fame and fortune very quickly on an issue such as busing."[3] For San Francisco mayor Joseph Alioto, the lesson from the school board hearing was clear. "No one in the community, including a large segment of the Negro community, really wanted to bus school children," he said.[4]

Inez Andry's strenuous attempt to make sure that a black mother was heard and seen in San Francisco's school battle and the efforts of media, school officials, and politicians to contain her comments as part of a "busing" debate illustrate at the local level a dynamic that played out nationally. Once the news media and politicians adopted "busing" as the dominant framework for discussing school desegregation, it became difficult for them to understand the diversity of black opinion on school desegregation or to recognize that "busing" was not the major issue for blacks that it was for whites who opposed school desegregation. Television news coverage of the southern civil rights movement informed the networks' approach to "busing," but this model proved poorly suited to the particular dynamics of the issue. On the one hand, "antibusing" activists appropriated the language and tactics of the civil rights movement rather than using explicitly racist language. On the other hand, the diversity of black opinion on "busing" made it difficult for broadcasters to present a single person or organization as representative of African American viewpoints, as they had with Martin Luther King Jr. and the Southern Christian Leadership Conference in the early 1960s.

Black politicians, activists, parents, and students articulated a wide range of views regarding "busing." Black nationalists like Roy Innis, director of the Congress of Racial Equality, opposed "busing" in favor of providing the black community with greater control of their schools; U.S. congresswoman Shirley Chisholm, activist Jesse Jackson, and the NAACP offered vocal criticism of racism in "antibusing" protests and legislation, and more cautious support for "busing" as a policy; and black parents took up a range of positions, raising concerns about the quality of schools, the distance of bus rides, and the safety of black children bused to white neighborhoods.

Rather than adapting their coverage to present the multiple and often conflicting black opinions on "busing," network newscasts structured their "busing" segments around white "antibusing" parents and politicians and presented black viewpoints as secondary. In Pontiac, for example, national broadcasts included a ten- to twenty-second sound bite from Pontiac

NAACP chairman Elbert Hatchett or a black parent in a three- to four-minute segment that focused on Irene McCabe and the National Action Group. In Boston, violent protests outside white high schools received far more coverage than viewpoints of black students, parents, or activists. This dynamic played out in television news coverage of "busing" in cities across the country. While school desegregation was the dominant civil rights issue of the era, there were no specific black people associated with the "busing" story, no worthy black students like the Little Rock Nine to delineate who was on the right side of history. Black students, parents, and activists fought tirelessly for decades to improve the educational options in majority-black schools, but the "busing" frame pushed these efforts to the background in favor of white protests. Without identifying the black students whose rights were at stake in the battle over school desegregation, "busing" appeared to be, as its critics charged, an inconvenient, unnecessary, and unjust intrusion on white families. That many black parents, including Inez Andry, spoke against "busing" only served to entrench this perspective.

This chapter examines what "busing" meant to black communities. Drawing on black newspapers as well as reports and commentary from black activists, parents, politicians, teachers, and students, three broad themes emerge. First, rather than accepting "busing" as the logical frame for debating school desegregation, black people argued that white opposition to "busing" was simply a new way of expressing antiblack racism, that "busing" was a phony issue which obscured the causes of educational inequality, and that "busing" had long been used to maintain segregated schools. Second, school desegregation plans frequently led to negative outcomes for black students and teachers, such as the closure of formerly black schools and the loss of employment for black teachers. Third, black students in recently desegregated schools were disproportionately suspended and pushed out of school. Each of these themes illuminates why black communities were often ambivalent to "busing." The various responses and alternatives black people offered were largely ignored by white media and politicians, who instead focused on more adamantly "antibusing" black viewpoints, such as the National Black Political Convention in Gary, Indiana, or Clay Smothers, who called himself "the most conservative black man in America" and appeared at "antibusing" rallies across the country. Like the San Francisco school officials and reporters who tried to contain Inez Andry's wide-ranging critique of educational inequality, national media and politicians preferred black voices that did not disrupt the predetermined "busing" frame. Many black parents would have concurred with Andry's comment, "We don't believe in busing either," but for them too, the reasons were complicated.

"IT'S US"

The aphorism "It's not the bus, it's us" served as a shorthand way for the black community to affirm that the "busing" debate was actually about antiblack racism. Speaking at Ohio State University in April 1972, Student Nonviolent Coordinating Committee (SNCC) cofounder and Georgia state legislator Julian Bond described the underlying motivations for opposing "busing" for school desegregation in clear terms. "What people who oppose busing object to," Bond told the audience, "is not the little yellow school buses, but rather to the little black bodies that are on the bus."[5] The following month, the NAACP Legal Defense Fund used a similar formulation as a title to a report, "It's Not the Distance, 'It's the Niggers,'" condemning President Nixon's call for a moratorium on "busing" orders and refuting the president's claims about "busing." "The proposed moratorium on busing threatens gains which have been made in the long and painful struggle to fulfill the constitutional rights of children to equal education opportunities," the report read. "These proposals, which would curtail only one kind of busing—busing to desegregate schools—and not any other kind of pupil transportation, barely camouflage their racist motivation."[6]

Like Bond and the NAACP Legal Defense Fund, black politicians and journalists dedicated a great deal of energy to exposing the underlying racism of "antibusing" measures. After New York's legislature approved the Lent-Kunzeman "neighborhood schools" bill prohibiting "busing" in 1969, Assemblyman Arthur Eve described the bill as the "worst kind of racism and very dangerous. It is hard for me to believe that I am standing in the chamber of the Assembly of the Empire State and not Alabama or South Africa."[7] For *Los Angeles Sentinel* columnist Stanley Robertson, "busing" made it clear that racism was not exclusively southern. "The year 1971 was the one during which bussing came to the North," Robertson wrote, "and suddenly the country discovered that there were a lot of Archie Bunkers who lived outside of Birmingham, Jackson and Lake Charles—lived in such sedate and supposedly discrimination-free areas as San Francisco, Forrest Hills and Boston."[8] National Urban League president Vernon Jordan struck a similar tone, drawing parallels between northern and southern racism. The "busing" controversy, he argued, was a "northernized" version of the southern resistance to desegregation in the 1950s. "I see little difference between the agitators who stood in front of public schools in Little Rock and New Orleans fifteen years ago and the distorted faces and hate-filled words of white parents in Canarsie a few weeks ago."[9] Writing in the *Chicago Defender,* Frank Stanley described the "furor" over "busing" as "baffling." "Pure and simple, it's the old issue of white supremacy fanned to a red heat again under the egis of busing," Stanley wrote.[10]

Black critics described "busing" as an early example of "dog whistle" politics, where racist sentiments were repackaged in coded language.[11] Following President Nixon's first major statement on school desegregation in 1970, U.S. congresswoman Shirley Chisholm said, "Nixon's statement this week was veiled in a dense fog of vague, fine sounding phrases. But it was also larded with code words like 'neighborhood school' and references to school busing that made it easy for southern segregationists to understand what it means. Nixon is paying off another installment of his 1968 debt to Dixie, and trying to store up credit for 1972."[12] Whitney Young, who preceded Jordan as president of the National Urban League, also saw coded appeals to racism at play in the "busing" debate. In an open letter to Jim Crow, Young wrote, "Part of the reason you came back in the schools is the phony smokescreen raised about integration. Code words like 'bussing' were much nicer to use than the straight out 'keep the schools white,' your supporters once used."[13] In an editorial on the eve of the 1972 election, the *Norfolk Journal and Guide* argued that black voters should oppose Nixon and his use of "code phrases." "The busing issue is one of the most divisive forces in America today," the editors argued. "It is an emotional issue that has been given respectability through such phrases as 'forced busing' and 'neighborhood schools.' Seemingly lost is the fact that 'neighborhood schools' actually mean segregated schools."[14]

While "busing" spoke to deeply entrenched antiblack prejudice, the focus on "busing" by white media and politicians masked the legal issues at play in school desegregation cases. "White Americans must understand that busing is a phony issue," Vernon Jordan said in comments that were replayed on the black public affairs television show *Black Journal.* "The real issue is the Constitutional rights of black people. The issue is so lethal that it is bound to seep outwards and poison the moral climate of our nation. Busing constitutes a 'domestic Vietnam.' It is the responsibility of white Americans to act now or face the probability of looking back a decade hence at a nation embracing full apartheid."[15] The ten black lawyers who resigned from the Justice Department in protest over President Nixon's call for a moratorium on "busing" for school desegregation wrote a letter to the *Washington Post* in which they argued that "busing" clouded which and whose rights were at stake. "Busing is not a real issue; it is instead a sham," the lawyers wrote. "We as ardent students of the civil rights struggle, have concluded that the recent fervor in the area of busing is nothing more than a thinly veiled attempt to sacrifice the rights of minority children to racist pressure groups and political expedience.... What we have been witnessing, when stripped of its shroud of innocence, is an attempted roll-back, a camouflaged effort to resurrect the concept of 'separate but equal,' and a deliberate effort to make the advancement of desegregation circular, beginning and ending with Plessy v. Ferguson."[16] In the heat of Boston's "busing crisis," the NAACP took out a full-page ad in the *New York Times* with the heading "The Law vs. the Mob": "The issue in Boston today is not whether 'busing' is good or bad; it is whether this nation's Constitution and laws are to be upheld and enforced or flagrantly violated.... The black parents of Boston don't enjoy sending their children out to face the mob any more than the black parents of Little Rock, New Orleans, Birmingham, Selma or Montgomery. But they know what happens when the mob makes the laws."[17]

In addition to calling out "busing" as a coded appeal to racist sentiments and an issue that obscured the constitutional rights of black students, black commentators also noted that buses had long been used to transport students, often to segregated schools. "What bothers me," Shirley Chisholm said, "is where were all those [antibusing] voices when black children were being bused right past their neighborhood schools in Mississippi, Georgia and Alabama ... riding old rat-trap buses down the back roads to dirty schools with tarpaper and no toilets? I've seen little children in Mississippi get up at 5 A.M. to take a bus one hour to a little shanty on the outskirts of town, and one back home again. If you believe in neighborhood schools, why didn't you talk about busing then?"[18] Historian John Hope Franklin described "busing" as "an example of the lengths to which people go to protect their racism," and tried to put the issue in historical perspective. "All of this talk about the evils of busing is almost amusing. Back in the 1930s and 40s children all over the country, especially in rural areas, were bused to new centralized rural schools. No one ever complained. It was acknowledged that the centralized schools could do a better job than the little one-room school houses and that a bus trip was a small price to pay for a better education...."

Now when busing is proposed as a partial remedy to segregation, everyone is clamoring about how awful it is for children to go to school outside their own community."[19] The *Norfolk Journal and Guide* featured an editorial cartoon with a school bus labeled "segregated busing for black children" driving past a white school, with a caption quoted from Vernon Jordan: "Black people need only think back a few years . . . to recall how they were bused far from home past nearby predominantly white schools to attend all-black ones."[20]

All these comments, printed in black newspapers or spoken at community meetings, were implicitly critical of white media for adopting "busing" as a frame for discussing school desegregation. These media critiques were made explicit on several occasions. "One of the biggest farces of the era is all the fighting about busing students," the *Baltimore Afro-American* editorialized in 1969. "The nation's press, which boasts of a keen eye on things which affect the public interest, seems somehow never to get around to putting the school busing hassle into proper perspective."[21] The paper's editors returned to this theme the following year, writing, "The remarkable thing about the nation-wide crusade against busing is that so much of the press accepts the arguments put forth without balancing their reports by citing the prevalence of busing in the country."[22] In response to a front-page *Los Angeles Times* headline regarding Judge Alfred Gitelson's ruling in *Crawford*, "Fear and Dismay: L.A. Bussing Rule Stuns Capital," the *Los Angeles Sentinel*'s Stanley Robertson asked, "Who created what is now being termed 'fear and dismay'?" Robertson went on to describe the willful ignorance that underlay the surprise with which the *Los Angeles Times* and other white media greeted school desegregation outside the South: "Were it not for racial bigotry, discrimination, and segregation in its most vile forms, right here in the land of sunshine and opportunity, dear old Los Angeles, Calif., the current 'fear and dismay' of which the Times speaks would not be occurring! Were it not for years and years of racism practiced by the majority community here—not in Birmingham, Memphis or Miami—the ideal concept of neighborhood schools would make busing unnecessary."[23]

"WE DON'T WANT YOUR RACIST INTEGRATION PLAN, WE WANT JUSTICE"

In many southern cities and towns, "busing" and school desegregation meant the closure of black schools and the demotion or firing of black administrators or teachers. When carried out in this way, "busing" and school desegregation represented a continuation of racist educational policies that black communities had fought against. "Negroes are tired of having to bear the burdens of integration," said HEW official A. J. Howell in response to protests of school closures in rural Hyde County, North Carolina. "Those Negro schools have been good enough for one race to use all these years. So, we don't see why they can't be utilized on a desegregated basis."[24]

In Chesapeake, Virginia, over two hundred black students crowded the school board meeting in May 1971 to protest the board's desegregation plan, which called for majority-black Crestwood High School to become a junior high school and for Crestwood's students to be transferred to formerly all-white schools in other neighborhoods. The students wanted the school board to devote more resources to Crestwood and to keep the institution as a high school. "We don't want Crestwood High to be a junior high school, we want justice," Crestwood student Jeffrey Sharpe told the board. "We don't want your 45–15 [year-round school] plan, we want justice; we don't want your four super high schools or your racist integration plans—we want justice. We want Crestwood High to remain a high school period."[25] Edward DeLeyatte Holley, a Crestwood High senior and the school's yearbook editor, explained to the *Norfolk Journal and Guide* that there was a "growing awareness of 'Blackness'" among the school's students and argued that Crestwood had not previously been integrated because "Crestwood is in a black community, and the white parents refuse to allow their children to attend a school in a black environment." "Are these the conditions which the blacks must perpetually live under?" Holley asked. "I, for one, do not believe so, and it is for this reason that I was and will remain wholeheartedly in this local protest movement."[26] Crestwood High students had protested several times since the board's plan was announced in late 1969.[27] "We want to make the general public see that the people of the Chesapeake public school system are pulling the wool over the eyes of the black people, and the adults should be aware of this fact," said Crestwood senior Johnnie Mae Cradle.[28] HEW also expressed suspicion about the board's plan. "It appears discriminatory to phase out this high school, since other high schools in the district are presently overcrowded and lacking the facilities available at Crestwood," HEW official Lloyd Henderson wrote in a letter to the Chesapeake School Board. "We must conclude that the decision to phase out Crestwood as a high school facility was based on race."[29]

Black students in neighboring Norfolk, Virginia, waged a similar battle against a school board plan to close Booker T. Washington High School and build a new Northside High School five miles away. The students, who presented a petition with two thousand signatures to the school board, asked for the new building to be built on the present site of Booker T. Washington High and to retain the school's name. "Why are new schools always built in white sections in the city and Negro students bused?" asked senior Clarence Garret, inquiring why it couldn't "be the other way around and white students be bused?"[30] Garret's classmate Dwight Davis agreed, saying, "I feel that busing black students to a white community to attend school and not busing the white students to a black community is unjust."[31] The *Norfolk Journal and Guide* supported the students' campaign to save the local black high school. "The [school board's desegregation] plan would leave Norfolk without a single high school in a predominately Negro section," the *Journal and Guide* editors wrote. "It would also deprive the city of the aspirations black students need in the name Booker T. Washington. The name, too, would be good for white students." The editors concluded, "The desegregation pattern in Norfolk is shaping up badly for the black community."[32]

The student campaigns to save Booker T. Washington High School and Crestwood High School met different fates. Booker T. Washington's students were successful, and the *Journal and Guide* praised the school board's decision to build a new Booker T. Washington High School on the existing site: "Happily, Booker T. Washington High School in Norfolk will remain and it must be remembered that names mean as much, if not more, to black people as to any other people in America during the current struggle to make school desegregation work."[33] As the *Journal and Guide*'s editors understood, the closure of black schools meant the loss of names, traditions, and mascots that had deep meanings for black communities.[34] In Wake Forest, North Carolina, for example, black students who attended W. E. B. DuBois High School were transferred to historically white Wake Forest High School, and the DuBois High School building became Wake Forest–Rolesville Middle School.[35] Similarly, in Louisiana school officials painted over murals of Booker T. Washington and George Washington Carver at recently desegregated and renamed schools.[36] The *Journal and Guide* noted that school closures were part of a larger burden of school desegregation that too often fell on black communities. "Somewhere in school desegregation, an effort should be made to accommodate Negro children and their parents," the editors argued. "In too many cases the burden of change has been deliberately placed on Negro families many of whom are least able financially and otherwise to accept the responsibility."[37]

Though the Booker T. Washington protests were successful, Crestwood High School became a junior high school in Fall 1971, and its students were reassigned. Like other black school closures across the South, the school board's decision meant demotions for black administrators. Crestwood High principal Clifton Wood became principal of the new junior high school, while Edward Cox, who had served as principal of the old Crestwood Junior High School, became supervisor of high school mathematics.[38] "It is a disgrace that a man who devoted 17 years to developing a first class high school as Mr. Wood has done is demoted to a junior high school," one black parent said in response to the announcement.[39] Most black principals in Virginia faced a fate similar to Wood's. Of 170 black high school principals in the state in 1965, only 16 were in the same position in 1970, and similar demotions took place in other southern states.[40]

Many black teachers, both in the South and in other parts of the country, also lost their jobs as a result of school desegregation. Barbara Sizemore, district superintendent of the Woodlawn Experimental Schools Project in Chicago, viewed the Supreme Court's 1971 *Swann* ruling from the perspective of black educators. "The models for desegregation have consistently displaced and plunged blacks into unemployment," Sizemore argued. "With no protection for the black incumbent educators, this will cause a great void . . . in the ranks of employed black professionals."[41] National Urban League president Vernon Jordan argued that the loss of teaching jobs would have a broad impact on black communities. Rather than talking only about the "phony issue of busing," Jordan suggested, "it is time now to turn the spotlight on the widespread discriminatory practices that have turned surface integration into a sham, harming black children and black educators, as well as the black economy."[42] These concerns were well founded, because over thirty thousand black teachers were displaced by school desegregation in southern states. An HEW survey of five southern states found that from 1968 to 1971, five thousand white teachers were hired while over one thousand black teachers lost their jobs.[43]

SUSPENDED AND PUSHED OUT

The firing and demotion of thousands of black teachers and principals directly affected black students who desegregated white schools. In their 1973 article on the significant job loses that black educators encountered, scholars

John Smith and Betty Smith warned, "The future offers the ghastly specter of black children totally at the mercy of a white-dominated school system."[44] For many black students, "busing" and desegregation meant leaving their communities to travel to schools where white students and parents were openly hostile and where white teachers and administrators blamed them for the whatever violence or disruptions accompanied desegregation in the schools. While "antibusing" protests dominated media coverage and dampened black enthusiasm for "busing," school suspensions and "pushouts" in recently desegregated schools represented a larger threat to black students.

In the early and mid-1970s, the Southern Regional Council and the Children's Defense Fund published reports revealing that black students across the country were being suspended, expelled, and pushed out of recently desegregated schools at alarming rates. During the 1972–73 school year, for example, one in eight black students was suspended at least once, double the rate of white student suspensions.[45] Office of Civil Rights (OCR) director Peter Holmes testified to the Subcommittee on Equal Opportunities of the Committee on Education and Labor in the House of Representatives that black students were suspended at rates disproportionate to their enrollment in nineteen of the twenty cities that his office had reviewed, including New York, Houston, Cleveland, Memphis, and Dallas.[46] "Just a cursory examination of our data suggests the probability of widespread discrimination in the application of disciplinary sanctions," Holmes said.[47] "In some cases, teachers were trigger-happy with suspensions after desegregation," a southern school administrator admitted to a Children's Defense Fund interviewer.[48]

School suspensions hindered black students' success and, in some cases, pushed them out of school permanently. The Southern Regional Council, which published *The Student Pushout: Victim of Continued Resistance to Desegregation*, encouraged policymakers to see black student "dropouts" from newly desegregated schools as "pushouts." Black students, the council argued, frequently encountered white teachers, administrators, and students who were not yet ready for desegregated schools. Peter Holmes at the Office of Civil Rights argued that these racially discriminatory disciplinary practices, in addition to being unfair, would lead to "the eventual erosion of confidence of many thousands of minority youth in the purposes of education so that the American school becomes for them less a means to personal achievement than a symbol of injustice."[49]

The problem of school suspensions also affected recently desegregated schools outside the South, in cities like Boston. A black teacher at South Boston

High School attested to this in an affidavit filed in 1975 seeking further relief in *Morgan v. Kerrigan*. "When an incident of apparent racial strife occurs, some white teachers see the black student as the original aggressor and as the source of the continuing threat to school order, even when neither perception is true," the teacher reported. "I have observed, for example, a white teacher challenge the possession by a black student of a 'pick'—a style of Afro comb used by many black students for grooming purposes. The teacher's attempt to confiscate the comb resulted in resistance by the student and a confrontation."[50] A member of the Citywide Coordinating Council assigned to monitor the implementation of Boston's desegregation order described in detail the connection between suspensions and resistance to "busing" for school desegregation:

> I have closely observed the Boston public school system since my arrival in 1973, including the reaction of the system to desegregation efforts in 1974–1975. I have become aware of tremendous disparities in the rates of suspension between black and white students in the Boston public school system. Based on professional work, it is my professional opinion that the root cause of such disparities is the disbelief in, and disrespect for, the findings of Judge Garrity as to the history of racial discrimination in the Boston public schools, that this disbelief and disrespect pervade the entire structure of the Boston public schools, under the active leadership of the Boston School Committee, and are reinforced by those aspects of the wider Boston community with whom members of the Boston public schools identify. This climate and milieu within which teachers and administrators function bear directly on the racial disparity in suspensions, for the entire system is saturated by hostility to the court's desegregation order and to the black students who are perceived as having caused the order.[51]

During the 1974–75 school year, Boston school officials suspended 5,076 black students and 3,367 white students.[52] This rate of suspension could have occurred by chance less than one in one billion times.[53]

Any attempt to understand what "busing" meant to black communities has to recognize that "busing" and school desegregation plans frequently led to negative outcomes for black students, parents, and educators. School closures, job loses for black teachers and principals, and a high rate of suspensions in recently desegregated schools all contributed to the ambivalence black people felt about "busing." These viewpoints, however, rarely made it into national television news reports or white magazines and newspapers. Instead, these media outlets focused their attention on black voices that fit more neatly within the prescribed "busing" framework.

Eight thousand activists, politicians, and students gathered at the National Black Political Convention in Gary, Indiana, in March 1972 to discuss the political future of black Americans. "Busing" was not the most important issue on their agenda, but an "antibusing" resolution, passed by acclamation on the third and final day of the gathering, dominated media coverage of the convention and offered white politicians and parents evidence that blacks shared their opposition to school desegregation. Describing "busing" as "obsolete and dangerous," the resolution read, "We condemn racial integration of schools as a bankrupt, suicidal method of desegregating schools, based on the false notion that black children are unable to learn unless they are in the same setting as white children."[54] The "antibusing" resolution reflected the views of the Congress of Racial Equality (CORE), whose delegates, led by CORE national chairman Roy Innis, brought the resolution to the convention floor and urged its adoption.[55] "The antibusing resolution was a mandate from black folks, proving they support this approach," Innis argued. "Now we know we're on the right road. We will go back into the South and redouble our efforts against busing from our new, moral position. We can now claim broad-based support for nationalism, and black people cannot be bulldozed any more by the integrationists."[56] Not everyone shared Innis's enthusiasm. "I'm appalled that the black community would even react to such a phony issue being injected into a serious convention," said Richard Newhouse, who attended the convention as an Illinois state senator representing Chicago's South Side. "The whole busing issue is a red herring, and for us to be caught up in that trap is absolutely crazy."[57]

While CORE's position reflected a long-standing desire of many black communities for control over their own schools, the white press interpreted the resolution strictly as a vote against "busing." "Blacks vote against busing," read the headline on the front page of the *Washington Post,* while the *Chicago Tribune*'s front page noted, "Black Parley Comes Out against Busing."[58] Black journalist Roger Wilkins wrote that after the "antibusing" resolution passed, "there were those in the hall who could see the next day's headlines and could have wept."[59] Ethel Payne wrote in the *Chicago Defender,* "The NAACP . . . saw 20 years of painstaking, exhaustive legal work go up in smoke when the section on opposition to busing was adopted."[60]

The National Black Political Convention ended a day before the closely watched Florida Democratic presidential primary, where George Wallace

FIGURE 29. Roy Innis, Congress of Racial Equality national chairman, speaking at the 1972 Republican National Convention in Miami, Florida. Innis pushed for an "antibusing" resolution at the National Black Political Convention in Gary, Indiana. He was one of the most visible black critics of "busing." Associated Press photo, August 17, 1972.

won a landslide victory and 74 percent of Floridians signaled their opposition to "busing" in a ballot straw poll. The Florida results made the black convention's "busing" resolution resonate with the national "busing" storyline. "In the midst of widespread white protest against school busing, significant antibusing sentiment has surfaced among blacks," the *Los Angeles Times* noted, pointing to the Gary "busing" resolution and Gallop polling.[61] The *New York Times* editorialized that "George Wallace could not have asked for better cooperation on the eve of the Florida balloting" than the Gary vote.[62] In a story on the Florida "busing" vote, the *Washington Post* cited the black convention's resolution as evidence of "the rising national sentiment against busing."[63]

Days after the National Black Political Convention and Florida primary votes, President Nixon gave a nationally televised address calling on Congress to pass a moratorium on new "busing" orders and pass new legislation establishing a national standard regarding school desegregation. "The great majority of Americans, white and black, feel strongly that the busing of schoolchildren away from their own neighborhoods for the purpose of achieving racial balance is wrong," Nixon argued.[64] Nixon's speech, in which he asserted that "large and increasing numbers of blacks" opposed "busing," drew criticism from the black press, which expressed frustration that the Gary vote made Nixon's claims seem more plausible. An article in the *Los Angeles Sentinel* read, "Millions of Americans believe that this unfortunate statement coming from the [National Black Political] convention had an impact on the Florida primary out of which Governor Wallace emerged as a great victor, saying the same thing about bussing and the pronouncement from President Nixon on bussing which he said many blacks and whites agreed with."[65] In an article in the *Chicago Defender* (reprinted in the *Pittsburgh Courier*), journalist Ethel Payne speculated, "The Nixon administration took a hand behind the scenes [in Gary] in promoting the vote against busing in order for the President to declare that the majority of blacks were not in favor of busing their children for the sake of integration."[66]

Louisville Defender editor and publisher Frank Stanley, writing in the *Chicago Defender*, described how the "busing" frame for school desegregation made it difficult for blacks to voice concerns about the policy. "American blacks are caught in a bind on the issue of busing," Stanley argued. "Our stand against it play[s] right into the hands of our ultra-conservative President who is more interested in swinging white votes on an emotional issue than he is in serving Blacks."[67] CORE also expressed misgivings about how the media and Nixon spun the Gary "antibusing" resolution. "The press has only mentioned the part of the resolution condemning busing," Roy Innis said in a press conference at CORE's Harlem headquarters, "and not the part supporting CORE's unitary school plan as a legitimate and desirable method of desegregating schools."[68] CORE's Mary Dennison said the Gary resolution condemned forced "busing" but "for different reasons than did the 'racist' Nixon administration."[69] Most press outlets, Dennison argued, failed to quote the part of the resolution that read, "As an alternative to busing of black children to achieve racial balance, we demand quality education in the black community by the controlling of our school districts and a guarantee of an equal share of the money."[70] CORE and the other black delegates who supported the "antibusing" resolution at the National Black Political Convention did not fully appreciate how little control they would have over the "blacks vote against busing" narrative that emerged from the convention. The *Washington Post,* for example, quoted Mary Dennison's critique of the "'racist' Nixon administration," next to a picture of Pontiac "antibusing" activist Irene McCabe on the first day of her mothers' march to Washington, DC.[71] The "busing" resolution made the Gary convention legible to the white media, but the "busing" frame did not allow any room for the history and context surrounding black opposition to "busing."

A month after the National Black Political Convention, the state chairman and several key players from the convention, including Gary mayor Richard Hatcher, Imamu (Amiri) Baraka, Congressman Charles Diggs Jr., black nationalist Queen Mother Moore, Beaulah Saunders of the National Welfare Rights Organization, Roy Innis, Dorothy Height of the National Council of Negro Women, and Jesse Jackson met at Howard University for a closed session to discuss and revise the draft agenda adopted at the convention.[72] With delegates from Mississippi, Alabama, and South Carolina insisting that "busing" was crucial to improving black educational opportunities in their states, the group clarified its position on "busing": "Our politics is that we must have control of our own education, with busing, and any other tool which guarantees quality, as an option, and also protects all rights guaranteed under the 14th Amendment."[73] This revised position did not receive the same attention as the original "antibusing" resolution. Whereas the *Chicago Tribune* ran "Black Parley Comes Out against Busing" as a front-page headline, the new story, "Busing Gets OK from Black Unit," was buried next to obituaries in the paper's second section.[74]

Black reporters Tony Batten and Ardie Ivie covered the Gary convention for *The 51st State,* a public affairs television show on New York's channel 13. "What was the convention about?" Ivie asked. "If you say it was about a stand on busing . . . then it was a failure." Ivie explained that he and Batten "weren't interested in the minutiae of the convention, but in a sense of mass."[75] From a different perspective, white media similarly looked to the National Black Political Convention to provide a "sense of mass." While black people articulated a range of often-conflicting positions on school desegregation that did not make for neat headlines or sound bites, the Gary convention seemed to provide a unified black voice speaking against "busing." Newspapers and television news programs could simply point to the Gary "antibusing" vote to represent black opinion on "busing," even if the reality of black sentiment did not fit easily in this frame.

CLAY SMOTHERS, "THE MOST CONSERVATIVE BLACK MAN IN AMERICA"

If the National Black Political Convention garnered attention as being representative of black opinion on "busing," Clay Smothers received media attention as one of the few black people at white "antibusing" rallies. Smothers was born and raised in rural Malakoff, Texas (seventy miles outside of Dallas), where his parents founded and ran the Saint Paul Industrial Training School, an orphanage for homeless black children based on the educational principles of Booker T. Washington. After graduating from Prairie View A&M University, Smothers worked briefly in Chicago as a teacher and a detective investigating youth gangs. Smothers returned to Dallas, where he served as news director for KNOK, a black-oriented radio station, and a newspaper columnist for the *Oak Cliff Tribune,* before emerging as an "antibusing" spokesman. His hometown newspaper described him as the "new voice of a Silent Majority" and wrote, "Clay Smothers is a black man. But when he speaks, white men listen."[76] Smothers embodied an old-fashioned version of black rural conservatism, but by speaking out against "busing," he found eager audiences well beyond his local newspaper and radio posts.

Smothers called himself "the most conservative black man in America" and traveled across the country speaking against "busing," making stops in Boston, Chicago, Memphis, West Virginia, Pontiac, Louisville, and suburban Washington, DC.[77] Protest organizers invited Smothers to speak because he was the best-known black "busing" opponent, and the news media printed and broadcast what he said for the same reason. When 150 parents affiliated with United Concerned Citizens of America (UCCA), a thirty-two-state "antibusing" organization, picketed in front of the Supreme Court and the White House, singing "God Bless America" and chanting, "Neighborhood schools," Smothers was the only protestor the United Press International story mentioned by name. "Among the pickets was a lone Negro," the story reported, "Clay Smothers ... who carried a sign saying 'Give Me Back My Black Child.'"[78] Smothers said he had joined the UCCA protest because "a federal judge ordered me to put my kids on a bus. I bought my home so my kids could walk down the street to school, and I don't like it."[79] While these stated reasons for protesting "busing" resembled the statements of countless white opponents of school desegregation, Smothers was deemed more newsworthy because he added a black voice to the chorus of resistance.

Smothers garnered further national attention when he joined over two hundred "antibusing" activists in Pontiac in February 1972 for a national conference organized and hosted by Irene McCabe and the National Action Group. NBC showed Smothers speaking to the white audience, with the names of U.S. congressmen who opposed "busing" handwritten on a large sign behind him. "To me it was just an insult when the judge came in my home, took my little boy from me," Smothers told the audience. "It was an insult. What he was saying to me was you black folks are so stupid and immoral and ignorant and indecent that you cannot develop your own institutions."[80] The *New York Times* and other papers carried an Associated Press account of the meeting that described Smothers receiving a "standing ovation when he spoke out against busing of schoolchildren."[81] *Newsweek* agreed that Smothers was the standout personality of the conference: "The star of the meeting, which featured speakers from the Tory center to the radical right, was Clay Smothers of Dallas, a black man who complained that 'I'm being used by white Federal judges. Some people don't understand that the hearts of black mothers and fathers bleed, too.'" *Newsweek* presented Smothers, along with polling data and a quote from CORE's Roy Innis, to highlight black opposition to "busing." "Smothers' presence at the NAG meetings pointed up a notable fact about the antibusing cause," *Newsweek* noted. "While membership in antibusing groups and participation in demonstrations is limited almost exclusively to whites, antibusing sentiment is not."[82]

Smothers attended the 1972 Democratic national convention as a George Wallace delegate and obtained the necessary signatures to nominate himself as a vice presidential candidate. The nomination allowed him to give a convention speech, which CBS and NBC broadcast to a national audience. In an interview after Smothers's speech, U.S. congressman John Conyers told CBS's Dan Rather, "To come here supporting George Wallace and all that he stands for is clearly not to be able to recognize who your enemy is. So men like [Clay Smothers] are given a great deal of airing on the media. I understand that he has been in the media a great deal, because he is the kind of phenomenon that unfortunately too many people want to see."[83] Smothers was never going to win the vice presidential nomination, but the convention speech enabled him to again speak out against "busing" to millions of television viewers across the country.

Smothers found a particularly warm welcome among school desegregation opponents in Boston. Smothers spoke in Boston at least three times and stayed in the homes of Restore Our Alienated Rights (ROAR) supporters.[84]

As Boston's "busing crisis" dominated headlines, Smothers continued to stand out as the lone black face and voice at "antibusing" rallies. The Associated Press reported on a December 1974 rally of over four thousand demonstrators at Boston Common. "Busing is the most idiotic thing I ever heard of in my life," Smothers told the crowd. "You here in Boston are the last hope. If you fail, we fail nationwide."[85] The *Los Angeles Times* described Smothers's speaking style when he was back in Boston for a ROAR rally at the start of the second phase of court-ordered "busing" in September 1975: "Speaking in the rhythms of the black pulpit, a style broadened to world fame by Martin Luther King Jr. in a different cause, Smothers attacked the federal judiciary in general and . . . busing."[86] Boston radio talk show host David Brudnoy saw Smothers as evidence of a "phenomenon that everyone [in Boston] knows to be true, but which the major media outlets do not care to dwell upon: black antibusing sentiment. Although few local Negroes have spoken out, at least on the airwaves or for attribution in print, and the major black voices raised in protest against Boston's forced busing have been those of outsiders, like Mr. Clay Smothers of Dallas, an occasional black voice materializes on a radio talk show, safe in his or her anonymity, expressing strong disapproval of the situation."[87] For Brudnoy, as for the "busing" protest organizers who invited Smothers to speak, Smothers could be the only black person at "antibusing" rallies and still be representative of widespread black "antibusing" sentiments.

The way "busing" opponents embraced Smothers is most evident in a photograph from the December 1974 rally at Boston Common. Smothers stands at the microphone, on a dais with two dozen white men, behind a sign reading, "Welcome to Boston, 1774–1994: The City Is Occupied, a Boycott Exists, a Tyrant Reigns, Law Is by Decree, the People Are Oppressed." The man to Smothers's right is leaning in, shaking Smothers's hand and giving him a hearty kiss on the check. The kiss looks spontaneous, as if the man was so overcome with joy at hearing Smothers, a black man, speak out against "busing" that he could not help but physically embrace him. This gesture of interracial same-sex intimacy looks very different from the photographs and televisual images of violence that marked Boston's "busing crisis," especially Stanley Forman's famous "The Soiling of Old Glory" photo of a white teenager using a flagpole with an American flag to attack black lawyer and civil rights activist Ted Landsmark. Spontaneous or not, the photo of a white "antibusing" activist embracing Smothers made visible the motivations that led white groups across the country to invite Smothers to speak. Smothers

FIGURE 30. Clay Smothers, who billed himself as the "most conservative black man in America," receives a warm welcome from "antibusing" activists in Boston. Associated Press, December 16, 1974.

appealed to "antibusing" groups (as well as members of the right-wing John Birch Society and American Party) because he shared some of their politics but also because they felt he offered visual proof that they were not racist. As a flamboyant speaker and the lone black face at "antibusing" rallies, Smothers appealed to newspaper reporters and television news producers who were looking for ways to represent black opinion on "busing."

. . .

Newspaper reporters and television news producers were drawn to Clay Smothers, as they were to Roy Innis and the National Black Political Convention, because they preferred people who spoke unambiguously about "busing." Neither the Gary convention's "antibusing" resolution nor Clay Smothers were representative of black opinion on school desegregation, but they received far more attention than the black parents, students, and activists who worked to improve educational opportunities for black students and who sought to ensure that "busing," when it was used, would benefit the black community. "Busing" meant many things to black communities, but these complex and nuanced sentiments about school closures, teacher and administrator firings, and student pushouts, did not fit neatly into newspaper articles or television news segments. Instead, the media preferred black voices like Clay Smothers and Roy Innis, who stayed on topic regarding "busing," and the media's "busing" frame pushed black educational activism to the background in favor of white protests.

EIGHT

Television News and the Making of the Boston "Busing Crisis"

The scene in Boston in recent weeks has been reminiscent of hundreds of others that flashed on TV screens at the opening of schools in years gone by. There were angry whites chanting their opposition to a Federal court order, throwing rocks at black school children and screaming defiance and hatred at a symbol of the Federal will to enforce the law. But, the city was not Little Rock or New Orleans . . . the city was Boston.

—ROGER WILKINS, New York Times,
September 24, 1974

Throughout the Nation the prevailing view is that court-ordered desegregation of the public schools in Boston proved to be a disaster during the school year 1974–75.

— UNITED STATES COMMISSION
ON CIVIL RIGHTS, *1975*

The Boston school desegregation crisis of 1974 is on its way to becoming a myth.

—JOHN LEUBSDORF, *1978*

WHEN BOSTON SCHOOLS OPENED on September 12, 1974, television news crews from ABC, CBS, and NBC were on hand to cover what transpired in the city's schools and neighborhoods. After years of civil rights protests, lawsuits, court cases, and acts of evasion by school officials, phase 1 of federal judge Arthur Garrity's order called for nearly seventeen thousand students to be transferred by bus to increase the racial integration of Boston's schools.[1] Few opening days had received so much national media attention, and the news anchors did their best to convey the scene. ABC's Harry Reasoner opened the newscast by comparing Boston to Little Rock, the last city to receive this level of crisis coverage on account of schools: "What did happen in Boston today was not as bad as what took place during the 1950s at places like Central High in Little Rock, but it wasn't very pleasant either."[2] On NBC, John Chancellor described how "thousands of white students stayed home to protest a new desegregation plan ordered by a federal judge." "There were a lot of empty seats on buses and in classrooms as schools opened in Boston today," Chancellor continued, before concluding, "There were a few demonstrations, arrests, and injuries but it was generally peaceful."[3] In his lead-in to the story, CBS's Roger Mudd said that "violence marked the beginning of court ordered busing in Boston today," while reporter Chris Kelly tweaked the formulation in the same segment: "Violence in South Boston marred what was otherwise a peaceful day."[4] In trying to balance scenes of violence and calm, each newscast illustrated the difficulty of summarizing a story that unfolded across a number of different schools and neighborhoods and had begun well before September 1974.

Opponents and supporters of court-ordered "busing" questioned the accuracy of media coverage, focusing most often on the city's leading newspaper, the *Boston Globe*. "Antibusing" parents and politicians argued that reporters downplayed violence in newly integrated schools and exaggerated racial prejudice as the root cause of "busing" protests. Desegregation supporters, on the other hand, contended that news reports overemphasized violence at a few schools rather than highlighting the relatively peaceful integration of many more schools. While this chapter touches on these media critiques, my goal is to shift the focus away from a narrow view of media accuracy and toward a broader consideration of the role of national television news in shaping Boston's "busing crisis." Political scientist Doris Graber describes media crises as "natural or manmade events that pose an immediate and serious threat to the lives and property or to the peace of mind of large numbers of citizens."[5] Television news programs cover some events, like floods or airplane crashes, as crises that interrupt the regular news cycle for a few hours or days. Other stories, such as political scandals or wars, play out over a longer time frame, and television news broadcasts frame these as ongoing crises that demand viewers' attention. The desegregation standoff at Little Rock's Central High School in 1957, for example, was the first civil rights "crisis" of the television era.[6] For southern civil rights activists, television news coverage made white mob violence in the Jim Crow South a national rather than regional issue. For television news producers in New York, bringing dramatic images from Little Rock to national audiences helped establish television journalism as a serious endeavor.

Television played a crucial role in defining Boston in 1974 as a "crisis" situation similar to Little Rock in 1957, but television broadcasts did not present the Boston story with the same moral clarity. Whereas Little Rock offered images of courageous and composed black youth (reluctantly backed by President Dwight Eisenhower and the U.S. Army's 101st Airborne Division) asserting their right to an equal education against white mobs and Arkansas governor Orval Faubus, television framed Boston as being about "busing" rather than school desegregation. The limitations of this "busing" frame were twofold. On the one hand, "busing" coverage focused on the white protestors who were most adamantly against court-ordered "busing" for school deseg-regation, and said remarkably little about students (black or white), schools, or education. On the other hand, "busing" coverage featured protests against court-ordered "busing" without regard for the history of school segregation that led to the court orders. By 1974, television news had already offered extensive coverage of protests against court-ordered "busing" in cites like Pontiac, San Francisco, and Denver. Coverage of these protests fueled "bus-ing" as a national issue, even though "busing" for desegregation involved a fraction of the students transported by school bus. As the *New York Times* reported in 1972, "little 'forced busing' has been put into effect by court or government order when compared to the nearly 20 million pupils trans-ported at public expense for all other purposes and the steady increase in busing that has taken place for decades without public opposition."[7] As this report suggests, in Boston and other cities, "busing" had long been used to transport students to large comprehensive high schools and also to maintain segregation. Arguments offered by parents and politicians against "busing" were particularly persuasive on television news because they voiced demands for neighborhood schools that circulated with little discussion of how these neighborhoods and schools became segregated.

By shifting the focus from print media to television, this chapter illumi-nates the production techniques of a medium that framed the "busing crisis" in Boston for millions of national viewers. First, I examine how the television coverage of Boston "busing" in the mid-1970s focused on reports, analysis, and predictions regarding "antibusing" protests and violence. This day-by-day focus on current and emergent scenes of crisis ignored the history of desegregation efforts since the 1960s, including those that had received televi-sion coverage in earlier years, like the community-funded Operation Exodus program to bus black children to schools in other neighborhoods and the U.S. Department of Health, Education, and Welfare's suspension of federal school aid to Boston for violating the 1964 Civil Rights Act. Second, I con-sider how television news framed the use of force in the Boston "busing" story. Much of the footage from Boston focused on confrontations between "antibusing" protestors and authorities from the Boston police and other law enforcement agencies. These confrontations provided television producers with compelling visuals to illustrate "forced busing," but this framing made it appear as though this was the first time local and federal force influenced school segregation. Enforcement of federal policies that shaped residential and school segregation, as well as the lack of enforcement of Massachusetts's Racial Imbalance legislation, remained out of view. Third, I look at how television news offered viewers background reports on two places at the center of the "busing" story, South Boston and Charlestown. These profiles foregrounded a spatial perspective that echoed protestors' calls to defend "neighborhood schools" and obscured the ordinariness of the racial attitudes in these neighborhoods. This emphasis on working-class neighborhoods also focused attention away from resistance to school desegregation in middle-class areas like Hyde Park or West Roxbury. Finally, I analyze how local television news programs in other cities presented "busing" in Boston as a failed policy and regularly replayed archived footage from Boston to underscore efforts to educate viewers on the importance of upholding the law and avoiding violence. Boston was neither the first nor the last city to witness violent resistance to school desegregation, but extensive television news coverage fixed Boston as the emblematic "busing" crisis and shaped popular conceptions of the history of "busing" for school desegregation.

ON THE SCENE

The substantial television news reporting of the Boston "busing" crisis in the mid-1970s both relied on and overlooked media coverage of earlier school desegregation battles in the city. Camera crews and reporters from the three national networks would not have been on the scene in Boston, prepared to film the first day of school in September 1974, if the city had not already been identified as a newsworthy site. Television cameras converged on Boston in September 1974 because television news had already visited Boston to cover earlier "busing" programs, "antibusing" protests, and legal maneuvering on civil rights policies. What is striking is how little of this recent historical context, broadcast in the 1960s and early 1970s, shows up in the reports from the mid-1970s. Once phase 1 of Judge Garrity's court order started in September 1974, television coverage focused on crisis reporting, offering day-by-day accounts of current and emergent signs of trouble. Reports portrayed fights among students and clashes between "antibusing" protestors and police, as well as predictions, offered by reporters and the parents, politicians, and community leaders they interviewed, about whether "busing" would go better or worse in the days, weeks, and months ahead. On one hand, this crisis coverage shifted the focus away from the historical context of school desegregation in Boston, instead framing the "busing" story like a television serial where viewers would need to tune in regularly to see the next development. At the same time, once television news established "busing" in Boston as an ongoing crisis and assigned news personnel to cover the story on a regular basis, almost any incident related to "busing" in the city was deemed newsworthy. After a fight among students at Hyde Park High School in January 1975, for example, ABC's Gregory Jackson noted that "a simple schoolboy fistfight here can have consequences unlike that of a fistfight almost anywhere else."[8] Jackson correctly identified television's power to amplify school conflicts in Boston, but left unstated television's role in broadcasting news of schoolboy fistfights to a national audience.

Television cameras were available to capture minor incidents like this because news media had covered the Boston school desegregation conflict intermittently over the prior decade. National television news and magazines reported on Louise Day Hicks's rise to political power amid the white "backlash" to "busing" in mid-1960s Boston, as well as Operation Exodus, where black parents and students organized use of the city's open enrollment policy to transfer to less crowded schools with better resources. In addition to following the "busing" and open enrollment battles of the 1960s, television news networks also covered the U.S. Department of Health, Education, and Welfare's (HEW) investigation of Boston in 1971. These reports detailed how the Boston School Committee maintained segregated schools and connected Boston to broader school segregation trends in the North. In December 1971, HEW charged Boston with violating the 1964 Civil Rights Act. Both CBS and ABC broadcast clips from the press conference, where J. Stanley Pottinger, director of the Office of Civil Rights in HEW said, "As a result of official actions taken since 1965, the Boston Public School System has adopted and administered student assignment and grade organization policies in such a manner as to create two separate, racially identifiable school subsystems. One predominately white and the other predominately nonwhite."[9] HEW's charges anticipated Judge Garrity's decision three years later and added weight to the arguments advanced by Boston's civil rights advocates. Television news framed HEW's investigation of Boston as having implications for other northern cities. ABC's Gregory Jackson concluded, "The question that remains is . . . where HEW moves next. The political overtones are clear. So is the fact that there is not a single major Northern school system that is basically any different from Boston."[10] Reporting on the early stages of the HEW investigation in April 1971, CBS's Daniel Schorr closed on a similar note: "It will probably be months before the federal government makes up its mind to decide whether to charge Boston with fostering discrimination by an open enrollment policy. . . . But the implied challenge to the oldest public school system in the nation is already having its unsettling effect. If Boston can be subject to civil rights surveillance, then what city is safe?"[11] While making important gestures toward the regional and national implications of HEW's censuring of Boston, these reports also highlight how the mainstream media, based in the North, covered northern school desegregation differently from the South. Whereas television and print journalists touted their role in exposing the deeply entrenched systems of segregation in the South, they were forever surprised to find evidence of school segregation in cities like Boston, New York, Chicago, or Philadelphia. Like Roger Wilkins in the *New York Times* ("The city was not Little Rock or New Orleans . . . the city was Boston") or Daniel Schorr on CBS ("If Boston can be subject to civil rights surveillance, then what city is safe?"), these journalists treated Boston's school segregation as anomalous and surprising, even as they reported on documented violations of students' constitutional rights. Still, these reports told a national audience of viewers about specific actions by the Boston School Committee regarding school siting and student transfer policies, all well before television returned to Boston to cover the "busing crisis" in 1974.

While this earlier media attention encouraged news outlets to be on the scene for phase 1 in September 1974, the crucial context they provided for Garrity's order faded out of view, replaced by day-to-day crisis coverage. This crisis coverage began on September 9, three days before the start of school, with reporting on a protest march to Boston Common. ABC's Harry Reasoner described how "some 4,000 demonstrators, all of them white, most of them women, booed [Senator Edward Kennedy] off a stage in downtown Boston," when he attempted to explain his views on "busing."[12] On CBS, which estimated the crowd at 8,000 to 10,000, reporter Jackie Castleberry described how "as Senator Kennedy retreated to his office, the crowd began to push, hurling eggs and insults. Just as the Senator reached shelter inside, the crowd rushed, pounding and then shattering a glass window."[13] The television footage of the confrontation is chaotic. The images are unsteady, filmed by camera operators jostled by the crowd, and the shouts of demonstrators are punctuated by the sound of shattering glass. The rally and confrontation cast Boston as a tense city, and ABC and CBS closed their segments on notes of anticipation and apprehension. "For many other communities the first weeks of school have been traumatic," ABC's Lem Tucker concluded. "Boston officials thought they had prepared well enough to prevent that here. Today's incident, however, leaves questions that cannot be answered until school opens on Thursday."[14] This feeling of anticipation and apprehension pervaded crisis coverage of "busing" in Boston, and television news presented the story as an unfolding drama that viewers could watch on a regular schedule. As NBC's Richard Hunt noted on the eve of the opening of schools, "The police are worried, the Mayor is worried, blacks are worried, and whites are worried. So the prospect is many thousands of parents will keep their children home tomorrow and until they feel the schools are safe. And that may take weeks."[15]

New media covered the confrontations and acts of violence that met school desegregation efforts, but what defined Boston as a crisis situation was the sense that conflicts would continue to develop in the coming days, weeks, months, and years. "Violence has flared again in the Boston school busing dispute," CBS's Walter Cronkite said as he introduced a December 11, 1974, segment on a stabbing at South Boston High School, while a few days later, NBC's John Chancellor described how "a federally ordered school busing plan has kept parts of the city in turmoil for months."[16] Reporting on the reopening of South Boston High School the following month, ABC's Gregory Jackson, speaking over film of students filing out of the school building past police in riot helmets, concluded, "It would be foolish to say the struggle is over."[17] The approach of phase 2 of Judge Garrity's plan in September 1975, which expanded the number of schools and students involved in "busing" for desegregation, brought similar reports regarding the continuation of violence in Boston. NBC's Robert Hager warned, "All through the last school year when whites in South Boston were in turmoil over school busing, the city's black communities were generally calm. But now there seems to be a new feeling of militance."[18] Opening with a tranquil image of the Boston skyline and sailboats on the Charles River, ABC's Charles Gibson said, "The appearance of Boston belies the city's troubles. Its schools open September 8th, no one is anywhere near ready." September 8 loomed as a dreaded date, but it arrived without any significant altercations. As NBC's Robert Hager described it, "A school day [that] began full of fears about trouble, ended without much trouble."[19] Without any major developments, the opening of schools on September 8, 1975, was not necessarily newsworthy, but it was made newsworthy by months of crisis coverage over the prior year. Television news kept a spotlight on Boston through the mid-1970s, with current and emergent scenes of trouble given center stage. Once the Boston "busing crisis" was an established news frame, the possibility of conflict and predictions about what might happen next became newsworthy subjects. This crisis coverage displaced reports on earlier desegregation efforts in the city, which had helped establish "busing" in Boston as worthy of close media attention in the first place.

FRAMING FORCE

Many of the best-known images of "busing" in Boston do not feature students or schools, but instead offer vivid displays of force in confrontations between "antibusing" protestors and law enforcement authorities. This media frame emphasized that the Boston "busing crisis" was about force. "Media frames," sociologist Todd Gitlin suggests, "are persistent patterns of cognitions, interpretation, and presentation, of selection, emphasis, and exclusion, by which symbol-handlers routinely organize discourse, whether verbal or visual."[20] Television news framed much of the reporting of the Boston "busing crisis" around clashes between white protesters and police but said little about the students or schools that were ostensibly at the center of the story. Television footage of these confrontations features an array of law enforcement tactics: police motorcades lead the way for buses while police helicopters hover overhead; police officers with riot helmets push protestors away from schools and out of the way of buses; and police officers on horseback lead charges to break up gatherings of protestors. In addition to Boston police, state police officers, U.S. federal marshals, National Guard soldiers, and FBI agents further enforcement power. ABC's Gregory Jackson described the arrayed authorities on hand for the reopening of South Boston High School in January 1975 as "a show of force more befitting a riot than a school opening."[21] Television rendered clashes between protestors and police with a visceral energy. In several cases, segments included film of the confrontations without voice-over commentary from reporters or anchors, production

FIGURES 31 AND 32. In covering Boston's "busing crisis," television news provided viewers with numerous images of police and other law enforcement authorities clashing with white "antibusing" protestors. *NBC Nightly News,* December 11, 1974.

techniques akin to the way network news presents footage from riots or war zones. NBC's report on December 11, 1974, for example, includes a forty-five-second clip without commentary. After reporter Phil Brady's terse introduction, "The Police moved in," the clip shows mounted police riding through a crowd in South Boston, a police officer with his knee on the back of a demonstrator, and other police officers holding protesters against squad cars. Without the reporter's commentary, the images are accompanied by loud crowd noise and indecipherable shouts.[22] Clips like these present police power in stark detail, but it is not clear who or what these police are protecting. Black children do not feature prominently in these clips, and school desegregation is rarely mentioned. There are many law enforcement authorities, but it is not clear which law they are in Boston to enforce.

When President Gerald Ford commented on Boston's "busing crisis" in fall 1974, he linked these televised images of violence to his opposition to "forced busing." "I deplore the violence that I have read about and seen on television," Ford told reporters at a news conference. "I think that it is most unfortunate. I would like to add this, however: the court decision in that case, in my judgment, was not the best solution to quality education in Boston. I have consistently opposed forced 'busing' to achieve racial balance as a solution to quality education, and, therefore, I respectfully disagree with the judge's order."[23] Ford's remarks drew mixed reactions from Bostonians. "Antibusing" activists applauded the president. "I was so happy when I heard his statement, I felt like screaming," said Fran Johnnene, a leader of Restore Our Alienated Rights (ROAR). "Thank God, someone is on our side." Paul Parks, a civil rights advocate who was soon to be appointed Massachusetts state secretary of education, was more critical of Ford. "The President talks about racial imbalance," Parks said. "This is not racial imbalance. This makes me think he's confused. The Boston situation is the School Committee's violation of the Fourteenth Amendment to the Constitution."[24]

While violent confrontations between police and protestors provided television news with a steady stream of images to illustrate and dramatize the "busing" issue, this framing presented the confrontations as the first instances of local or federal force in the school segregation issue. The authorities tasked with maintaining peace outside the schools were extremely visible, and this visibility made their force seem like the first action in the "busing" dispute, more immediate than the federal, state, and local policies that shaped residential and school segregation. Judge Garrity's decision in *Morgan v. Hennigan,* in contrast, identified the use of force by the Boston School

Committee and superintendent: "The court concludes that the defendants took many actions in their official capacities with the purpose and intent to segregate the Boston public schools and that such actions caused current conditions of segregation in the Boston public schools."[25] These actions were massive in scale and duration but not easily captured by television cameras or slotted into network news segments. "Plaintiffs have proved that the defendants intentionally segregated schools at all levels," Garrity wrote, "built new schools for a decade with sizes and locations designed to promote segregation; maintained patterns of overcrowding and underutilization which promoted segregation at 26 schools; and expanded the capacity of approximately 40 schools by means of portables and additions when students could have been assigned to other schools with the effect of reducing racial imbalance."[26]

In their actions and failures to act, school officials built on discrimination in the housing market that contributed to residential and school segregation. A 1963 report on housing discrimination in Boston found that "despite the enactment of a fair housing law, widespread discriminatory housing practices continue to occur in Massachusetts," adding that "techniques of discrimination employed by real estate brokers, developers, home owners, and landlords are varied, sometimes blunt, sometimes subtle."[27] These repeated acts of discrimination limited the apartments, houses, and neighborhoods available to black Bostonians and combined with official actions by school administrators regarding school siting, zoning, and enrollment policies to produce Boston's segregated schools. These acts of force are crucial to understanding school segregation, but they remained out of site for viewers watching the Boston "busing crisis" unfold on their television screens. Instead, television news offered viewers intense images of force in confrontations between police and protestors. In this view, Judge Garrity's "busing" order and the police presence required to ensure its safe implementation are framed as the first acts of force rather than a response to the forces that segregated Boston's schools.

EXPLAINING PLACE

The long duration of the Boston "busing crisis" meant that television news offered viewers frequent reports on the neighborhoods at the center of the "busing" story. Given the time constraints of television news, these three- to five-minute background reports on South Boston and Charleston signaled a significant effort to explain the places where "busing" conflicts were most visible. The reports focus on neighborhood boundaries, traditions, fears, and prejudices as leading to the failure of "busing," while obscuring the widespread opposition to school integration in the Boston metropolitan area and nationally.

Television reports on South Boston and Charlestown are most interesting for how they explain these neighborhoods as being apart from Boston. NBC's Richard Hunt highlighted this separation in introducing a background report on South Boston in October 1974: "On three sides the sea protects South Boston from the rest of the world, and that helps explain why it's different. On the land a six-lane highway shields the whites of South Boston from the blacks across the road, and that helps explain it. But the people of South Boston are also set apart by their state of mind."[28] CBS's Chris Kelly offered a similar analysis in a December 1974 background report: "To the people who live here its called 'Southie,' a placid community on the surface, geographically isolated from the rest of the city, virtually an island. It is Irish, Roman Catholic, blue collar, and tough. South Boston High towers over this enclave like a monument and now this monument has become a symbol, a symbol of Southie resistance to change. On the opening day of school, South Boston looked like a city in the deep South years ago reacting to the arrival of its first black students."[29] These descriptions, combined with maps that highlighted South Boston, helped present the neighborhood as distinct from Boston, as "a place with a special character all its own," as NBC described it.[30] South Boston's residents certainly had their share of racial prejudice, but the language of these reports—"different," "virtually an island," "set apart by their state of mind," "like a city in the deep South years ago"—perpetuated the idea that South Boston was a pocket of racism in an otherwise progressive city (Boston) and region (the North).

History and traditions provided another way to accentuate the uniqueness of South Boston and Charlestown. NBC's profile of Charlestown in 1975, for example, framed the area's opposition to "busing" as a product of protecting neighborhood traditions. "When the buses roll into Charlestown on September 8th, they'll be rolling into one of the oldest neighborhoods in America," Robert Hager reported, "a neighborhood fiercely proud of its heritage and independence. Sixteen thousand people live in this crowded, working class section of Boston. Most of them are Irish Catholic. Charlestown is barely one mile square, you can walk from one end to the other in barely

FIGURE 33. NBC's John Chancellor introduces a profile on South Boston. *NBC Nightly News,* October 15, 1974.

fifteen minutes. . . . In the past few years, the 'Townies,' as they like being called, have seen great change in their community. . . . [B]uses represent more change for Charlestown, change this time the people say they just can't understand."[31] This profile concluded with images of marchers carrying a sign reading, "Charlestown against Forced Busing." Like South Boston, profiles of Charlestown presented the neighborhood's boundaries as sacrosanct, and this privileging of neighborhood echoed the arguments of school integration opponents who advanced "neighborhood schools" as the most important "busing" battleground.

For all their local history and pride, schools in South Boston and Charlestown were part of the Boston public school system, not autonomous school districts. Geographical neighborhood boundaries, moreover, were not the primary factor in determining student attendance in Boston. Judge Garrity's decision details how elementary school "district lines weave in and out," with the effect that "the predominantly black areas are cut away from predominantly white areas."[32] Likewise, high-school enrollments were determined by feeder patterns from specific junior high schools, with black students generally entering high schools after eighth grade and white students

FIGURE 34. NBC's profile of Charlestown concluded with footage of a march against "busing" for school desegregation. *NBC Nightly News,* August 31, 1975.

after completing ninth grade. "The only consistent basis for the feeder pattern designations, changes and deletions was the racial factor," Garrity wrote. "Neither distances between schools, capacities of receiving schools, means of transportation or natural boundaries explain them."[33]

Profiles of South Boston and Charlestown offered appraisals of places that figured prominently in Boston's "busing" story, but they also presented these neighborhood battlegrounds as enclaves of white racism removed from Boston and the rest of the country. Judge Garrity's desegregation plan only affected schools in Boston, not the larger Boston metropolitan area. Suburban communities like Concord, Lincoln, and Lexington, as historian Lily Geismer shows, welcomed a small number of black students from Boston city schools through the Metropolitan Council for Educational Opportunity (METCO), but opposed affordable housing programs, two-way "busing" (that is, sending suburban students to Boston schools and vice versa), and other policies that would have threatened their white suburban privilege.[34] Opponents of Judge Garrity's order were also frustrated by what they saw as artificial metropolitan boundaries that kept the suburbs from having to participate in court-ordered "busing" for school desegregation. "In five minutes

I can go to Dedham, Needham or Newton," argued West Roxbury parent K. Marie Clarke. "I can walk to Dedham."[35] Nationally, protesters in Seattle, Pasadena, and Denver expressed their opposition to school integration with different accents but the same intent as those in Boston's working-class neighborhoods. In short, presenting South Boston and Charleston as uniquely racist let the rest of the Boston metropolitan area and the nation off the hook.

THE LONG SHADOW OF BOSTON

The visibility of the Boston "busing crisis" made the city a cautionary tale for other cities that implemented court-ordered or voluntary "busing" plans for school desegregation after 1974. In Louisville, a citizens' group called CALM (Concerned About Louisville's Mood) prepared radio and television advisements and distributed bumper stickers reading, "Nobody Wins when You Lose Your Cool." In Stockton, California, assistant superintendent Leopoldo Gloria saw the negative example of Boston as encouraging a cooperative atmosphere: "Everybody, even most of the parents, decided early that we did not want another Boston—not here."[36] As the Los Angeles police and school officials prepared for "busing" to start in 1978, they too looked to Boston. "We don't expect a Boston," school district security chief Richard Green said. "But our plans are prepared—just in case we have a Boston."[37] The specter of "another Boston" cast a long shadow over "busing" for school desegregation. Boston became synonymous with "busing" in large part because local television news programs regularly replayed the archived footage of violence in Boston. For local television stations, clips from Boston underscored efforts to educate viewers on the importance of upholding the law and avoiding violence. At the same time, these segments reiterated many of the themes from the national television news coverage and cemented the association of "busing" in Boston with violence and the failure of school desegregation.

It took less than a year for other cities to attempt to find transferable lessons from the Boston "busing crisis." Just before Louisville's "busing" program started in 1975, Louisville's WAVE-TV (NBC) sent reporter Dave Nakdimen to Boston for several days to report on "why desegregation in that city has been so violent" and "why what happened there doesn't have to happen here." Nakdimen saw the ethnic neighborhoods in Boston as different from Louisville: "The ethnic lines in Boston are very sharply drawn: the

Irish, the Poles, the Italians, the Chinese, the Black communities, there's a very strong sense of ethnic and neighborhood identification. If you're from South Boston, you're from 'Southie,' if you're from Charlestown, you are called a 'Townie,' and busing was disruptive to this sense of neighborhood identification. In Louisville and Jefferson County, while you have community pride in the various communities . . . these strong ethnic divisions do not exist."[38] Like the network's background reports on South Boston and Charlestown, this analysis pointed to Boston's ethnic neighborhoods as limiting the success of "busing."

Footage of confrontations between police and protestors in South Boston figured prominently in the Louisville report, as well as in features from stations in Dallas, Cleveland, Los Angeles, and Indianapolis. Dallas's WFFA-TV (ABC) emphasized the show of force by law enforcement: "Those who wanted to start trouble couldn't get out from under the eyes of nearly 2,000 city, state, and metropolitan police, along with a couple hundred federal marshals. Along bus routes, surrounding neighborhood schools, lining the streets there are men in blue; on foot, on horseback, on motorcycles, in cruisers."[39] Cleveland's WKYC (NBC) contrasted the violence in Boston with the relatively peaceful integration of schools in Springfield, Massachusetts. The report opened with film of police pushing and arresting protestors in the streets of South Boston: "Several hundred cities in the United States have been ordered to integrate their schools by busing. In a few, the order was met by anger, force, rebellion. It happened that way in Boston. The violence occurred at only four schools in Boston but adults threw stones at children and that grabbed the attention of anyone who had the slightest interest in what has been called 'forced busing.'"[40] Los Angeles's KNXT (CBS) played similar footage of South Boston conflicts, as reporter Mike Parker said: "The problems in Boston and similar problems in other cities across the country have frightened many parents here locally into looking for alternatives to the mandatory busing plan due to start on Tuesday." Profiles of "frightened" San Fernando Valley parents, who were enrolling their children in private schools or moving to avoid "busing," followed the Boston footage, suggesting a clear televisual link between opposition to school integration in South Boston and suburban Los Angeles.[41] Eleven years after the start of "busing" in Boston, Indianapolis's WTHR-TV (NBC) introduced its segment on Boston with a title card, white letters on a black screen, reading, "The Anger: Boston, September 1974," and the voices of protesting mothers chanting, "Here we go Southie, here we go." The station explicitly contrasted

Boston and the successful start of "busing" in Indianapolis. "In places like Boston," the anchor's voice-over intoned, "there was opposition to busing, and they fought it. In Indianapolis, there was opposition to busing and the law was obeyed."[42] Boston, for each of these local television stations, signified the violent failure of "busing" and school integration. Archived television footage from the Boston "busing crisis" showed local viewers why it was important to make sure that their city did not become "another Boston." At the same time, continually replaying clips of "busing" in Boston left the city looped in time, with the confrontations in South Boston in 1974 and 1975 replayed over and over again. If national network news established "busing" in Boston as a crisis, local news reports drew from the same film footage to make the Boston busing crisis the definitive standard for understanding "busing" for school desegregation.

Testifying about the media coverage of the Boston "busing crisis" to the U.S. Commission on Civil Rights in August 1975, Boston deputy mayor Robert Kiley reflected,

> The essential difference between the national media, particularly television, and the local media, I believe, is that a complex situation has to be telescoped into a maximum 90 seconds' presentation over a national network, and you don't sell automobiles by having the desultory aspect of these activities. So my sense is that the national media must go toward the sensational, the easily photographed, the dramatic.[43]

Three months later, WLBT, a station that had aggressively opposed civil rights in Mississippi in the 1950s and 1960s, aired an hour-long special titled "A Southern Perspective on School Busing in Boston," which offered an analysis of television news similar to Kiley's. "For years the South was faced with a perplexing question," the report begins. "How to integrate its schools by the use of court ordered busing. It was a dilemma and the national press watched and filed their reports. Today it is a dilemma and the press is now looking in their own backyard [with film of the Charles River and the Boston skyline on the screen]." Later in the segment, reporter Rae Dillon noted, "Because of the national news media, most people would agree that busing in Boston has not worked. However, only in 7 or 8 of the 140 schools was there any trouble, and these received all of the publicity."[44] As both critiques suggest, when national television news programs discussed "busing" in Boston in the mid-1970s, they focused an extraordinary level of attention on violent confrontations taking place in only a few of the city's schools and neighborhoods. Television news, as this chapter has argued, played a crucial role in framing Boston's "busing crisis" for a national audience. Television news'

FIGURE 35. Young black student explains her feelings on school desegregation to an NBC reporter. Television's "busing crisis" rendered black Bostonians as bit players in their own civil rights story. *NBC Nightly News,* September 7, 1975.

dominant frames for the "busing crisis" presented the story as a conflict between white protestors and police that played out in working-class ethnic neighborhoods, rather than a decades-long fight for the constitutional rights of black students taking place not only in Boston but in cities all over the country. While not overtly sympathetic to the white protestors, national television coverage legitimated the view that "busing" was the problem in Boston.

· · ·

Unlike earlier civil rights struggles in the South, media coverage of Boston presented no specific black students—like Elizabeth Eckford and the Little Rock Nine, Vivian Malone Jones and James Hood at the University of Alabama, or James Meredith at the University of Mississippi—whose rights seemed to be at stake. The closest network television news came to presenting black protagonists in the "busing" story was an NBC special report on Roxbury and Dorchester (similar to earlier reports on South Boston and Charlestown) that aired in September 1975. Whereas most broadcasts featured a short sound bite from one black parent or civil rights activist, this report solicited almost a dozen opinions from black business owners, homeowners, parents, and students. The last student to speak was a young girl with braided hair who told the reporter, "I don't think it's fair, cause when they come up here to go to school we don't mess with them, but why when we go to school down there they mess with us? That ain't fair to me. That ain't fair to me at all."[45] The girl, perhaps eight or nine years old, is one of the city's black students whose rights, which were at the center of Judge Garrity's desegregation order, were elided in media coverage of the "busing crisis." This young black student presented a different image of the Boston "busing" story, but even here television news presented only a narrow spectrum of her views. *Eyes on the Prize,* the celebrated documentary on the civil rights movement, closes its segment on "busing" in Boston with this same young girl, using a portion of NBC's interview that the network did not broadcast. Before her appeal to fairness, the young girl replies to the reporter's question about what will happen when she goes to school in South Boston by looking toward the camera and saying, "When we go up there we gonna be stoned."[46] This blunt prediction, with its mixture of anger and fear, complicates the appeal to fairness that follows. NBC's decision to edit out the young girl's anger and fear, even in a detailed national television news report on Roxbury and Dorchester, illuminates how television's "busing crisis" rendered black Bostonians as bit players in their own civil rights story.

Speaking at Boston College at a conference on the "New Boston" in 1984, community organizer and politician Mel King explained how describing "busing" as a "burden" was detrimental to black people. "Black people are not a burden," King said. "That is a mean and vicious way of saying something about black people and people of color in this city.... We were, and in fact are, an opportunity." School desegregation, King argued, offered an opportunity for whites "to open up and act in the most humane way possible. And they blew it."[47]

Conclusion

A YEAR BEFORE BOSTON'S "BUSING CRISIS" became a national story, Stephen Horn, United States Commission on Civil Rights vice chair and president of California State University Long Beach, expressed frustration with how "busing" had come to define school desegregation in America. "Somehow the busing for desegregation debate has become clouded in its own language and expressions in which the word busing is always preceded by such labels as massive and forced, and the defenders of busing are pictured as wanting children bused simply for the experience of being bused," Horn said. "People have been misled and they are confused." Reverend Theodore Hesburgh, Civil Rights Commission chair and president of the University of Notre Dame, shared these concerns. "In contrast to the newspaper headlines and television newscasts, our [Commission on Civil Rights] investigators did not find parents blocking the entrances, or teachers resigning in masses, or pupils engaged in continuous disorders," Hesburgh argued. "On the contrary, we found schools being conducted in an atmosphere of relative peace, harmony and efficiency and in an atmosphere consistent with the nation's ideals."[1] Horn and Hesburgh spoke to the findings of Civil Rights Commission reports on Charlotte, Las Vegas, Pasadena, Pontiac, Tampa, and other cities, which found that "school desegregation is working, that most of the fears and anxieties, such as those concerning busing, have proven groundless."[2] The Civil Rights Commission's thorough studies of best practices in school desegregation received a fraction of the attention garnered by " antibusing" protests. Fifteen months after the Civil Rights Commission argued, "Busing is not an insurmountable problem," television and print news media descended on Boston and told a very different story. For millions of viewers and readers across the county, Boston's "busing crisis" cemented the popular view that "busing" was a failed and misguided policy.

"Busing" continued in dozens of cities after 1974, but Boston's "busing crisis," the Supreme Court's *Milliken* decision, and the Reagan administration's opposition to mandatory school integration ensured that "busing" would not lead to widespread and sustainable school desegregation. After the 1974 *Milliken* decision, only school districts in Indianapolis, Saint Louis, and Wilmington, Delaware, were compelled to create metropolitan school desegregation plans after findings of discrimination across city and suburban lines.[3] The majority of suburban districts remained untouched by the nation's school desegregation battles. By the 1990s, a series of the Supreme Court rulings made it easier for school districts to be released from court supervision. In *Board of Education of Oklahoma City v. Dowell* (1991), the Supreme Court ruled that school boards could be released from court supervision if "vestiges of past de jure segregation had been eliminated to the extent practicable."[4] The next year, the court ruled in *Freeman v. Pitts* (1992) that "a district court has the authority to relinquish supervision and control of a school district in incremental stages, before full compliance has been achieved in every area of school operations," with the goal of "returning schools to the control of local authorities at the earliest practicable date."[5] In *Missouri v. Jenkins* (1995), the court ended eighteen years of court supervision in Kansas City and found that, once de jure segregation has been fixed, state officials have no constitutional duty to fund efforts to promote minority student achievement, such as teacher salary increases and compensatory education programs.[6] In the wake of these cases, a number of school districts successfully appealed to be released from judicial oversight, including Boston, Buffalo, Cleveland, Denver, Jacksonville, Las Vegas, Miami, Minneapolis, Mobile, Nashville, San Francisco, San Jose, and Seattle.[7]

More recently, in *Parents Involved v. Seattle* (2007), the Supreme Court ruled against voluntary school desegregation plans in Seattle and Louisville. Writing for the majority, Chief Justice John Roberts argued, "For schools that never segregated on the basis of race, such as Seattle, or that have removed the vestiges of past segregation, such as Jefferson County . . . the way to stop discrimination on the basis of race is to stop discriminating on the basis of race."[8] The court's majority drew a sharp distinction between de jure and de facto segregation, a framework that developed its political and cultural power during the battles over "busing." In his dissenting opinion, Justice Stephen Breyer called this de jure–de facto framework into question. "The histories [of these school districts] also make clear the futility of looking simply to whether earlier school segregation was *de jure* or *de facto* in order to draw firm lines separating the constitutionally permissible from the constitutionally forbidden use of 'race-conscious' criteria," Breyer argued. "No one here disputes that Louisville's segregation was *de jure*. But what about Seattle's? Was it *de facto? De jure?* A mixture? Opinions differed. Or is it that a prior federal court had not adjudicated the matter? Does that make a difference? Is Seattle free on remand to say that its schools were *de jure* segregated, just as in 1956 a memo for the School Board admitted?"[9] Despite the large body of scholarship which demonstrates that residential and school segregation developed from government polices—that it was not accidental or innocent—the *Parents Involved* decision reinforced the myth of de facto segregation. For their part, school officials and parents in Louisville (Jefferson County) remained committed to integrated education and brought in desegregation expert Gary Orfield to help design a plan for integration that would meet the court's criteria.[10]

As the courts turned away from school desegregation, the Reagan administration also sought to curtail the government's role in school desegregation. Even more than during the Nixon administration, during President Reagan's administration the Justice Department stopped filing school desegregation lawsuits and sided with school districts that sought to be released from court orders.[11] William Bradford Reynolds, the assistant attorney general for civil rights who directed the Justice Department, told a congressional committee in 1981 that "compulsory busing of students in order to achieve racial balance in the public schools is not an acceptable remedy" and that this position "has been endorsed by the President, the Vice President, the Secretary of Education, and me."[12] The Reagan administration also weakened school desegregation through budget cuts to federal education programs. Funding reductions eliminated three-fourths of the Desegregation Assistance Centers, which provided technical assistance to school districts in developing and implementing desegregation plans. More importantly, Reagan won congressional support to end the Emergency School Aid Act of 1972, which had provided funding for school districts undergoing school desegregation (this Nixon-era legislation already prohibited using funds for "busing").[13] While some funds remained available for "magnet schools," the elimination of the Emergency School Aid Act of 1972 effectively ended federal financial support for school desegregation in most districts.

Scholars have shown that school desegregation was an educational success in that it provided opportunities to black students without diminishing opportunities for white students.[14] These potential gains were limited, however, because "busing" came to dominate the national debate on school desegregation. While "busing" is commonly associated with the 1970s, organized opposition to "busing" started in the mid-1950s in response to small-scale, voluntary, one-way programs to reduce school overcrowding in black and Puerto Rican schools. Parents and politicians rallied against "busing," and the news media helped establish "busing" as the common-sense way to debate and oppose school desegregation. The battle over "busing" was never primarily a debate over which policy would lead to the best educational outcomes but rather a debate about how school desegregation would be defined in public discourse, and about how much actual desegregation would take place in the nation's schools, especially in schools outside the South. Framing school desegregation as being about "busing" rather than unconstitutional racial discrimination privileged white parents' fears over legal evidence. Ultimately, "busing" failed to more fully desegregate public schools because school officials, politicians, courts, and the news media valued the desires of white parents more than the rights of black students.

My goal in writing this book is to change how we talk about and teach the history of "busing" for school desegregation. Rather than starting the story in the 1970s, we need to understand that the battles over "busing" started two decades earlier in the wake of the *Brown* decision and in the context of civil rights activism in the North. Rather than focusing exclusively on Boston or seeing South Boston's Irish residents as uniquely prejudiced, we need to understand how white parents and politicians in cities across the country rallied to defend racially segregated schools. And rather than using *busing* as a politically neutral word, we need to understand that this term developed as a selective way to label and oppose school desegregation. The long history of "busing" for school desegregation is more nuanced, complicated, and important than any one city's "busing crisis." My hope is that by seeing the history of "busing" clearly and speaking honestly about the history of civil rights, people who care about educational equality can chart a more just future.

NOTES

INTRODUCTION

1. "Boston's Unfinished Journey," *Boston Globe,* June 19, 1994.

2. Storer Rowley, "Busing 'Failed': Reagan Aide," *Chicago Tribune,* September 28, 1981.

3. "Ronald Reagan Presidential Campaign Ad on Busing," 1976, Julian P. Kanter Commercial Archive, University of Oklahoma, Norman, OK.

4. Eric Wentworth, "Sen. Biden: A Busing Foe Who Wears Liberal Clothing," *Pittsburgh Press,* October 4, 1975.

5. "Diversity in Gary," *New York Times,* March 14, 1972; Angela Parker, "Black Parley Comes Out against Busing," *Chicago Tribune,* March 13, 1972.

6. Richard Halloran, "Nixon Vows to Aid Catholic Schools, but Asks Caution," *New York Times,* April 7, 1972.

7. United States Commission on Civil Rights, "Your Child and Busing," May 1972, 7.

8. "Cradle of the Confederacy" letter [ca. 1957], Rosa Parks Collection, Box 18, Folder 10, Library of Congress.

9. Michael O'Brien, *Hesburgh: A Biography* (Washington, DC: Catholic University of America Press, 1998), 131.

10. Interview with Linda Brown Smith, conducted by Blackside, Inc., on October 26, 1985, for *Eyes on the Prize: America's Civil Rights Years (1954–1965),* Washington University Libraries, Film and Media Archive, Henry Hampton Collection.

11. "80 Miles & 11 Hours," *New York Times,* December 1, 1959.

12. Robert Dentler and Marvine Scott, *Schools on Trial: An Inside Account of the Boston Desegregation Case* (Cambridge, MA: Abt Books, 1981), 28.

13. "Boycotts Cut into 3 Detroit Grade Schools," *Chicago Tribune,* November 1, 1960.

14. Robert Levey, "Consistency's Hobgoblin," *Boston Globe,* January 16, 1965.

15. John Berthlesen, "Calif. Busing Action Is Near," *Washington Post,* April 20, 1970.

16. Civil Rights Act of 1964, 88th Cong., 2d sess., July 2, 1964.

17. United States Commission on Civil Rights, "School Desegregation: The Courts and Suburban Migration," 1975, 182.

18. United States Commission on Civil Rights, "Desegregation of the Nation's Public Schools: A Status Report," 1979, iv.

19. Among the many policy studies and debates regarding "busing" and school desegregation in this era, see David Armor, "The Evidence on Busing," *Public Interest* (Summer 1972): 90–126; David Armor, "The Double Double Standard: A Reply," *Public Interest* (Winter 1973): 119–133; Gary Orfield, *Must We Bus? Segregated Schools and National Policy* (Washington, DC: Brookings Institution, 1978); Thomas Pettigrew, *A Study of School Integration,* U.S. Department of Health, Education, and Welfare, 1970; Thomas Pettigrew, Elizabeth Useem, Clarence Normand, and Marshall Smith, "Busing: A Review of 'the Evidence,'" *Public Interest* (Winter 1973): 88–118; Nicolaus Mills, ed., *Busing U.S.A.* (New York: Teachers College Press, 1979), 119–256. On the use of social science in school desegregation more broadly, see Mark Chesler, Joseph Sanders, and Debra Kalmuss, *Social Science in Court: Mobilizing Experts in the School Desegregation Cases* (Madison: University of Wisconsin Press, 1988); Betsy Levin and Willis Hawley, eds., *The Courts, Social Science and School Desegregation* (New Brunswick, NJ: Transaction Books, 1975).

20. According to several United States Commission on Civil Rights reports, the percentage of students transported by school buses for court-ordered desegregation ranged in the 1970s between 2 and 5 percent. Some communities also experimented with voluntary busing for desegregation. Black students made up the majority of students bused in both court-ordered and voluntary plans. See "Your Child and Busing," 1972, 7; "Public Knowledge and Busing Opposition," 1973, 12; "Statement on Metropolitan School Desegregation," 1977, 71n34; "Reviewing a Decade of School Desegregation," 1977, 51; "With All Deliberate Speed: 1954–19??," 1981, 37.

21. In his influential chapter on the limitations of the de jure–de facto framework, historian Matthew Lassiter argues, "The label of de facto segregation is so historically loaded—so wrapped up in artificial binaries between South and North, between the educational and residential areas, between deliberate state action and private market forces, between white culpability and white innocence—that historians should discard it as an analytical and descriptive category and evaluate it instead as a cultural and political construct." Matthew Lassiter, "De Jure/De Facto Segregation: The Long Shadow of a National Myth," in *The Myth of Southern Exceptionalism,* ed. Lassiter and Joseph Crespino (New York: Oxford University Press, 2010), 28.

22. Quoted in *Integrated Education* (February–March 1965), 9.

23. On the intertwined histories of racial discrimination and civil rights activism in the North, Midwest, and West, see Alan Anderson and George Pickering, *Confronting the Color Line: The Broken Promise of the Civil Rights Movement in Chicago* (Athens: University of Georgia Press, 1987); Martha Biondi, *To Stand and Fight: The Struggle for Civil Rights in Postwar New York City* (Cambridge, MA: Harvard University Press, 2003); Mark Brilliant, *The Color of America Has Changed:*

How Racial Diversity Shaped Civil Rights Reform in California, 1941–1978 (New York: Oxford University Press, 2010); Christopher Bonastia, *Knocking on the Door: The Federal Government's Attempt to Desegregate the Suburbs* (Princeton, NJ: Princeton University Press, 2006); Robert Bullard, J. Eugene Grigsby III, and Charles Lee, eds., *Residential Apartheid: The American Legacy* (Los Angeles: CAAS Publication, 1994); Matthew Countryman, *Up South: Civil Rights and Black Power in Philadelphia* (Philadelphia: University of Pennsylvania Press, 2006); Matthew Delmont, *The Nicest Kids in Town: American Bandstand, Rock 'n' Roll, and the Struggle for Civil Rights in 1950s Philadelphia* (Berkeley: University of California Press, 2012); David Freund, *Colored Property: State Policy & White Racial Politics in Suburban America* (Chicago: University of Chicago Press, 2007); Kevin Fox Gotham, *Race, Real Estate, and Uneven Development: The Kansas City Experience, 1900–2000* (Albany: State University of New York Press, 2002); Lisa Levenstein, *A Movement without Marches: African American Women and the Politics of Poverty in Postwar Philadelphia* (Chapel Hill: University of North Carolina Press, 2009); A. Scott Henderson, *Housing & the Democratic Ideal: The Life and Thought of Charles Abrams* (New York: Columbia University Press, 2000); Jeffrey Gonda, *Unjust Deeds: The Restrictive Covenant Cases and the Making of the Civil Rights Movement* (Chapel Hill: University of North Carolina Press, 2015); Colin Gordon, *Mapping Decline: St. Louis and the Fate of the American City* (Philadelphia: University of Pennsylvania Press, 2008); Arnold Hirsch, *Making the Second Ghetto: Race and Housing in Chicago 1940–1960* (New York: Cambridge University Press, 1983); Daniel Martinez HoSang, *Racial Propositions: Ballot Initiatives and the Making of Postwar California* (Berkeley: University of California Press, 2010); Kenneth Jolly, *Black Liberation in the Midwest: The Struggle in St. Louis, Missouri, 1964–1970* (New York: Routledge, 2006); Patrick Jones, *The Selma of the North: Civil Rights Insurgency in Milwaukee* (Cambridge, MA: Harvard University Press, 2010); Clarence Lang, *Grassroots at the Gateway: Class Politics & Black Freedom Struggle in St. Louis, 1936–1975* (Ann Arbor: University of Michigan Press, 2009); Douglas Massey and Nancy Denton, *American Apartheid: Segregation and the Making of the Underclass* (Cambridge, MA: Harvard University Press, 1993); Evan McKenzie, *Privatopia: Homeowners Associations and the Rise of Residential Private Government* (New Haven, CT: Yale University Press, 1994); Stephen Meyer, *As Long As They Don't Move Next Door: Segregation and Racial Conflict in American Neighborhoods* (New York: Rowman and Littlefield, 2000); Karen Miller, *Managing Inequality: Northern Racial Liberalism in Interwar Detroit* (New York: New York University Press, 2014); Carl Nightingale, *Segregation: A Global History of Divided Cities* (Chicago: University of Chicago Press, 2012); Antero Pietila, *Not in My Neighborhood: How Bigotry Shaped a Great American City* (Chicago: Ivan R. Dee, 2010); Brian Purnell, *Fighting Jim Crow in the County of Kings: The Congress of Racial Equality in Brooklyn* (Lexington: University of Kentucky Press, 2013); James Ralph Jr., *Northern Protest: Martin Luther King, Jr., Chicago, and the Civil Rights Movement* (Cambridge, MA: Harvard University Press, 1993); Daria Roithmayr, *Reproducing Racism: How Everyday Choices Lock in White Advantage* (New York: New York

University Press, 2014); Robert Self, *American Babylon: Race and the Struggle for Postwar Oakland* (Princeton, NJ: Princeton University Press, 2003); Josh Sides, *L.A. City Limits: African American Los Angeles from the Great Depression to the Present* (Berkeley: University of California Press, 2006); Beryl Satter, *Family Properties: How the Struggle over Race and Real Estate Transformed Chicago and Urban America* (New York: Picador, 2010); Amanda Seligman, *Block by Block: Neighborhoods and Public Policy on Chicago's West Side* (Chicago: University of Chicago Press, 2005); Patrick Sharkey, *Stuck in Place: Urban Neighborhoods and the End of Progress toward Racial Equality* (Chicago: University of Chicago Press, 2013); Emily Straus, *Death of a Suburban Dream: Race and Schools in Compton, California* (Philadelphia: University of Pennsylvania Press, 2014); Thomas Sugrue, *The Origins of the Urban Crisis: Race and Inequality in Postwar Detroit* (Princeton, NJ: Princeton University Press, 1996); Thomas Sugrue, *Sweet Land of Liberty: The Forgotten Struggle for Civil Rights in the North* (New York: Random House, 2008); Clarence Taylor, *Knocking at Our Own Door: Milton A. Galamison and the Struggle to Integrate New York City Schools* (New York: Lexington Books, 2001); Clarence Taylor, ed., *Civil Rights in New York City: From World War II to the Giuliani Era* (New York: Oxford University Press, 2011); Jeanne Theoharis, "'We Saved the City': Black Struggles for Educational Equality in Boston," *Radical History Review* 81 (2001): 61–93; Jeanne Theoharis and Komozi Woodard, eds., *Freedom North: Black Freedom Struggles outside the South, 1940–1980* (New York: Palgrave Macmillan, 2003); Jeanne Theoharis and Komozi Woodard, eds., *Groundwork: Local Black Freedom Movements in America* (New York: New York University Press, 2005); Craig Wilder, *A Covenant with Color: Race and Social Power in Brooklyn* (New York: Columbia University Press, 2001).

24. For works that are particularly critical of the de jure–de facto framework, see Ansley Erikson, "Building Inequality: The Spatial Organization of Schooling in Nashville, Tennessee, after Brown," *Journal of Urban History* 38, no. 2 (2012): 247–270; Brett Gadsden, *Between North and South: Delaware, Desegregation, and the Myth of American Sectionalism* (Philadelphia: University of Pennsylvania, 2012); Lassiter, "De Jure/De Facto Segregation," in *The Myth of Southern Exceptionalism;* Lassiter, *The Silent Majority: Suburban Politics in the Sunbelt South* (Princeton, NJ: Princeton University Press, 2007); George Lipsitz, *How Racism Takes Place* (Philadelphia: Temple University Press, 2011); Andrew Highsmith, *Demolition Means Progress: Flint, Michigan, and the Fate of the American Metropolis* (Chicago: University of Chicago Press, 2015); Richard Rothstein, "Why Our Schools Are Segregated," *Educational Leadership* 70, no. 8 (2013): 50–55.

25. *Taylor v. Board of Education of City School District,* 191 F. Supp. 195 (1961).

26. Minute Order of Court's Intended Findings of Fact, Conclusions of Law, Judgment, and for Peremptory Writ of Mandate (February 11, 1970), 30–31; Jack McCurdy, "Deadline: Sept. 1971," *Los Angeles Times,* February 12, 1970.

27. *Davis v. School District of City of Pontiac,* 309 F. Supp. 734, 741–742 (1970).

28. *Morgan v. Hennigan,* 379 F. Supp. 144 (1974).

29. *Morgan v. Hennigan* (1974); *Keyes v. School District No. 1, Denver, Colo.* (1973); *Milliken v. Bradley* (1971); *HEW v. Kansas City, Missouri, School District* (1976); *Kelly v. Guinn* (1972); *Crawford v. Board of Educ. of the City of Los Angeles* (1970); and *Davis v. School District of City of Pontiac* (1970).

30. Leon Panetta, *Bring Us Together: The Nixon Team and the Civil Rights Retreat* (New York: Lippincott, 1971), 312; "Top Nixon Aids Feel North Getting off Hook," *Tuscaloosa News,* December 25, 1969; "Chronicle of Race and Schools," *Equity & Excellence in Education* 8, no. 2 (1970): 57–58.

31. NAACP Legal Defense and Educational Fund, "Conversation with Veteran Organizer June Shagaloff," July 15, 2014, http://www.naacpldf.org/event/conversation-veteran-organizer-june-shagaloff. On the NAACP's approach to school segregation in the South, see Mark Tushnet, *The NAACP's Legal Strategy against Segregated Education, 1925–1950* (Chapel Hill: University of North Carolina Press, 1987).

32. Gunnar Myrdal, *An American Dilemma: The Negro Problem and Modern Democracy* (New York: Harper & Row, 1962 [1944]), 47–48.

33. United States National Advisory Commission on Civil Disorders, *Report of the National Advisory Commission on Civil Disorders* (New York: Bantam Books, 1968), 366.

34. United States National Advisory Commission on Civil Disorders, *Report of the National Advisory Commission on Civil Disorders,* 203.

35. Nicholas Johnson, *How to Talk Back to Your Television Set* (Boston: Little Brown, 1970), 104–105.

36. I am influenced here by George Lipsitz's and Charles Mills's writings on the idea of an "epistemology of ignorance"; see George Lipsitz, "Getting around *Brown:* The Social Warrant of the New Racism," in *Remembering Brown at Fifty: The University of Illinois Commemorates Brown v. Board of Education,* ed. Orville Burton and David O'Brien (Urbana: University of Illinois Press, 2009), 38–63; Charles Mills, "White Ignorance," in *Race and Epistemologies of Ignorance,* ed. Shannon Sullivan and Nancy Tuana (Albany: State University of New York, 2007), 11–38.

37. Mary Blue and Vanessa Murphree, "'Stoke the Joke' and His 'Self-Appointed White Critics': A Clash of Values on Network Television News, 1966–70," *Media History* 15, no. 2 (2009): 208.

38. Quoted in Robert Donovan and Ray Scherer, *Unsilent Revolution: Television News and American Public Life* (New York: Cambridge University Press, 1992), 3.

39. William Monroe, "Television: The Chosen Instrument of the Revolution," in *Race and the News Media,* ed. Paul Fisher and Ralph Lowenstein (New York: Praeger, 1967),, 85.

40. William Peters, "The Visible and Invisible Images," in *Race and the News Media,* ed. Fisher and Lowenstein, 81–82. Peters and Monroe are quoted in Aniko Bodroghkozy, *Equal Time: Television and the Civil Rights Movement* (Urbana: University of Illinois Press, 2012), 41.

41. Aniko Bodroghkozy and Martin Berger, in their respective studies of television news and photojournalism, have emphasized that in covering southern civil rights the news media favored particular black subjects. Bodroghkozy describes how

television news programs searched for a "moderate middle" and that "over and over again network news elevated Southern white moderates, as reporters and news producers searched for some figures of consensus. Paired with these white moderates, network news programs gave viewers not Southern black civil rights activists working within collective social and political movements to demand their rights, but rather individualized, often mute, worthy black victims of discrimination brutality. In general, television news was uneasy, if not hostile, to black demonstrators and activists acting as part of social change campaigns, even if nonviolently." In his analysis of the iconic images of civil rights confrontations, Berger argues, "White reporters and editors downplay[ed] the bravery and accomplishments of blacks as they conjured a fantasy of black passivity in the face of white aggression." Bodroghkozy, *Equal Time,* 9; Martin Berger, *Seeing through Race: A Reinterpretation of Civil Rights Photography* (Berkeley: University of California Press, 2011), 22. On civil rights and visual culture, see also Elizabeth Abbel, *Sign of the Times: The Visual Politics of Jim Crow* (Berkeley: University of California Press, 2010); Maurice Berger, *For All the World to See: Visual Culture and the Struggle for Civil Rights* (New Haven, CT: Yale University Press, 2010); Steven Kasher, *The Civil Rights Movement: A Photographic History, 1954–68* (New York: Abbeville Press, 1996); Leigh Raiford, *Imprisoned in a Luminous Glare: Photography and the African American Freedom Struggle* (Chapel Hill: University of North Carolina Press, 2013).

42. Robert Donovan and Raymond Scherer, *Unsilent Revolution: Television News and American Public Life, 1948–1991* (New York: Cambridge University Press, 1992), 6.

43. Bodroghkozy, *Equal Time,* 2.

44. Quoted in George P. Hunt, "The Racial Crisis and the News Media: An Overview," in *Race and the News Media,* ed. Paul Fisher and Ralph Lowenstein (New York: Praegar, 1967), 15.

45. On the *Montgomery Advertiser* and other southern newspapers, see Jeanne Theoharis, *The Rebellious Life of Mrs. Rosa Parks* (Boston: Beacon, 2013); Gene Roberts and Hank Klibanoff, *The Race Beat: The Press, the Civil Rights Struggle, and the Awakening of a Nation* (New York: Vintage Books, 2006).

46. Daniel Zwerdling, "Block Those Buses: White Militance in Michigan," *New Republic,* October 23, 1971, 16.

47. NBC News, "NYC Parents Demonstrate against Forced Busing," March 12, 1964, NBC Universal Archives.

48. Howard Rosenberg, "TV and Busing," *Los Angeles Times,* April 3, 1981.

49. Nathan Irvin Huggins, "Opportunities for Minorities in Television and Movies: Façade of Humor Can Obscure Substance of Subject," *Washington Post,* April 13, 1978.

50. *Red Lion Broadcasting Co., Inc. v. FCC,* 395 U.S. 369 (1969).

51. *CBS v. Democratic National Committee,* 412 U.S. 111 (1973).

52. Among the analyses of television news in this era, see Edith Efron, *The News Twisters* (Los Angeles: Nash Publishing, 1971); Robert Stevenson et al., "Untwisting the News Twisters: A Replication of Efron's Study," *Journalism & Mass Communi-*

cation Quarterly 50 (Summer 1973): 211–219; Nicholas Johnson, *How to Talk Back to Your Television Set* (Boston: Little, Brown and Company, 1970); David Altheide, *Creating Reality: How TV News Distorts Events* (Beverly Hills: Sage, 1976); Michael Arlen, *Living Room War* (New York: Viking, 1969); Robert Bower, *Television and the Public* (New York: Holt, 1973); Les Brown, *Televi$ion: The Business behind the Box* (New York: Harcourt, 1971); Harry Clor, ed., *The Mass Media and Modern Democracy* (Chicago: Rand McNally, 1974); Edward Jay Epstein, *News from Nowhere: Television and the News* (New York: Random House, 1973), Irving Fang, *Television News* (New York: Hastings House, 1972); Fred Friendly, *Due to Circumstances beyond Our Control. . .* (New York: Random House, 1967); Herbert Gans, *Deciding What's News: A Study of CBS Evening News, NBC Nightly News, Newsweek, and Time* (New York: Random House, 1979); George Gordon and Irving Falk, *TV Covers the Action* (New York: Julian Messner, 1968); Robert MacNeil, *The People Machine: The Influence of Television on American Politics* (New York: Harper & Row, 1968); Martin Mayer, *About Television* (New York: Harper & Row, 1972); Sig Mickelson, *The Electronic Mirror: Politics in an Age of Television* (New York: Dodd, Mead, 1972); Michael Robinson, "American Political Legitimacy in an Era of Electronic Journalism: Reflections on the Evening News," in *Television as a Social Force: New Approaches to TV Criticism,* ed. Richard Adler (New York: Praeger, 1975), 97–140; Tony Schwartz, *The Responsive Chord* (New York: Anchor Press/ Doubleday, 1973); Harry Skornia, *Television and the News: A Critical Appraisal* (Palo Alto, CA: Pacific Books, 1968); William Small, *To Kill a Messenger: Television News and the Real World* (New York: Hastings House, 1970); Gaye Tuchman, *Making News: A Study in the Construction of Reality* (New York: Free Press, 1978); Av Westin, *Newswatch: How TV Decides the News* (New York: Simon and Schuster, 1982).

53. Paul Simpson, *Network Television News: Conviction, Controversy, and a Point of View* (Franklin, TN: Legacy Communications, 1995); Lucas Hilderbrand, *Inherent Vice: Bootleg Histories of Videotape and Copyright* (Durham, NC: Duke University Press, 2009), 121–122.

54. On the Nixon administration's relationship to the news media, see Tim Kiska, "Nixon and the Media," in *Blackwell Companions to American History: A Companion to Richard M. Nixon,* ed. Melvin Small (Oxford: Blackwell, 2011), 292–310; Nicholas Johnson, "Government by Television: A Case Study, Perspectives, and Proposals," *Journal of Aesthetic Education* 5 (July 1971): 11–37; Herbert Klein, *Making It Perfectly Clear: An Inside Account of Nixon's Love-Hate Relationship with the Media* (New York: Doubleday, 1980); Marilyn Lashner, *The Chilling Effect in TV News: Intimidation by the Nixon White House* (New York: Praeger, 1984); Fred Powledge, *The Engineering of Restraint: The Nixon Administration and the Press* (Washington, DC: Public Affairs Press, 1971).

55. Epstein, *News from Nowhere,* 105.

56. Ibid., 102.

57. Ibid., 107.

58. Ibid., 139–142.

59. Westin, *Newswatch*, 57.

60. U.S. Commission on Civil Rights, "Your Child and Busing," 10.

61. *Milliken v. Bradley*, 418 U.S. 717 at 814.

62. This national history of "busing" builds on local and regional histories of school desegregation, such as Adina Back, "Exposing the 'Whole Segregation Myth': The Harlem Nine and New York City's Schools Desegregation Battles," *Freedom North: Black Freedom Struggles outside the South, 1940–1980*, ed. Jeanne Theoharis and Komozi Woodard (New York: Palgrave Macmillan, 2003), 65–92; Liva Baker, *The Second Battle of New Orleans: The Hundred-Year Struggle to Integrate the Schools* (New York: Harper Collins, 1996); Joyce Baugh, *The Detroit School Busing Case: Milliken v. Bradley and the Controversy over Desegregation* (Lawrence: University Press of Kansas, 2011); Howell Baum, *Brown in Baltimore: School Desegregation and the Limits of Liberalism* (Ithaca, NY: Cornell University Press, 2010); Charles Bolton, *The Hardest Deal of All: The Battle over School Integration in Mississippi, 1870–1980* (Jackson: University of Mississippi Press, 2005); Edna Bonacich and Robert Goodman, *Deadlock in School Desegregation: A Case Study of Inglewood, California* (New York: Praeger, 1972); William Chafe, *Civilities and Civil Rights: Greensboro, North Carolina, and the Black Struggle for Freedom* (New York: Oxford University Press, 1980); Robert Crain, *The Politics of School Desegregation: Comparative Case Studies of Community Structure and Policy-Making* (Chicago: Aldine, 1968); Joseph Cronin, *Reforming Boston Schools, 1930 to the Present: Overcoming Corruption and Racial Segregation* (New York: Palgrave Macmillan, 2008); Robert Dentler and Marvin Scott, *Schools on Trial: An Inside Account of the Boston Desegregation Case* (Cambridge: Abt Books, 1981); Paul Dimond, *Beyond Busing: Inside the Challenge to Urban Segregation* (Ann Arbor: University of Michigan Press, 1985); Rubén Donado, *The Other Struggle for Equal Schools: Mexican Americans during the Civil Rights Era* (Albany: State University of New York Press, 1997); Jack Dougherty, *More Than One Struggle: The Evolution of Black School Reform in Milwaukee* (Chapel Hill: University of North Carolina Press, 2004); Davison Douglas, *Reading, Writing & Race: The Desegregation of the Charlotte Schools* (Chapel Hill: University of North Carolina Press, 1995); T. Bentley Edwards and Frederick Wirt, eds., *School Desegregation in the North: The Challenges and the Experience* (San Francisco: Chandler Publishing, 1967); Doris Fine, *When Leadership Fails: Desegregation and Demoralization in the San Francisco Schools* (New Brunswick, NJ: Transaction Books, 1986); Ronald Formisano, *Boston against Busing: Race, Class, and Ethnicity in the 1960s and 1970s* (Chapel Hill: University of North Carolina Press, 2003); Brett Gadsden, *Between North and South: Delaware, Desegregation, and the Myth of American Sectionalism* (Philadelphia: University of Pennsylvania, 2012); Jon Hillson, *The Battle of Boston: Busing and the Struggle for School Desegregation* (New York: Pathfinder Press, 1977); Gregory Jacobs, *Getting around Brown: Desegregation, Development, and the Columbus Public Schools* (Columbus: Ohio State University Press, 1998); Tracy K'Meyer, *From Brown to Meredith: The Long Struggle for School Desegregation in Louisville, Kentucky, 1954–2007* (Lexington: University of Kentucky Press, 2013); Glenn Linden, *Desegregating Schools in Dallas: Four Decades in the Federal Courts* (Dallas: Three Forks

Press, 1995); Alan Lupo, *Liberty's Chosen Home: The Politics of Violence in Boston* (Boston: Little, Brown, 1977); Vivian Gunn Morris and Curtis Morris, *The Price They Paid: Desegregation in the African American Community* (New York: Teachers College Press, 2002); Robert Pratt, *The Color of their Skin: Education and Race in Richmond, Virginia, 1954–89* (Charlottesville: University Press of Virginia, 1992); Richard Pride and J. David Woodard, *The Burden of Busing: The Politics of Desegregation in Nashville, Tennessee* (Knoxville: University of Tennessee Press, 1985); Jeffrey Raffel, *The Politics of School Desegregation: The Metropolitan Remedy in Delaware* (Philadelphia: Temple University Press, 1980); Jonathan Rieder, *Canarsie: The Jews and Italians of Brooklyn against Liberalism* (Cambridge, MA: Harvard University Press, 1985); J. Michael Ross and William Berg, *"I Respectfully Disagree with the Judge's Order": The Boston School Desegregation Controversy* (Washington, DC: University Press of America, 1981); Lilian Rubin, *Busing and Backlash: White against White in a California School District* (Berkeley: University of California Press, 1972); Steven Taylor, *Desegregation in Boston and Buffalo: The Influence of Local Leaders* (Albany: State University Press of New York, 1998); Guadalupe San Miguel, Jr., *Brown, Not White: School Integration and the Chicago Movement in Houston* (College Station: Texas A&M University Press, 2001); Jeanne Theoharis, "Hidden in Plain Sight: The Civil Rights Movement outside the South," in *The Myth of Southern Exceptionalism,* ed. Lassiter and Crespino, 49–73; Jeanne Theoharis, "'I'd Rather Go to School in the South': How Boston's School Desegregation Complicates the Civil Rights Paradigm," in *Freedom North: Black Freedom Struggles outside the South, 1940–1980,* ed. Jeanne Theoharis and Komozi Woodard (New York: Palgrave Macmillan, 2003), 125–151; Charles Willie and Susan Greenblatt, eds., *Community Politics and Education Change: Ten School Systems under Court Order* (New York: Longman, 1981); Eleanor Wolf, *Trial and Error: The Detroit School Segregation Case* (Detroit, MI: Wayne State University Press, 1981).

63. Robert Dentler, "Boston School Desegregation: The Fallowness of Common Ground," *New England Journal of Public Policy* 2, no. 1 (1986): 81.

64. Kai Erikson, "A City Convulsed by History," *New York Times,* September 15, 1985.

65. Dentler, "Boston School Desegregation," 96, 90.

66. On the controversy over *Mississippi Burning,* see Kristen Hoerl, "Burning Mississippi into Memory? Cinematic Amnesia as a Resource for Remembering Civil Rights," *Critical Studies in Media Communication* 26, no. 1 (2009): 54–79.

67. Ruth Batson, *The Black Educational Movement in Boston: A Sequence of Historical Events: A Chronology* (Boston: Northeastern University School of Education, 2001), 15.

CHAPTER 1

1. Fred Powledge, "More Than 10,000 March in Protest on School Pairing," *New York Times,* March 14, 1964.

2. "15,000 Demonstrate at N.Y. City Hall: Parents Protest School 'Pairing' Plan," *Stars and Stripes,* March 14, 1964.

3. *Huntley-Brinkley Report,* NBC, March 12, 1964, NBC Universal Archives.

4. Benjamin Fine, "Northern Cities Confront the Problem of De Facto," *New York Times,* February 10, 1957; "The School Boycott," *New York Times,* February 2, 1964.

5. Martin Arnold, "Rights Rally at City Today Sets '15,000 and One' as Goal," *New York Times,* May 18, 1964.

6. Quoted in Tomas Sugrue, *Sweet Land of Liberty: The Forgotten Struggle for Civil Rights in the North* (New York: Random House, 2008), 467.

7. Legal scholar Cheryl Harris describes these settled expectations as one way that whiteness functions as property in United States law and culture: "Because the law recognized and protected expectations grounded in white privilege (albeit not explicitly in all instances), these expectations became tantamount to property that could not permissibly be intruded upon without consent." Cheryl Harris, "Whiteness as Property," *Harvard Law Review* 106 (June 1993): 1731.

8. In her study of the relationship between taxpayer rights language and education, historian Camille Walsh writes, "The use of taxation and 'taxpayer rights' as a principle to uphold segregation was implicitly premised on the idea . . . that African Americans must proportionally pay less in taxes, and therefore were not entitled to the same benefits as whites. . . . A sense of paternalism toward African Americans was often connected to the belief among whites that the public tax funds really belonged to whites to distribute. Whites repeatedly asserted that they paid 'more' taxes than blacks and therefore had the right to be heard by courts and legislatures. This sense of 'buying' services from the government through tax payments was connected to an idea that African Americans were 'lesser' taxpayers and therefore 'lesser' citizens." Camille Walsh, "Guardians of Inequality: Class, Race and the Struggle over Education in U.S. Courts, 1899–1974" (PhD diss., University of Oregon, 2010), 176–177.

9. *Congressional Record,* 88th Cong., 2d sess., March 12, 1964, 5081.

10. *Congressional Record,* 88th Cong., 2d sess., March 24, 1964, 6084.

11. *Congressional Record,* 88th Cong., 2d sess., April 10, 1964, 7563.

12. *Congressional Record,* 88th Cong., 2d sess., June 2, 1964, 12440.

13. *Congressional Record,* 88th Cong., 2d sess., June 17, 1964, 14220.

14. *Congressional Record,* 88th Cong., 2d sess., June 17, 1964, 14229.

15. U.S. Census Bureau, *Historical Census Statistics on Population Totals by Race, 1790 to 1990: New York—Race and Hispanic Origin for Selected Cities and Other Places: Earliest Census to 1990* (table 33), Population Division, Working Paper No. 76, February 2005.

16. Abraham Lederman, "Pulse of the Public: Union Head Takes Issue with Supt. Jansen," *New York Amsterdam News,* July 3, 1954.

17. On school segregation in New York in the first half of the twentieth century, see David Ment, "Patterns of Public School Segregation, 1900–1940: A Comparative Study of New York City, New Rochelle, and New Haven," in *Schools in Cities:*

Consensus and Conflict in American Educational History, ed. Ronald Goodenow and Diane Ravitch (New York: Holmes, 1983), 67–110.

18. Quoted in Adina Back, "School Segregation—Naming a Northern Problem" (unpublished chapter), 2. On Baker's work in New York and the North, see Ellen Cantarow, *Moving the Mountain: Women Working for Social Change* (New York: Feminist Press, 1980), 55–69; Joanne Grant, *Ella Baker: Freedom Bound* (New York: John Wiley, 1998), 1–104; Barbara Ransby, *Ella Baker and the Black Freedom Movement: A Radical Democracy Vision* (Chapel Hill: University of North Carolina Press, 2003), 64–169.

19. Gerald Markowitz and David Rosner, *Children, Race, and Power: Kenneth and Mamie Clark's Northside Center* (New York: Routledge, 1999).

20. Kenneth Clark, "Speech to Urban League of Greater New York," February 15, 1954, New York City Board of Education Records, Series 911: United Parents Associations Records, Subseries 10, Folder 52, New York City Municipal Archives; Gerald Fraser, "Citizens Should Demand Study of School System," *New York Amsterdam News,* February 27, 1954.

21. Kenneth Clark, "Segregated Schools in New York City," April 24, 1954, New York City Board of Education Records, Series 911: United Parents Associations Records, Subseries 10, Folder 52, New York City Municipal Archives; "Some City Schools Held Segregated," *New York Times,* April 25, 1954.

22. Adina Back, "Up South in New York: The 1950s School Desegregation Struggle" (Ph.D. diss., New York University, 1997), 99–100.

23. Leonard Buder, "City Schools Invite Inquiry of 'Jim Crow' Allegations," *New York Times,* July 14, 1954.

24. Irving Goldaber, "The Treatment by the New York City Board of Education of Problems Affecting the Negro, 1954–1963" (Ph.D. diss., New York Unuiversity, 1965), 59; "School Situation in New York," *New York Amsterdam News,* August 21, 1954.

25. "Siamese Twins?" editorial cartoon, *New York Amsterdam News,* November 6, 1954.

26. "Racial Unity Set for City Schools," *New York Times,* December 24, 1954.

27. Back, "Up South," 107.

28. Kenneth Clark, "Segregation and Desegregation in Our Schools," in *Ethnical Frontiers: The City's Children and the Challenge of Racial Discrimination,* ed. Algernon Black, Kenneth Clark, and James Dumpson (New York: Society for Ethical Culture, 1958), 15.

29. Back, "Up South," 109.

30. Public Education Association, "The Status of the Pubic School Education of Negro and Puerto Rican Children in New York City," October 1955, 14.

31. Public Education Association, "The Status of the Pubic School Education of Negro and Puerto Rican Children in New York City," 18.

32. Peter Bart, "School Migration," *Wall Street Journal,* January 29, 1957.

33. "New York Tension High over School Integration," *Hartford Courant,* April 30, 1957.

34. Peter Kihss, "Jansen Will Face Critics in Queens," *New York Times,* March 23, 1957.

35. Back, "Up South," 216.

36. Back, "Up South," 214.

37. Back, "Up South," 216.

38. Back, "Up South," 215.

39. Kihss, "Jansen Will Face Critics in Queens."

40. "Jansen Clarifies Findings on Bias," *New York Times,* April 11, 1957. See also "Jansen Clarifies Integration Plan," *New York Times,* April 20, 1957.

41. "Text of Jansen Report on School Zoning," *New York Times,* July 27, 1957; Benjamin Fine, "Jansen Program for Integration Leads to Dispute," *New York Times,* July 27, 1957.

42. Benjamin Fine, "Critics of Jansen Ask to Query Him," *New York Times,* August 5, 1957.

43. Clark, "Segregation and Desegregation in Our Schools," 18–19.

44. George Cornell, "Tension Runs High in N.Y. Race Plan," *Big Springs Daily Herald* (Big Springs, Texas), May 3, 1957; "William Weart, "Mixing Held Key to Racial Amity," *New York Times,* November 29, 1956.

45. Anthony Lewis, "President Bars U.S. Move in South at Present Time," *New York Times,* September 6, 1956; "President Speaks on Race Relations," *Washington Post,* September 6, 1956.

46. James Naughton, "President Backs a 'Middle Course' on Desegregation," *New York Times,* September 27, 1969; Warren Weaver, "School Integration 'at Once' Is Ordered by Supreme Court," *New York Times,* October 30, 1969.

47. Adina Back, "Blacks, Jews and the Struggle to Integrate Brooklyn's Junior High School 258: A Cold War Story," *Journal of American Ethnic History,* no. 2 (Winter 2001): 44.

48. "N.A.A.C.P. Rebukes City Board for All-Negro Brooklyn School," *New York Times,* November 2, 1956.

49. Back, "Blacks, Jews and the Struggle to Integrate Brooklyn's Junior High School 258," 47.

50. Jennifer de Forest, "The 1958 Harlem School Boycott: Parental Activism and the Struggle for Educational Equity in New York City," *Urban Review,* no. 1 (2008): 26.

51. Adina Back, "Exposing the 'Whole Segregation Myth': The Harlem Nine and New York City's School Desegregation Battles," in *Freedom North: Black Freedom Struggles Outside of the South, 1940–1980,* ed. Jeanne Theoharis and Komozi Woodard (New York: Palgrave Macmillan, 2003), 72.

52. "Parents Picket City Hall over Delay in Integration," *New York Times,* September 20, 1957.

53. Sara Slack, "Don't Forget N.Y. Has Its Own School Problem," *New York Amsterdam News,* September 28, 1957.

54. Loren Pope, "21 Negro Pupils Are Kept Home on Charge of Segregation Here," *New York Times,* September 9, 1958.

55. De Forest, "The 1958 Harlem School Boycott," 39.

56. *Matter of Skipwith,* 14 Misc. 2d 325, 345 (N.Y. Misc. 1958).

57. Gene Currivan, "Pact Is Reached on Harlem Schools," *New York Times,* February 11, 1959.

58. "4 Negro Mothers Freed in Boycott," *New York Times,* February 19, 1959.

59. "The Polier Decision," *New York Amsterdam News,* January 17, 24, 31, and February 7, 1959.

60. Quoted in de Forest, "The 1958 Harlem School Boycott," 39.

61. Back, "Up South," 39

62. Clarence Taylor, *Knocking at Our Own Door: Milton A. Galamison and the Struggle to Integrate New York City Schools* (New York: Lexington Books, 2001), 91–104.

63. On "freedom of choice" plans in the South, see Matthew Lassiter, *The Silent Majority: Suburban Politics in the Sunbelt South* (Princeton, NJ: Princeton University Press, 2006); Charles Bolton, *The Hardest Deal of All: The Battle over School Integration in Mississippi, 1870–1980* (Jackson: University Press of Mississippi, 2005), 117–166; Kevin Kruse, "The Fight for 'Freedom of Association': Segregationist Rights and Resistance in Atlanta," in *Massive Resistance: Southern Opposition to the Second Reconstruction,* ed. Clive Webb (New York: Oxford University Press, 2005), 99–116.

64. Robert Alden, "2 Groups of Pickets Score City's Plans to Transfer Pupils," *New York Times,* June 26, 1959.

65. John Wicklein, "Realty Scare Hit by Queens Clergy," *New York Times,* August 6, 1959.

66. Homer Bigart, "Whites in Queens Keep Pupils Home in Transfer Fight," *New York Times,* September 15, 1959.

67. Bigart, "Whites in Queens Keep Pupils Home in Transfer Fight."

68. Sara Slack, "Search Negro Pupils," *New York Amsterdam News,* February 6, 1960.

69. Leonard Buder, "City Board Backs Negro Pupil Shift," *New York Times,* August 15, 1959.

70. "Shift of Pupils Taken to Court," *New York Times,* September 5, 1959.

71. "Free Choice in City Schools," *New York Times,* September 1, 1960; Fred Hechinger, "School Integration," *New York Times,* September 1, 1960.

72. "Deserves a Chance," *New York Amsterdam News,* September 10, 1960.

73. David Rogers, *110 Livingston Street: Politics and Bureaucracy in the New York City School System* (New York: Vintage Books, 1969), 306.

74. Rogers, *110 Livingston Street,* 307.

75. Taylor, *Knocking on Our Own Door,* 104.

76. Jacob Landers, *Improving Ethnic Distribution of New York City Pupils* (New York: City School District of the City of New York, 1966), 25, 27.

77. Rogers, *110 Livingston Street,* 31.

78. Theodore Jones, "25 Arrested Here in School Protest," *New York Times,* December 17, 1963.

79. June Shagaloff and Frederick Jones, "NAACP on New York Situation," *Integrated Education*, February 1964, 36.

80. Milton Galamison, "The Pace Must Quicken," *Integrated Education*, February 1964, 24.

81. Galamison, "The Pace Must Quicken."

82. Taylor, *Knocking on Our Own Door*, 121.

83. Leonard Buder, "Boycott Cripples City Schools," *New York Times*, February 4, 1964.

84. Buder, "Boycott Cripples City Schools."

85. Taylor, *Knocking on Our Own Door*, 144.

86. Fred Powledge, "Leaders of Protest Foresee a New Era of Militancy Here," *New York Times*, February 4, 1964.

87. Powledge, "Leaders of Protest Foresee a New Era of Militancy Here."

88. Powledge, "Leaders of Protest Foresee a New Era of Militancy Here."

89. Back, "Up South," 416.

90. "A Boycott Solves Nothing," *New York Times*, January 31, 1964.

91. James Donovan, "We Are the Leaders," *Integrated Education*, February 1964, 30.

92. Landers, *Improving Ethnic Distribution of New York City Pupils*, 21–31.

93. Quoted in George P. Hunt, "The Racial Crisis and the News Media: An Overview," in *Race and the News Media*, ed. Paul Fisher and Ralph Lowenstein (New York: Frederick Praeger, 1967), 15.

94. Hodding Carter, "The Wave beneath the Froth," in *Race and the News Media*, ed. Fisher and Lowenstein, 54.

95. Margaret Halsey, "White Papers and Negro Readers," *New Republic*, October 16, 1965, 20.

96. Rogers, *110 Livingston Street*, 233.

97. Back, "Up South," 423; Lisa Yvette Waller, "Holding Back the Dawn: Milton A. Galamison and the Fight for School Integration in New York City, A Northern Civil Rights Struggle, 1948–1968 (PhD diss., Duke University, 1998), 414–416.

98. Sonia Song-Ha Lee, *Building a Latino Civil Rights Movement: Puerto Ricans, African Americans, and the Pursuit of Racial Justice in New York City* (Chapel Hill: University of North Carolina Press, 2014), 165–210.

99. Back, "Up South," 426.

100. "WSB-TV newsfilm clip of demonstrators protesting against de facto school segregation and of African American leaders Malcolm X and Adam Clayton Powell speaking in favor of the school boycott in New York City, New York," March 16, 1963, Walter J. Brown Media Archives and Peabody Awards Collection, University of Georgia, Athens, GA.

101. "1949 Fairness Report," 13 FCC 1246 (1949).

102. Public Notice, "Controversial Issue Programming, Fairness Doctrine," FCC 63–734 (July 26, 1963), 25 RR 1899 (1963); Marvin Wexler, "Women on Televi-

sion: Fairness and the 'Fair Sex,'" *Yale Review of Law and Social Action* 2, no. 1 (1972): 63.

103. Leonard Buder, "275,638 Pupils Stay Home in Integration Boycott," *New York Times,* September 15, 1964; "The Boycott's 'Success,'" *New York Times,* September 15, 1964.

104. Fred Powledge, "Poll Shows Whites in City Resent Civil Rights Drive," *New York Times,* September 21, 1964.

105. H.R. 7152, 88th Cong., 1st sess., November 20, 1963, 19–20.

106. H.R. 7152, 88th Cong., 1st sess., November 20, 1963, 18–26.

107. Charles and Barbara Whalen, *The Longest Debate: A Legislative History of the 1964 Civil Rights Act* (Washington, DC: Seven Locks Press, 1985) 33. On the history of the legislative debate over the Civil Rights Act, see also David Filvaroff and Raymond Wolfinger, "The Origin and Enactment of the Civil Rights Act of 1964," in *Legacies of the 1964 Civil Rights Act,* ed. Bernard Grofman (Charlottesville: University Press of Virginia, 2000); Todd Purdum, *An Idea Whose Times Has Come: Two Presidents, Two Parties, and the Battle for the Civil Rights Act of 1964* (New York: Henry Holt, 2014).

108. *Congressional Record,* 88th Cong., 2d sess., February 1, 1964, 1598.

109. *Congressional Record,* 88th Cong., 2d sess., February 6, 1964, 2280.

110. *Congressional Record,* 88th Cong., 2d sess., February 6, 1964, 2280.

111. *Congressional Record,* 88th Cong., 2d sess., March 21, 1964, 5861.

112. *Congressional Record,* 88th Cong., 2d sess., May 1, 1964, 9796.

113. *Congressional Record,* 88th Cong., 2d sess., April 13, 1964, 7745.

114. *Congressional Record,* 88th Cong., 2d sess., April 23, 1964, 8915.

115. Back, "Blacks, Jews and the Struggle to Integrate Brooklyn's Junior High School 258," 58, 69

116. *Lee v. Nyquist,* 318 F. Supp. 710, Dist. Court, New York (1970).

117. "Antibusing Law Is Ruled Unconstitutional," *Atlanta Daily World,* October 4, 1970.

118. On the Stennis Amendment, see Joseph Crespino, "The Best Defense Is a Good Offense: The Stennis Amendment and the Fracturing of Liberal School Desegregation Policy, 1964–1972," *Journal of Policy History* 18, no. 3 (2006), 304–325.

119. *Congressional Record,* 88th Cong., 2d sess., April 11, 1964, 7688.

CHAPTER 2

1. U.S. Congress, House of Representatives, Special Subcommittee of the Committee on Education and Labor, *De Facto School Segregation,* 89th Cong., 1st sess., July 27–28, 1965, 152, 162.

2. Coordinating Council of Community Organizations (CCCO) to Francis Keppel, July 4, 1965, Douglass Cater collection, box 52, folder "Complaints under Title VI," Lyndon Baines Johnson Presidential Library, Austin, TX (henceforth LBJPL).

3. CCCO to Keppel, July 4, 1965, Cater Collection; Alan Anderson and George Pickering, *Confronting the Color Line: The Broken Promise of the Civil Rights Movement in Chicago* (Athens: University of Georgia Press, 1987), 160.

4. "Title VI: Southern Education Faces the Facts," *Saturday Review,* March 20, 1965, 60.

5. Gary Orfield, *The Reconstruction of Southern Education: The Schools and the 1964 Civil Rights Act* (New York: Wiley & Sons, 1969), 196.

6. "Carrot and Stick," *Chicago Tribune,* February 22, 1964; "Neighborhood Schools Upheld," *Chicago Tribune,* May 5, 1964; Mary Pakenham, "Bow to Demand of Negroes for School Inquires," *Chicago Tribune,* July 18, 1965; "End Neighborhood Schools?" *Chicago Tribune,* June 26, 1966; "Racial 'Imbalance' in the Schools," *Chicago Tribune,* February 27, 1967; "A Far Reaching Rule on Integration," *Chicago Tribune,* April 18, 1967; "School Integration in the Election," *Chicago Tribune,* September 16, 1968.

7. "NAACP Wants Chicago Schools Desegregated," *Chicago Defender,* December 15, 1956.

8. James Sparkman, "NAACP Pushes Bid for Chicago Mixed Schools," *Christian Science Monitor,* March 20, 1957.

9. "De Facto Segregation in the Chicago Public Schools," *Crisis,* February 1958, 90.

10. "De Facto Segregation in the Chicago Public Schools," 89.

11. "Board Orders Probe of School Bias," *Chicago Defender,* December 14, 1957.

12. Reverend Carl Fuqua replaced Willoughby Abner as leader of the Chicago branch of the NAACP. Alan Anderson and George Pickering note that black congressman William Dawson played a key role in Abner's ouster and that "as a result, the local NAACP developed a reputation for being politically controlled and thereafter was suspect among civil rights activists for years to come." Alan Anderson and George Pickering, *Confronting the Color Line: The Broken Promise of the Civil Rights Movement in Chicago* (Athens: University of Georgia Press, 1987), 77.

13. "NAACP Steps Up Fight on School Bias," *Chicago Defender,* April 13, 1961.

14. Adolph Slaughter, "'Operation Transfer' Hits Chicago School Bias," *Chicago Defender,* September 7, 1961.

15. "Lawyer Says Schools Bias Not Due to Segregated Housing," *Chicago Defender,* September 2, 1961.

16. Kenneth Field, "School Suit Puts Blame on Superintendent Willis," *Chicago Defender,* September 19, 1961.

17. Anderson and Pickering, *Confronting the Color Line,* 85–86.

18. Anderson and Pickering, *Confronting the Color Line,* 84, 118, 134.

19. "200 Jam Courtroom for 'Truth Squad' Trial," *Chicago Defender,* May 8, 1962.

20. "Resume 'Study-In' Protest over Burnside Transfers," *Chicago Defender,* January 4, 1962; "School Officials Warn 'Study-In' Parents," *Chicago Defender,* January 8, 1962; "Judge Butler Frees 17 'Walk-Ins' in Burnside School Demonstration," *Chicago Defender,* January 18, 1962; "Clergy Joins in Protest to Pupils' Shift," *Chicago Tribune,* January 6, 1962.

21. "Dumb School Principal," *Chicago Defender,* January 22, 1962.

22. Anderson and Pickering, *Confronting the Color Line,* 90.

23. "March Protests 'Willis Wagons,'" *Chicago Defender,* June 19, 1962; "Willis Wagons 'Indefinite,'" *Chicago Defender,* May 31, 1962; "Urge Boycott of 'Willis Wagons,'" *Chicago Defender,* August 22, 1963.

24. "The Willis Wagons," *Chicago Defender,* May 29, 1962.

25. "C.O.R.E. Plans Petitions for Willis' Firing," *Chicago Tribune,* September 21, 1963.

26. "WE ACCUSE!" *Chicago Defender,* August 15, 1963.

27. The protest sign reading "Whitson voted good like a segregationist should" was a play on a well-known cigarette ad of this era, "Winston tastes good like a cigarette should." James Ritch, "Home of Willis Picketed," *Chicago Tribune,* August 16, 1963.

28. Sarah Lyall, "B. C. Willis, 86; Led Chicago Schools for 13 Years," *New York Times,* August 31, 1988.

29. "Chronicle of School Integration," *Integrated Education,* December 1963–January 1964, 10.

30. "Picketing Continues at Bogan High," *Chicago Defender,* September 11, 1963.

31. "Parents Protest," *Chicago Tribune,* September 11, 1963; James Ritch, "Overcrowding an Old Thorn at Bogan High," *Chicago Tribune,* September 16, 1963; "Willis Limits Transfers to 9 Schools," *Chicago Tribune,* September 20, 1963; "Willis Favors Bogan Parents over Negroes," *Chicago Defender,* September 16, 1963.

32. Anderson and Pickering, *Confronting the Color Line,* 117.

33. "Dr. Willis Resigns," *Chicago Tribune,* October 5, 1963; "Dr. Willis Will Stay," *Chicago Tribune,* September 28, 1963.

34. "Appeals for Supt. Willis Flood School Board and Mayor Daley," *Chicago Tribune,* October 8, 1963.

35. Special Subcommittee of the Committee on Education and Labor, *De Facto School Segregation,* 103. On Willis and the Chicago School Board in this era, see Joseph Pois, *The School Board Crisis: A Chicago Case Study* (Chicago: Educational Methods, 1964).

36. See chapters 1 and 3 for discussion of school boycotts in New York and Boston. On other school boycotts, see "Chronicle of School Integration," *Integrated Education,* June–July 1964, 4; "Chronicle of School Integration," *Integrated Education,* August–September 1964, 4; "Chronicle of School Integration," *Integrated Education,* June–July 1966, 6–7.

37. "Chicago's Lawrence Landry Is Typical of 'New Breed' in U.S. Negro Revolt," *Chicago Defender,* November 5, 1963.

38. Anderson and Pickering, *Confronting the Color Line,* 118–119.

39. "School Boycott Success," *Chicago Defender,* October 23, 1963.

40. "School Boycott Success," *Chicago Defender;* "Negro Leaders in Chicago Hail Impact of Mass School Boycott," *New York Times,* October 24, 1963.

41. "Boycott a Thumping Success! 225,000 Kids Make Willis Eat Jim Crow," *Chicago Defender,* October 23, 1963.

42. "Civil Commotion—to What Purpose?" *Chicago Tribune,* October 24, 1963.

43. Peggy Robinson, "2 Big Upsets: Boycott Wins! Clay Does, Too!" *Chicago Defender,* February 26, 1964.

44. "125,000 in School Boycott," *Chicago Tribune,* February 26, 1964.

45. "Boycott a Flop Declares Daley," *Chicago Defender,* February 27, 1964.

46. James Sullivan, "Roddewig Opposes 'Pupil Busing' Plan," *Chicago Tribune,* February 17, 1964.

47. John Coons, "Chicago, Illinois," in *Civil Rights U.S.A.: Public Schools Cities in the North and West 1962* (Washington, DC: U.S. Government Printing Office, 1962), 175–248; City of Chicago Board of Education, Advisory Panel on Integration of the Public Schools, "Integration of the Public Schools: Chicago, 1964," March 31, 1964; Robert Havinghurst, *The Public Schools of Chicago: A Survey for the Board of Education of the City of Chicago* (Chicago: Board of Education of the City of Chicago, 1964).

48. Anderson and Pickering, *Confronting the Color Line,* 139.

49. The Title VI model of denying federal funds to discriminatory projects grew out of similarly worded amendments U.S. congressman Adam Clayton Powell of Harlem introduced to federal expenditure bills since the 1950s. On the history and legacies of Title VI, see Stephen Halpern, *On the Limits of the Law: The Ironic Legacy of Title VI of the 1964 Civil Rights Act* (Baltimore, MD: Johns Hopkins University Press, 1995).

50. James Kerr, "Ben Willis after Chicago," *Chicago Tribune,* October 31, 1971.

51. *Congressional Record,* 88th Cong., 2d sess., June 4, 1964, 12717.

52. *Congressional Record,* 88th Cong., 2d sess., June 4, 1964, 12717; *Bell v. School City of Gary, Indiana,* 213 F. Supp. 819 (1963).

53. Mary Pakenham, "Bow to Demand of Negroes for School Inquires," *Chicago Tribune,* July 18, 1965.

54. "From Excess to Excess," *Chicago Tribune,* July 7, 1965.

55. Telephone interview with John Coons, November 25, 2014.

56. "Prof's Letter Cites Failure to See Willis," *Chicago Tribune,* September 4, 1965.

57. Special Subcommittee of the Committee on Education and Labor, *De Facto School Segregation,* 135.

58. "Prof's Letter Cites Failure to See Willis."

59. "Local Leaders Praise School Fund Cutoff," *Chicago Defender,* October 2, 1965.

60. "Our School Board," *Chicago Defender,* October 5, 1965.

61. James Yuenger, "City School Aid Halted," *Chicago Tribune,* October 2, 1965.

62. "Pucinski Hits Halt to Aid as Arbitrary," *Chicago Tribune,* October 2, 1965.

63. Anderson and Pickering, *Confronting the Color Line,* 180.

64. "Humiliating and Outrageous," *Chicago Tribune,* October 5, 1965.

65. On Daley's political power, see Roger Biles, *Richard J. Daley: Politics, Race and the Governing of Chicago* (De Kalb: Northern Illinois University Press, 1995); Mike Royko, *Boss: Richard J. Daley of Chicago* (New York: Plume, 1971).

66. Orfield, *The Reconstruction of Southern Education,* 193.

67. Orfield, *The Reconstruction of Southern Education,* 193–194.

68. Ruby Martin interview by Thomas Baker, February 24, 1969, transcript, p. 17, Lyndon Baines Johnson Library Oral History Collection, LBJPL.

69. James Yuenger, "Chicago School Fund Released," *Chicago Tribune,* October 6, 1965.

70. "Raby Applies New Heat to Schools," *Chicago Defender,* October 7, 1965.

71. Austin Wehrweins, "Chicago Story—City Hall and Civil Rights," *New York Times,* October 17, 1965.

72. Marjorie Hunter, "Chicago Schools Face U.S. Inquiry," *New York Times,* December 31, 1965.

73. "A Man among Midgets," *Chicago Tribune,* October 6, 1965.

74. Rowland Evens and Robert Novak, "Inside Report . . . : The Chicago Fiasco," *Washington Post,* October 18, 1965.

75. Wehrweins, "Chicago Story—City Hall and Civil Rights."

76. Irving Spiegel, "Powell Critical of Aid to Chicago," *New York Times,* October 16, 1965.

77. Both Keppel and Quigley left HEW in the months after the fund reversals, with their departures attributed to President's Johnson's anger over their handling of the Chicago case. Orfield, *The Reconstruction of Southern Education,* 198, 206.

78. Leonard Buder, "School Aid by U.S. Is Raising Fears," *New York Times,* October 29, 1965.

79. James Yuenger, "School Fund Action Defender by Keppel," *Chicago Tribune,* December 4, 1965.

80. Douglas Cater to F. Peter Libassi, January 21, 1965, Cater Collection, Box 52, folder "Proposed Guidelines and Summary—Title VI," LBJPL.

81. Martin interview by Baker, 21–22.

82. Harold Howe II to the Secretary (Joseph Califano), December 16, 1966, Joseph Califano Collection, box 8, folder "School Desegregation," LBJPL; Orfield, *The Reconstruction of Southern Education,* 203.

83. "Redmond Plan Is Protested by Motorcade," *Chicago Tribune,* August 27, 1967.

84. "Labels Busing 'Ivory Tower' School Plan," *Chicago Tribune,* August 28, 1967.

85. "Whites Oppose Busing Plan," *Chicago Defender,* January 11, 1968.

86. Casey Banas, "Busing Foes Picket City Hall, Cardinal," *Chicago Tribune,* January 31, 1968.

87. "School Busing," *Chicago Defender,* January 11, 1968.

88. ABC News, "Mothers Demo in Front of Chicago Board of Ed," January 10, 1968, Assignment number A42296O, Library number 029464A, ABC VideoSource; ABC News, "Anti-Bussing Demo," January 10, 1968, Assignment number A42296C, Library number 029464C, ABC VideoSource.

89. James Ralph, Jr., *Northern Protest: Martin Luther King, Jr., Chicago, and the Civil Rights Movement* (Cambridge, MA: Harvard University Press, 1993), 123.

90. ABC News, "Anti-Bussing Demo," January 10, 1968, Assignment number A42296C, Library number 029464C, ABC VideoSource. On taxpayer rights, see Clarence Lo, *Small Property Versus Big Government: Social Origins of the Property Tax Revolt* (Berkeley: University of California Press, 1990); Camille Walsh, "Guardians of Inequality: Class, Race and the Struggle over Education in U.S. Courts, 1899–1974" (Ph.D. diss., University of Oregon, 2010).

91. Casey Banas, "Asks O.K. for Pupil Busing," *Chicago Tribune,* December 27, 1967.

92. "Charges Controversy Blocking Real Issue," *Chicago Defender,* February 12, 1968.

93. "Crowds Jam 15 Hearings on Pupil Busing," *Chicago Tribune,* February 9, 1968.

94. "Crowds Jam 15 Hearings on Pupil Busing"; "Busing Foes Vow Campaign at the Polls," *Chicago Tribune,* February 10, 1968; Peter Negronida and Casey Banks, "Antibusing Valentines for Johnson," *Chicago Tribune,* February 14, 1968; "Group Holds Second Boycott for Busing," *Chicago Tribune,* February 15, 1968; "1,700 Attend Busing Parley at Steinmetz," *Chicago Tribune,* February 16, 1968; "School Board Opposition to Busing Grows," *Chicago Tribune,* February 20, 1968; "Hanson Pk. Busing Protest Draws 2,000," *Chicago Tribune,* February 26, 1968; Peter Negronida, "Nearly 1,000 Stand By for Busing Vote," *Chicago Tribune,* February 29, 1968; "Both Friends, Foes of Busing Unhappy at School Board Vote," *Chicago Tribune,* February 29, 1968; Donald Mosby and Betty Washington, "Busing Plan Goes Bust at Volatile Board Meeting," *Chicago Defender,* February 29, 1968.

95. "Spineless School Board," *Chicago Defender,* March 4, 1968.

96. "249 Pupils Bused on 1st Day of Plan," *Chicago Tribune,* March 12, 1968.

97. "296 to Begin Busing Monday," *Chicago Tribune,* March 8, 1968.

98. Bob Hunter, "School Officials Rap White Austin Parents," *Chicago Defender,* March 12, 1968.

99. Donald Mosby, "2 Antibusing Women Arrested in Fracas at Northwestside School," *Chicago Defender,* March 27, 1968.

100. ABC News, "Footage of School Bussing," Assignment number A43760B, Library number 031076B, ABC VideoSource.

101. Bob Hunter, "School Officials Rap White Austin Parents," *Chicago Defender,* March 12, 1968.

102. Vernon Jarrett, "Finally, We Are Facing the Facts," *Chicago Tribune,* April 15, 1979.

103. Dionne Danns, *Desegregating Chicago's Public Schools: Policy Implementation, Politics, and Protest, 1965–1985* (New York: Palgrave MacMillan, 2014), 120–186. On the management of Chicago's schools, see Dorothy Shipps, *School Reform, Corporate Style: Chicago, 1880–2000* (Lawrence: University of Kansas Press, 2006).

104. Michael Casserly, "Council of the Great City Schools," in *Encyclopedia of Educational Reform and Dissent,* ed. Thomas Hunt and Thomas Lasley II (New York: Sage, 2010), 230–232.

105. "And Boston Begins to Sweat," *Boston Globe,* October 2, 1965.

CHAPTER 3

1. David Oyama, "8000 Marchers in Roxbury Protest Segregation in City's Public Schools," *Harvard Crimson,* September 23, 1963.

2. Robert Levey, "6000 March for Rights in Boston," *Boston Globe,* September 23, 1963.

3. Levey, "6000 March for Rights in Boston."

4. Oyama, "8000 Marchers in Roxbury Protest Segregation in City's Public Schools."

5. On the Racial Imbalance Act, see Frank Levy, *Northern Schools and Civil Rights: The Racial Imbalance Act of Massachusetts* (Chicago: Markham, 1971).

6. "George Parker," *Boston Globe,* October 27, 1965.

7. On educational activism by black Bostonians, see Jeanne Theoharis, "'I'd Rather Go to School in the South': How Boston's School Desegregation Complicates the Civil Rights Paradigm," in *Freedom North: Black Freedom Struggles Outside of the South, 1940–1980,* ed. Jeanne Theoharis and Komozi Woodard (New York: Palgrave Macmillan, 2003), 125–152; "'They Told Us Our Kids Were Stupid': Ruth Batson and the Educational Movement in Boston," in *Groundwork: Local Black Freedom Movements in America,* ed. Jeanne Theoharis and Komozi Woodard (New York: New York University Press, 2005), 17–45; Jeanne Theoharis, "'We Saved the City': Black Struggles for Educational Equality in Boston, 1960–1976," *Radical History Review* (Fall 2001): 61–93;

8. Ruth Batson interview by Jackie Shearer, November 8, 1988, transcript, *Eyes on the Prize II Interviews,* Washington University Digital Gateway, http://digital.wustl.edu/e/eii/eiiweb/bat5427.0911.011ruthbatson.html.

9. Theoharis, "We Saved the City," 65.

10. Henry Hampton and Steve Fayer, *Voices of Freedom: An Oral History of the Civil Rights Movement from the 1950s through the 1980s* (New York: Bantam, 1990), 588–589.

11. Theoharis, "We Saved the City," 66.

12. "Anti-Bias March on City Hall," *Boston Globe,* June 12, 1963.

13. Batson interview by Shearer.

14. Jim Vrabel, *A People's History of the New Boston* (Amherst: University of Massachusetts Press, 2014), 52.

15. Seymour Linscott, "8260 Stay Out—but All Calm," *Boston Globe,* June 19, 1963.

16. Seymour Linscott, "Negroes to Go Ahead with Stay-Out," *Boston Globe,* June 18, 1963.

17. "It Was a Victory . . . It Was a Failure," *Boston Globe,* June 19, 1963.

18. Robert Levey, "School Board—NAACP Parley Short, Unhappy," *Boston Globe,* August 16, 1963.

19. Levey, "School Board—NAACP Parley Short, Unhappy."

20. Levey, "School Board—NAACP Parley Short, Unhappy."

21. Batson interview by Shearer.

22. Theoharis, "We Saved the City," 69.

23. Massachusetts State Board of Education, "Because It Is Right—Educationally: Report of the Advisory Committee on Racial Imbalance," April 1965, 2.

24. Bryant Rollins, "Kiernan Orders Racial Count Oct. 1," *Boston Globe,* August 19, 1965.

25. Rollins, "Kiernan Orders Racial Count Oct. 1."

26. Ian Forman, "No Crisis End in Sight," *Boston Globe,* September 12, 1965.

27. Robert Levey, "School Report Stirs New Storm," *Boston Globe,* April 16, 1965.

28. Levey, "School Report Stirs New Storm."

29. Levey, "School Report Stirs New Storm."

30. "I'm Not Anti-Negro, Mrs. Hicks Says," *Boston Globe,* October 2, 1967.

31. Bertram Waters, "Ban New School Busing," *Boston Globe,* August 7, 1965.

32. "50% Cut If Imbalance Continues?" *Boston Globe,* August 8, 1965.

33. "The Imbalance Issue," *Boston Globe,* October 17, 1967.

34. "Boston," *Integrated Education,* December 1965/January 1966, 6.

35. "Public Schools: Boston's Busing Battle," *Time,* September 24, 1965.

36. *Look* also cast a suspicious eye on the "neighborhood school" rhetoric that accompanied opposition to school integration: "As officials talk of redistricting, redistributing grades and reshuffling students, white parents have suddenly noticed a tugging at their heartstrings for the little school around the corner—the neighborhood school." Ira Mothner, "Boston's Louise Day Hicks: Storm Center of the Busing Battle," *Look,* February 22, 1966, 72.

37. "Backlash in Boston—and Across the U.S.," *Newsweek,* November 1967, 29–34.

38. ABC News, "Louise Day Hicks," September 27, 1967, Assignment number A39798, Library number 026752, ABC News Video Source.

39. "Mrs. Hicks to Address Campbell Graduating Class: Protest Demonstrations Planned," *Bay State Banner,* June 11, 1966.

40. "Rev. Mendelsohn: Calls Hicks 'Sick,'" *Bay State Banner,* July 2, 1966.

41. *Morgan v. Hennigan,* 379 F. Supp. 144 (1974).

42. "Backlash in Boston—and Across the U.S."

43. Robert Levey, "Consistency's Hobgoblin," *Boston Globe,* January 16, 1965.

44. Tom Atkins interview by Jackie Shearer, October 11, 1988, transcript, *Eyes on the Prize II Interviews,* Washington University Digital Gateway, http://digital.wustl.edu/e/eii/eiiweb/atk5427.0976.006tomatkins.html.

45. Robert Levey, "Lee, Eisenstadt or Mrs. Hicks?" *Boston Globe,* December 22, 1965.

46. Robert Levey, "Berkeley Shows Way on School Busing," *Boston Globe,* January 23, 1968.

47. George Collins, "Sullivan Blasts Hub School Committee, Legislature as He Quits," *Boston Globe,* July 6, 1972.

48. Bertram Waters, "Ban New School Busing," *Boston Globe,* August 7, 1965.

49. Elizabeth Weymouth, "Ellen Jackson: Housewife-Crusader, *Boston Globe,* January 30, 1966.

50. "Ellen Jackson Hits Middle Class Apathy," *Bay State Banner,* March 19, 1966; Ellen Jackson Rocks St. Mark's Audience," *Bay State Banner,* May 28, 1966.

51. "Woman in the News: Ellen Jackson of Operation Exodus," *Bay State Banner,* August 27, 1966.

52. "Ellen Jackson Stresses Better Communications," *Bay State Banner,* November 26, 1966.

53. "Mrs. Jackson Shares Newton Pulpit, Discusses Issues of 'Black Power,'" *Bay State Banner,* February 11, 1967. On the origins of Operation Exodus, see James Teele, Ellen Jackson, Clara Mayo, *Family Experiences in Operation Exodus: The Bussing of Negro Children* (New York: Behavioral Publications, 1967); James Teele, *Evaluating School Busing: Case Study of Boston's Operation Exodus* (New York: Praeger, 1973).

54. "Woman in the News: Ellen Jackson of Operation Exodus," *Bay State Banner,* August 27, 1966.

55. "Framer Hits Hub in Rights Speech," *Boston Globe,* October 20, 1965.

56. John Fenton, "Boston Negroes Invade 4 Schools: Pupils from Crowded Units Defy City by Transferring," *New York Times,* September 10, 1965; "200 Negroes Enroll in Schools in White Boston Neighborhoods," *Chicago Tribune,* September 11, 1965.

57. *Frank McGee Report: Boston Busing,* NBC, January 22, 1967, NBC Universal Archives.

58. *Frank McGee Report: Boston Busing.*

59. "Ellen Jackson Stresses Better Communications," *Bay State Banner,* November 26, 1966.

60. Ellen Jackson, "Mrs. Jackson Explains," *Boston Globe,* January 14, 1969; Holcomb Noble, "Operation Exodus: A Costly but Worthwhile Effort," *Boston Globe,* July 6, 1966.

61. "Exodus to Stop Busing Program," *Bay State Banner,* January 16, 1969.

62. Lily Geismer, *Don't Blame Us: Suburban Liberals and the Transformation of the Democratic Party* (Princeton, NJ: Princeton University Press, 2014). On METCO, see also Susan Eaton, *The Other Boston Busing Story: What's Won and Lost Across the Boundary Line* (New Haven, CT: Yale University Press, 2001).

63. "Exodus to Sue School Board for Bus Costs," *Boston Globe,* September 5, 1968.

64. "Exodus to Stop Busing Program."

65. Timothy Leland, "Imbalance Law Repeal Drive Launched," *Boston Globe,* August 3, 1967.

66. James Bolner and Robert Shanley, *Busing: The Political and Judicial Process* (New York: Praeger, 1974), 212–233.

67. Jack Dougherty, *More Than One Struggle: The Evolution of Black School Reform in Milwaukee* (Chapel Hill: University of North Carolina Press, 2004), 105.

68. "St. Louis," *Integrated Education,* June 1963, 48–49.

69. Al Sweeney, "News Desk: Lest We Forget about the Cleveland Incident," *Cleveland Call and Post,* March 20, 1965.

CHAPTER 4

1. "Text of Senator Goldwater's Address at Madison Sq. Garden in Only Campaign Appearance in City," *New York Times,* October 27, 1964.

2. Peter Kihss, "Goldwater Exhorts 18,000 in Garden 'Victory' Rally; Hits Johnson 'Daddyism,'" *New York Times,* October 27, 1964.

3. James Booker, "A Negro at the Goldwater Rally," *New York Amsterdam News,* October 31, 1964.

4. George Tagge, "Barry Tells Rights Goal," *Chicago Tribune,* October 17, 1964; "Barry Calls for Equality thru Freedom," *Chicago Tribune,* October 17, 1964; Rick Perlstein, *Before the Storm: Barry Goldwater and the Unmaking of the American Consensus* (New York: Nation Books, 2009), 424.

5. "G.O.P. Relying on TV in Barry Stretch Drive," *Chicago Tribune,* October 30, 1964.

6. "Transcript of the President's News Conference on Foreign and Domestic Matters," *New York Times,* September 13, 1963; James Bolner and Robert Shanley, *Busing: The Political and Judicial Process* (New York: Praeger, 1974), 134.

7. R. W. Apple Jr., "Kennedy Says He Opposes Distant Busing of Students," *New York Times,* September 9, 1964; "The Wisdom to Be Silent," *New York Times,* September 10, 1964.

8. Robert Terte, "Donovan Assails Busing as Issue," *New York Times,* September 9, 1964.

9. "Humphrey Opposes Long Pupil Busing," *New York Times,* September 15, 1964.

10. Bolner and Shanley, *Busing,* 83; *Congressional Record,* 91st Cong., 2d sess., February 17, 1970, 3582.

11. *Congressional Record,* 89th Cong., 2d sess., October 14, 1966, 26948; U.S. Congress, House of Representatives, Committee on Banking and Currency, 89th Cong., 2d sess., November 4, 1966, *Demonstration Cities and Metropolitan Development Act of 1966,* 52; Bolner and Shanley, *Busing,* 59.

12. *Congressional Record,* 89th Cong., 2d sess., October 6, 1966, 25549; Bolner and Shanley, *Busing,* 60.

13. *Congressional Record,* 89th Cong., 2d sess., October 6, 1966, 25549.

14. *Congressional Record,* 89th Cong., 2d sess., October 6, 1966, 25553.

15. *Congressional Record,* 89th Cong., 2d sess., October 6, 1966, 25553; *Congressional Record,* 89th Cong., 2d sess., October 14, 1966, 26949; Bolner and Shanley, *Busing,* 60.

16. *Congressional Record,* 89th Cong., 2d sess., October 14, 1966, 26949.

17. *Congressional Record,* 90th Cong., 2d sess., June 26, 1968, 18933; Bolner and Shanley, *Busing,* 63.

18. *Congressional Record,* 90th Cong., 2d sess., September 4, 1968, 25661; Bolner and Shanley, *Busing,* 64.

19. *Congressional Record,* 90th Cong., 2d sess., October 14, 1968, 31694; Bolner and Shanley, *Busing,* 64.

20. Joseph Crespino, "The Best Defense Is a Good Offense: The Stennis Amendment and the Fracturing of Liberal School Desegregation Policy, 1964–1972," *Journal of Policy History*, no. 3 (2006): 312.

21. *Congressional Record,* 91st Cong., 1st sess., December 16, 1969, 39341–39342.

22. *Congressional Record,* 91st Cong., 2d sess., February 5, 1970, 2552; Bolner and Shanley, *Busing,* 85.

23. *Congressional Record,* 91st Cong., 2d sess., February 9, 1970, 2892.

24. Crespino, "The Best Defense Is a Good Offense," 313.

25. "Conferees Ease Integration Curb," *New York Times,* March 20, 1970; Crespino, "The Best Defense Is a Good Offense," 318.

26. George Metlcalf, *From Little Rock to Boston: The History of School Desegregation* (Westport, CT: Greenwood Press, 1983), 79.

27. Bill Kovach, "Governor Signs Antibusing Bill," *New York Times,* May 3, 1969.

28. "Busing Order 'Ridiculous,' Reagan Says," *Los Angeles Times,* February 14, 1970; Tom Goff, "State to Support L.A. Schools Plea," *Los Angeles Times,* February 20, 1970.

29. "We Have the Right to Learn," *Los Angeles Sentinel,* February 19, 1970.

30. "Governors against the Law," *Time,* February 2, 1970, 13.

31. Jon Nordheimer, "Kirk Is the Name of the Man in the Door," *New York Times,* April 12, 1970.

32. Nordheimer, "Kirk Is the Name of the Man in the Door."

33. Richard Nixon, "Statement about Desegregation of Elementary and Secondary Schools," March 24, 1970.

34. Robert Sherrill, "A Political Happening Named Claude Kirk," *New York Times Magazine,* November 26, 1967, 34.

35. David Halberstam, "Claude Kirk and the Politics of Promotion," *Harper's,* May 1968, 37.

36. Kenneth Slocum, "Florida's Gov. Kirk Assigns Himself Task of Stopping Wallace," *Wall Street Journal,* January 31, 1968.

37. "7 Governors Shun Alabama Meeting," *New York Times,* April 14, 1967.

38. Marshall Frady, "'It Is a Joyous Thing to Be a Kirk Republican,'" *Saturday Evening Post,* July 29, 1971, 78.

39. "Mr. Nixon's 'New Alignment,'" *New York Times,* May 21, 1968.

40. Claude Kirk, "Direction of 'New South' Leadership," *New York Times,* May 25, 1968.

41. Halberstam, "Claude Kirk and the Politics of Promotion," 38.

42. Halberstam, "Claude Kirk and the Politics of Promotion," 39.

43. Darryl Paulson and Milly St. Julien, "Desegregating Public Schools in Manatee and Pinellas Counties, 1954–71," *Tampa Bay History* 7 (Spring/Summer 1985): 32–34.

44. *Green v. County School Board of New Kent County,* 391 U.S. 430 (1968); *Alexander v. Holmes County Board of Education,* 396 U.S. 19 (1969).

45. Fred Graham, "High Court Bids Six States Integrate Schools by Feb. 1," *New York Times,* January 15, 1970.

46. *ABC Evening News,* January 19, 1970, Vanderbilt Television News Archive (hereafter VTNA); *CBS Evening News,* January 19, 1970, VTNA.

47. *ABC Evening News,* January 19, 1970.

48. *ABC Evening News,* January 23, 1970, VTNA.

49. John MacKenzie, "Kirk Asks Standard for Desegregation," *Washington Post,* January 24, 1970.

50. *CBS Evening News,* January 23, 1970, VTNA.

51. "Four Dixie States Ask Uniform Desegregation Rules for Nation," *Los Angeles Times,* January 24, 1970.

52. Crespino, "The Best Defense Is a Good Offense," 304.

53. William Safire, *Before the Fall: An Inside View of the Pre-Watergate White House* (New York, Doubleday, 1975), 238; quoted in Randy Sanders, "Rassling a Governor: Defiance, Desegregation, Claude Kirk, and the Politics of Richard Nixon's Southern Strategy," *Florida Historical Quarterly* 80 (Winter 2002): 344–45.

54. Raymond Rapp, "The Failure of Massive Resistance: The Law and Social Change in Manatee, Florida" (MA thesis, University of South Florida, 1972), 173; "Kirk Takes Over a School System," *New York Times,* April 6, 1970.

55. *ABC Evening News,* April 6, 1970, VTNA.

56. *CBS Evening News,* April 6, 1970, VTNA.

57. Bruce Galphin, "Florida: Tackling the Busing Problem," *Washington Post,* April 14, 1970.

58. *ABC Evening News,* April 9, 1970, VTNA.

59. Spiro Agnew, "Television News Coverage," November 13, 1969, www.americanrhetoric.com/speeches/spiroagnewtvnewscoverage.htm.

60. These letters and telegrams were decidedly more positive than newspaper and magazine coverage of Kirk's school standoff. Most of the print coverage criticized Kirk for taking the law into his own hands and violating the "law-and-order" values he (and Nixon) previously championed. These critics pointed out that Kirk's behavior hewed too closely to black militants and student radicals. "Claude Kirk has reminded the nation that the challenge to law and order is not the exclusive preserve of the New Left," the *Cincinnati Enquirer* argued. The *Wall Street Journal* described Kirk's school takeover as "patently dubious" and called him an "albatross" for the law-and-order ideal. These columnists, however, focused their complaints on Kirk's tactics and took the wrongness of "busing" for granted. *Cincinnati Enquirer,* April 11, 1970; "Law and Order Albatross," *Wall Street Journal,* April 10, 1970.

61. Charles Lipps to Claude Kirk, telegram, April 9, 1970, Claude R. Kirk Jr. Papers (henceforth CK), series 923, box 16, folder 3, State Archives of Florida (henceforth SAF); James Polisso to Claude Kirk, January 31, 1970, CK, series 923, box 15, folder 3, SAF; "A Concerned Senior Citizen" to Claude Kirk [n.d., ca. February 1970], CK, series 923, box 15, folder 9, SAF; Beverly Wicks to Claude Kirk, January

24, 1970, CK, series 923, box 15, folder 10, SAF; Judith Bates to Claude Kirk, telegram, April 10, 1970, CK, series 923, box 16, folder 3, SAF; "Silent Majority" to Claude Kirk, February 1, 1970, CK, series 923, box 15, folder 3, SAF.

62. Rapp, "The Failure of Massive Resistance," 213.

63. Benjamin Houston, "Voice of the Exploited Majority: Claude Kirk and the 1970 Manatee County Forced Busing Incident," *Florida Historical Quarterly* 83 (Winter 2005): 282.

64. Sanders, "Rassling a Governor," 357.

65. Edmund Kallina, Jr., *Claude Kirk and the Politics of Confrontation* (Gainesville: University Press of Florida, 1993), 177.

66. Sanders, "Rassling a Governor," 345–346.

67. Kallina, *Claude Kirk and the Politics of Confrontation,* 178.

68. Houston, "Voice of the Exploited Majority," 285.

69. *Lee v. Nyquist,* 318 F. Supp. 710, Dist. Court, New York (1970).

70. "Antibusing Law Is Ruled Unconstitutional," *Atlanta Daily World,* October 4, 1970.

71. On the Stennis Amendment, see Crespino, "The Best Defense Is a Good Offense."

72. Miles Benson, "Secret House Petition Signed by 146, Pushes Lent Antibusing Plan," *Long Island Press,* March 11, 1972.

73. "House Joint Resolution 620," U.S. House of Representatives, School Busing: Hearings before Subcommittee No. 5 of the Committee on the Judiciary, 92d Cong., 1972, 1879.

74. "Busing Does Not Equal Quality Ed: So Contends Busing Forum Speakers," *Bell-Merr Home News,* February 24, 1972.

75. "Alexander Bickel letter to Emanuel Celler," U.S. House of Representatives, School Busing: Hearings before Subcommittee No. 5 of the Committee on the Judiciary, 92d Cong., February 29, 1972, 60; "Statement of Theodore M. Hesburgh, Chairman, U.S. Commission on Civil Rights," U.S. House of Representatives, School Busing: Hearings before Subcommittee No. 5 of the Committee on the Judiciary, 92d Cong., March 1, 1972, 236; "Statement of Hon. Norman F. Lent, A Representative in Congress from the State of New York," U.S. House of Representatives, School Busing: Hearings before Subcommittee No. 5 of the Committee on the Judiciary, 92d Cong., March 1, 1972, 163.

76. "Statement of Hon. Norman F. Lent, A Representative in Congress from the State of New York," 165.

77. *Parents Involved in Community Schools v. Seattle School District No. 1 et al.,* 551 U.S. 701 (2007).

CHAPTER 5

1. "Nixon on 'a Question Which Divides Many Americans,'" *Washington Post,* March 18, 1972.

2. John Ehrlichman, *Witness to Power: The Nixon Years* (New York: Simon and Schuster, 1982), 221.

3. NAACP Legal Defense and Education Fund, *It's Not the Distance, 'It's the Niggers': Comments on the Controversy over School Busing* (New York: NAACP Legal Defense and Educational Fund, Division of Legal Information and Community Service, 1972).

4. Arthur Chotin, letter to the editor, *Washington Post*, March 24, 1972; "7 Rights Lawyers Quit Justice Unit," *New York Times*, May 11, 1972.

5. "Humphrey Has Change of Mind," *Chicago Defender*, March 22, 1972; "Wilkins Asks Equal TV Time," *Pittsburgh Courier*, April 8, 1972.

6. Robert Mason, *Richard Nixon and the Quest for a New Majority* (Chapel Hill: University of North Carolina Press, 2004), 48.

7. John Anthony Mastese, *Spin Control: The White House Office of Communications and the Management of Presidential News* (Chapel Hill: University of North Carolina Press, 1994), 13–116.

8. Lydon (Mort) Allin interviewed by Susan Yowell, September 4, 1974, transcript, p. 14, Richard Nixon Presidential Archive.

9. Spiro Agnew, "Television News Coverage," November 13, 1969, www.americanrhetoric.com/speeches/spiroagnewtvnewscoverage.htm.

10. Walter Annenberg, who founded and published *TV Guide,* was a political supporter of President Nixon and was appointed by Nixon to be ambassador to the United Kingdom. Historians Glenn Altschuler and David Grossvogel write that "the *TV Guide* of the seventies became a self-proclaimed truth squad, exposing bias and endorsing 'balance.'" On the *TV Guide* "New Watch" column, see Glenn Altschuler and David Grossvogel, *Changing Channels: America in TV Guide* (Urbana: University of Illinois Press, 1992), 178–190.

11. On the Nixon administration's relationship to the news media, see Tim Kiska, "Nixon and the Media," in *Blackwell Companions to American History: A Companion to Richard M. Nixon,* ed. Melvin Small (Oxford: Blackwell, 2011), 292–310; Nicholas Johnson, "Government by Television: A Case Study, Perspectives, and Proposals," *Journal of Aesthetic Education* 5 (July 1971): 11–37; Herbert Klein, *Making It Perfectly Clear: An Inside Account of Nixon's Love-Hate Relationship with the Media* (New York: Doubleday, 1980); Marilyn Lashner, *The Chilling Effect in TV News: Intimidation by the Nixon White House* (New York: Praeger, 1984); Fred Powledge, *The Engineering of Restraint: The Nixon Administration and the Press* (Washington, DC: Public Affairs Press, 1971).

12. Ehrlichman, *Witness to Power,* 285

13. "Nixon Replies," *New Republic,* October 26, 1968, 15.

14. "Nixon Replies."

15. James Bolner and Robert Shanley, *Busing: The Political and Judicial Process* (New York: Praeger, 1974), 141.

16. Roy Reed, "Finch School Aim Held Compromise," *New York Times,* January 31, 1969.

17. Benjamin Mays, "The South Triumphs Again," *Pittsburgh Courier*, February 15, 1969.

18. Reed, "Finch School Aim Held Compromise."

19. John Herbers, "School Desegregation Opponents Intensify Pressure on President," *New York Times*, March 12, 1969.

20. Herbers, "School Desegregation Opponents Intensify Pressure on President."

21. Herbers, "School Desegregation Opponents Intensify Pressure on President."

22. Rowland Evans and Robert Novak, "Finch Blocked Administration Bid to Reverse Desegregation Drive," *Washington Post*, July 11, 1969.

23. "Text of Statement by Finch and Mitchell on School Desegregation Policy," *New York Times*, July 4, 1969.

24. "Text of Statement by Finch and Mitchell on School Desegregation Policy."

25. Peter Milius, "Schools Get Leeway on Integration," *Washington Post*, July 4, 1969.

26. Milius, "Schools Get Leeway on Integration."

27. Milius, "Schools Get Leeway on Integration."

28. Lawrence McAndrews, *The Era of Education: The Presidents and the Schools, 1965–2001* (Urbana-Champaign: University of Illinois Press, 2008), 63; Matthew Lassiter, *The Silent Majority: Suburban Politics in the Sunbelt South* (Princeton, NJ: Princeton University Press, 2006), 243.

29. McAndrews, *The Era of Education*, 64.

30. "On August 25, 1969," *New York Times*, September 3, 1969.

31. James Naughton, "President Backs a 'Middle Course' on Desegregation," *New York Times*, September 27, 1969; Warren Weaver, "School Integration 'at Once' Is Ordered by Supreme Court," *New York Times*, October 30, 1969.

32. Fred Graham, "Nixon Aide Warns Quick Integration Can't Be Enforced," *New York Times*, September 30, 1969; Eve Edstrom, "Leonard Says Desegregation Can't Be Sped," *Washington Post*, September 30, 1969.

33. James Wooten, "Agnew Declares He's Antibusing," *New York Times*, September 17, 1969.

34. Bruce Galphin and Peter Milius, "White House Backs Agnew on Busing," *Washington Post*, September 18, 1969.

35. Anthony Lewis, "President Bars U.S. Move in South at Present Time," *New York Times*, September 6, 1956; "President Speaks on Race Relations," *Washington Post*, September 6, 1956.

36. Robert Jensen, "Mrs. King Criticizes Nixon on Policy toward Blacks," *Washington Post*, September 29, 1969.

37. "The President and 'the Extremists,'" *Washington Post*, October 3, 1969.

38. "Rebel Rights Aide Forced to Resign," *New York Times*, October 2, 1969; Don Irwin, "Federal Attorney Says He Was Forced to Quit," *Los Angeles Times*, October 3, 1969.

39. "Rights Chief Backs Integration Policies of Administration," *New York Times,* October 3, 1969. "Second Rights Aide Resigns U.S. Post," *New York Times,* October 17, 1969.

40. Peter Milius, "School Integration Delay Barred," *Washington Post,* October 30, 1969.

41. Anthony Lewis, "End It 'at Once,' Says the Supreme Court," *New York Times,* November 2, 1969.

42. Peter Mililus, "Decision Denounced in South," *Washington Post,* October 31, 1969.

43. Dean Kotlowski, *Nixon's Civil Rights: Politics, Principle, and Policy* (Cambridge, MA: Harvard University Press, 2002), 31; Kevin McMahon, *Nixon's Court: His Challenges to Judicial Liberalism and Its Political Consequences* (Chicago: University of Chicago Press, 2011), 97.

44. Peter Mililus, "Decision Denounced in South," *Washington Post,* October 31, 1969.

45. Bob Woodward and Scott Armstrong, *The Brethren: Inside the Supreme Court* (New York: Simon & Schuster, 2005), 63.

46. Lassiter, *The Silent Majority,* 244.

47. McMahon, *Nixon's Court,* 97.

48. Leon Panetta, *Bring Us Together: The Nixon Team and the Civil Rights Retreat* (New York: Lippincott, 1971), 312; "Top Nixon Aids Feel North Getting Off Hook," *Tuscaloosa News,* December 25, 1969; "Chronicle of Race and Schools," *Equity & Excellence in Education* 8, no. 2 (1970): 57–58.

49. "Rights Zealots Look Northward," *Human Events,* December 13, 1969.

50. "Exit Leon Panetta," *Washington Post,* February 19, 1970.

51. Ehrlichman, *Witness to Power,* 226; McMahon, *Nixon's Court,* 98.

52. "Raps Nixon on Schools," *Chicago Defender,* March 2, 1970.

53. *Mary Ellen Crawford v. Board of Education of the City of Los Angeles*: Minute Order of Court's Intended Findings of Fact, Conclusions of Law, Judgment, and for Peremptory Writ of Mandate (Los Angeles: The Court, 1970), 30–31; Jack McCurdy, "Deadline: Sept. 1971," *Los Angeles Times,* February 12, 1970.

54. *Swann v. Charlotte-Mecklenburg Board of Education,* 300 F. Supp. 1358 (1969), 1359, 1369.

55. Lassiter, *The Silent Majority,* 157–158.

56. "The Retreat on Urban Busing," *Washington Post,* April 19, 1970.

57. William Deutscher, "President Nixon and School Busing" (Ph.D. diss, University of Maryland, 1999), 66.

58. Lassiter, *The Silent Majority,* 157.

59. *Northcross et al. v. Board of Education of the Memphis, Tennessee, City Schools et al.,* 397 U.S. 232, 237 (1970).

60. "The Retreat on Urban Busing," *Washington Post,* April 19, 1970.

61. McMahon, *Nixon's Court,* 99; William Safire, *Before the Fall: An Inside View of the Pre-Watergate White House* (New York: Doubleday, 1975), 238.

62. Raymond Price to John Ehrlichman, March 17, 1970, http://blog
.nixonfoundation.org/files/2013/08/Price-Memo-to-Ehrlichman.pdf.

63. Don Oberdorfer, "Nixon Put in Long House on School Statement," *Washington Post,* March 25, 1970.

64. McMahon, *Nixon's Court,* 99.

65. "Text of President's Statement Explaining His Policy on School Desegregation," *New York Times,* March 25, 1970.

66. "President Accused of Distorting School Facts," *Los Angeles Sentinel,* April 2, 1970.

67. "'Paying Southern Debts' Says Shirley," *New York Amsterdam News,* April 4, 1970.

68. "Text of President's Statement Explaining His Policy on School Desegregation," *New York Times,* March 25, 1970.

69. "Text of President's Statement Explaining His Policy on School Desegregation."

70. The White House sent a memo to Republican senators supporting the Stennis amendment: "It is the view of this administration that every law of the United States should apply equally in all parts of the country. To the extent that the uniform application amendment offered by Senator Stennis would advance equal application of law, it has the full support of this administration." "'All Parts of Country': Nixon Backs Dixie View in School Desegregation," *Norfolk Journal and Guide,* February 14, 1970.

71. *Keyes v. School District No. 1, Denver, Colorado,* 413 U.S. 189, 206, 254 n12 (1973).

72. Lassiter, *The Silent Majority,* 245.

73. Ehrlichman, *Witness to Power,* 225, 228; McMahon, *Nixon's Court,* 98.

74. Raymond Price, memo for the President, March 22, 1970, http://blog
.nixonfoundation.org/files/2013/08/Price-Memo-to-President-Nixon-School-Statement.pdf.

75. McMahon, *Nixon's Court,* 101.

76. Ehrlichman, *Witness to Power,* 133; McMahon, *Nixon's Court,* 102.

77. "Chief Justice Knocks TV Camera to Ground," *New York Times,* December 17, 1981.

78. *CBS Evening News,* April 20, 1971.

79. *NBC Evening News,* April 20, 1971.

80. "Supreme Court, 9–0, Backs Busing to Combat South's Dual Schools, Rejecting Administration Stand," *New York Times,* April 21, 1971.

81. John MacKenzie, "Court Backs School Busing, 9–0," *Washington Post,* April 21, 1971; Ronald Ostrow, "High Court Upholds Cross-City Bussing," *Los Angeles Times,* April 21, 1971.

82. Ostrow, "High Court Upholds Cross-City Bussing."

83. McMahon, *Nixon's Court,* 103.

84. McMahon, *Nixon's Court,* 103.

85. *Swann v. Charlotte-Mecklenburg Board of Education,* 402 U.S. 1. 24, 32 (1971).

86. *Swann v. Charlotte-Mecklenburg Board of Education,* 402 U.S. 1. at 30.

87. Gary Orfield, *Must We Bus? Segregated Schools and National Policy* (Washington: Brookings Institution, 1978), 11–27; William Gordon, "The Implementation of Desegregation Plans since Brown," *Journal of Negro Education* 63 (Summer 1994): 313.

88. "Secy. Richardson Caught in the Middle on Busing," *Boston Globe,* August 15, 1971.

89. "Text of Nixon Statement," *New York Times,* August 4, 1971; Peter Milius, "Nixon Repudiates HEW Busing Plan on Desegregation," *Washington Post,* August 4, 1971; Glen Elsasser, "Nixon Orders Use of Busing Minimized," *Chicago Tribune,* August 4, 1971.

90. Martin Nolan, "Law Laid Down on Nixon Integration Policy," *Boston Globe,* August 12, 1971.

91. "Secy. Richardson Caught in the Middle on Busing."

92. Leroy Aarons, "Texas Busing Crisis Hurts President," *Washington Post,* August 22, 1971.

93. Aarons, "Texas Busing Crisis Hurts President."

94. Peter Milius, "Wallace Bars Some Busing, Prods Nixon," *Washington Post,* August 13, 1971.

95. Jack Thomas, "The Busing Battle—2," *Boston Globe,* September 3, 1973.

96. Rowland Evans and Robert Novak, "Nixon Bus Issue Aids Wallace," *Washington Post,* August 23, 1971.

97. John Herbers, "Desegregation in North," *New York Times,* August 31, 1971.

98. Milius, "Wallace Bars Some Busing, Prods Nixon."

99. Tom Wicker, "The Harrisburg Story," *New York Times,* August 8, 1971.

100. Don Irwin, "Nixon Busing Plan Florida Link Denied," *Los Angeles Times,* March 28, 1972.

101. J. V. Reistrup, "Critics Call Proposal Too Little," *Washington Post,* March 18, 1972.

102. "Nixon on 'a Question Which Divides Many Americans.'"

103. "Ray Price," March 16, 1972, H. R. Haldeman Collection, box 165, folder "Follow-up (TV Appearances by P)," Richard Nixon Presidential Library, Yorba Linda, CA (henceforth RNPL).

104. "Clark MacGregor," March 16, 1972, Haldeman Collection, box 165, folder "Follow-up (TV Appearances by P)," RNPL.

105. Mark Goode memo, March 16, 1972, Haldeman Collection, box 165, folder "Follow-up (TV Appearances by P)," RNPL.

106. Gordon Strachan to John Ehrlichman, March 8, 1972, box 104, folder "John Ehrlichman March 1972," RNPL.

107. Gordon Strachan to H. R. Haldeman, March 17, 192, box 105, folder "Gordon Strachan March 1972," RNPL.

108. "Humphrey Has Change of Mind," *Chicago Defender,* March 22, 1972; "Wilkins Asks Equal TV Time," *Pittsburgh Courier,* April 8, 1972.

109. Robert Semple, Jr., "A Plan by Nixon That Will Test the Constitution," *New York Times,* March 19, 1972.

110. "Unofficial Returns of Florida Primary," *Washington Post,* March 16, 1972.

111. Anthony Lewis, "A Moment of Belief," *New York Times,* March 20, 1972.

112. Nicholas Peck, "Some Praise, Others Blast Nixon's Busing View," *Boston Globe,* March 17, 1972.

113. "A Satanic Plea," *Chicago Defender,* March 20, 1972.

114. "Nixon Cheapens Presidency with Antibusing Plan," *Baltimore Afro-American,* April 1, 1972.

115. Bolner and Shanley, *Busing,* 157.

116. McMahon, *Nixon's Court,* 108.

117. Lambda Corporation, "School Desegregation with Minimum Busing: A Report to the Assistant Secretary for Planning and Evaluation, U.S. Department of Health, Education, and Welfare," December 10, 1971, 4; Joseph Kraft, "Little Busing Goes a Long Way, Lambda Study Discloses," *Boston Globe,* April 5, 1972; Joseph Kraft, "The Lambda Study," *Washington Post,* April 4, 1972; Alton Frye, "One Way Out: A Ceiling on Busing," *Washington Post,* April 23, 1972.

118. Lambda Corporation, "A Survey of Urban School Desegregation: Summary Report Prepared for the Office for Civil Rights and the Office of the Assistant Secretary for Planning and Evaluation, U.S. Department of Health, Education, and Welfare," May 9, 1974.

119. Bolner and Shanley, *Busing,* 162.

120. John Herbers, "Basis of Nixon Pupil Aid Shift Doubted," *New York Times,* March 24, 1972.

121. "Hodgson" [n.d., ca. March 1972], Haldeman Collection, box 166, folder "Speech by P. Busing 3/16/72 Cabinet/Staff," RNPL.

122. Thomas Oliphant, "President Avoided Crux of Busing Issue in TV Soliloquy," *Boston Globe,* March 17, 1972.

123. Arthur Chotin, "Letter to the Editor," *Washington Post,* March 24, 1972.

124. Austin Scott, "Justice Dept. Lawyers Urge Hill Not to Restrict Courts on Busing," *Washington Post,* April 25, 1972.

125. "Dissent in the Ranks at Justice," *Washington Post,* April 26, 1972.

126. John W. Davis et al., "10 Black Lawyers at Justice," *Washington Post,* April 25, 1972.

127. "7 Rights Lawyers Quit Justice Unit," *New York Times,* May 11, 1972.

128. Eric Wentworth, "Black Appointees Assail Busing Curbs," *Washington Post,* April 27, 1972.

129. Wentworth, "Black Appointees Assail Busing Curbs"; Moses Newson, "Nixon Will Enforce Busing He May Feel Excessive," *Baltimore Afro-American,* May 6, 1972.

130. "Dirty Harry," *Time,* May 1972, 18.

131. *Milliken v. Bradley,* 418 U.S. 717. 757, 815 (1974).

132. *Milliken v. Bradley,* 418 U.S. 717. at 814.

133. McMahon, *Nixon's Court,* 210.

CHAPTER 6

1. The vast majority of "antibusing" groups referred to themselves with acronyms. Shortly after Judge Damon Keith handed down the integration order for Pontiac in February 1970, parents on the predominately white north side of the city formed a group called "Concerned Parents." In spring 1971, Irene McCabe led a faction that broke off from Concerned Parents to form Northside Action Group, which changed its name to National Action Group soon thereafter. "Statement of John K. Irwin, President, Pontiac School Board," U.S. Senate, Select Committee on Equal Education Opportunity, 92d Cong., November 4, 1971, 9842; "Entourage Heads toward Carroll County," *Times Reporter* (Dover, Ohio), March 31, 1972.

2. Marsha Low, "1970s Busing Activist Is Dead," *Detroit Free Press,* November 5, 2004.

3. On "mother" and "housewife" as political identities, see Annelise Orleck, "'We Are That Mythical Thing Called the Public': Militant Housewives during the Great Depression," in *Unequal Sisters: An Inclusive Reader in U.S. Women's History,* ed. Vicki Ruiz (New York: Routledge, 1990); Alexis Jetter, Annelise Orleck, and Diana Taylor, eds., *The Politics of Motherhood: Activist Voices from Left to Right* (Hanover, NH: University Press of New England, 1997); and Catherine Rymph, *Republican Women: Feminism and Conservatism from Suffrage through the Rise of the New Right* (Chapel Hill: University of North Carolina Press, 2006). On the ways American families were politicized in this era, see James T. Patterson, *Freedom Is Not Enough: The Moynihan Report and America's Struggle over Black Family Life—from LBJ to Obama* (New York: Basic Books, 2010); Robert Self, *All in the Family: The Realignment of American Democracy since the 1960s* (New York: Hill and Wang, 2012); and Natasha Zaretsky, *No Direction Home: The American Family and the Fear of National Decline, 1968–1980* (Chapel Hill: University of North Carolina Press, 2007).

4. Patricia Hill Collins, "Shifting the Center: Race, Class, and Feminist Theorizing about Motherhood," in *Mothering: Ideology, Experience, and Agency,* ed. Evelyn Nakano Glenn, Grace Change, and Linda Rennie Forcey (New York: Routledge, 1994), 45–66; Elaine Tyler May, *Homeward Bound: American Families in the Cold War Era* (New York: Basic, 1988); Ruth Frankenberg, *White Women, Race Matters: The Social Construction of Whiteness* (Minneapolis: University of Minnesota Press, 1993).

5. "Antibusing Mothers," *Chicago Defender,* May 10, 1972.

6. Nathan Irvin Huggins, "Opportunities for Minorities in Television and Movies: Façade of Humor Can Obscure Substance of Subject," *Washington Post,* April 13, 1978.

7. Maryanne Conheim, "Irene McCabe: Soul Sister of the Antibusing Set," *St. Petersburg Times* (Saint Petersburg, Florida), September 24, 1971.

8. "State Busing Foes Begin 46-Day Trek," *News-Palladium* (Benton Harbor, Michigan), March 15, 1972; Tom Huth, "Michigan–D.C. March Protests Busing," *Washington Post,* April 16, 1972.

9. In their study of representations of women in television news, Lana Rakow and Kimberlie Kranich suggest, "Women generally fall into the category of 'ordinary people,' who appear in the news and typically stand for a social aggregate." "Ordinary women," Rakow and Kranich argue, "are used to make a connection between the private sphere of home, family, emotions, neighborhood, and personal experience and the public world of politics, policy, and authority." Lana Rakow and Kimberlie Kranich, "Woman as Sign in Television News," *Journal of Communication* 41 (Winter 1991): 13, 16.

10. "School Buses in Pontiac, Mich.. Are Destroyed by Fire Bombs," *New York Times,* August 31, 1971; "Former Klan Chief among Six Seized in Pontiac Bus Bombing," *Los Angeles Times,* September 10, 1971; and Agis Salpukas, "Wider Plot Laid to Pontiac Klan," *New York Times,* September 11, 1971.

11. "Judge Dismisses Attempt in Michigan to Bar Busing," *New York Times,* September 2, 1971.

12. *CBS Evening News,* CBS, September 6, 1971, Vanderbilt Television News Archive (hereafter VTNA).

13. *ABC Evening News,* September 6, 1971, VTNA.

14. Bonnie Dow describes 1970 as the "key year for media coverage" for the second-wave feminist movement. Bonnie Dow, "Spectacle, Spectatorship, and Gender Anxiety in Television News Coverage of the 1970s Women's Strike for Equality," *Communication Studies* 50, no. 2 (1999): 143.

15. Dow, "Spectacle, Spectatorship, and Gender Anxiety," 148.

16. "Wiry Mrs. Irene McCabe Sparks Antibusing Group," *Holland Evening Sentinel* (Holland, Michigan), September 8, 1971.

17. *ABC Evening News,* September 7, 1971, VTNA.

18. *NBC Nightly News,* September 9, 1971, VTNA.

19. *CBS Evening News,* September 9, 1971, VTNA.

20. Daniel Zwerdling, "Block Those Buses: White Militance in Michigan," *New Republic,* October 23, 1971, 16.

21. Huth, "Michigan–D.C. March Protests Busing."

22. Quoted in Tamar Jacoby, *Someone Else's House: America's Unfinished Struggle for Integration* (New York: Basic Books, 1998), 260.

23. *CBS Evening News,* September 14, 1971, VTNA; and *NBC Nightly News,* September 14, 1971, VTNA.

24. *CBS Evening News,* September 23, 1971, VTNA.

25. Conheim, "Irene McCabe;" "Antibusing Forces Seek Boycott," Abilene Reporter-News (Abilene, TX), September 12, 1971; "Columbus School Supt. Asked to Resign Office," *Atlanta Daily World,* September 21, 1971.

26. *NBC Nightly News,* October 25, 1971, VTNA.

27. Spiro Agnew, "Television News Coverage," November 13, 1969, www.americanrhetoric.com/speeches/spiroagnewtvnewscoverage.htm.

28. Irving Fang, *Television News* (New York: Hastings House, 1972), 11.

29. Rueven Frank, *Out of Thin Air: The Brief Wonderful Life of Network News* (New York: Simon & Schuster, 1991), 296; William Small, *To Kill a*

Messenger: Television News and the Real World (New York: Hastings House, 1970), 244.

30. Edith Efron, "The 'Silent Majority' Comes into Focus," *TV Guide,* September 27, 1969, 6–9; Edith Efron, *The News Twisters* (Los Angeles: Nash Publishing, 1971), 179–180.

31. Edward Jay Epstein, *News from Nowhere: Television and the News* (New York: Random House, 1973), 150.

32. Agnew, "Television News Coverage."

33. "Pontiac Disservice," *Christian Science Monitor,* September 11, 1971.

34. Conheim, "Irene McCabe."

35. Peter Arnett, "Woman Continues Fight," *Avalanche Journal* (Lubbock, Texas), December 27, 1971; Powell Lindsay, "Moms March, but Change in Constitution Far Off," *Albuquerque Tribune,* April 28, 1972; "Michigan Housewives Plan Protest March on School Bus Plan," *Cumberland Evening Times* (Cumberland, Maryland), March 16, 1972; Mark Arnold, "Busing Battler," *Emporia Gazette* (Emporia, Kansas), reprint of *National Observer,* November 9, 1971; and Conheim, "Irene McCabe."

36. On the gendering of the assumed television news viewer as male, see Bernadette Barker-Plummer, "News and Feminism: A Historic Dialog," *Journalism and Mass Communication Monographs* 12 (Autumn/Winter 2010): 145–203; Bonnie Dow, "Fixing Feminism: Women's Liberation and the Rhetoric of Television Documentary," *Quarterly Journal of Speech* 90 (February 2004): 53–80; Dow, "Spectacle, Spectatorship, and Gender Anxiety"; Rakow and Kranich, "Woman as Sign in Television News"; and Gaye Tuchman, *Making News: A Study in the Construction of Reality* (New York: Free Press, 1978).

37. Julia Wrigley, "From Housewives to Activists: Women and the Division of Political Labor in the Boston Antibusing Movement," in *No Middle Ground: Women and Radical Protest,* ed. Kathleen Blee (New York: New York University Press, 1997), 251–288.

38. Harvey Molotch, "The News of Women and the Work of Men," in *Hearth and Home: Images of Women in the Mass Media,* ed. Gaye Tuchman, Arlene Kaplan Daniels, and James Benet (New York: Oxford University Press, 1978), 180.

39. *Davis v. School District of City of Pontiac,* 309 F. Supp. 734, 741–742 (1970).

40. Quoted in United States Commission on Civil Rights, *Five Communities: Their Search for Equal Education,* 1972, 16; Maryanne Conheim and John Oppedahl, "School Buses Built in Pontiac Turn into Symbols of Fear," *Detroit Free Press,* September 7, 1971.

41. United States Commission on Civil Rights, *Five Communities,* 16

42. Author interview with Elbert Hatchett, February 15, 2013.

43. "Statement of Mrs. Jo Ann Walker, Reading Teachers, Pontiac City School System," U.S. Senate Select Committee on Equal Education Opportunity, 92d Cong., November 4, 1971, 9882–9884.

44. "Statement of Elbert Hatchett, President, Pontiac Chapter, NAACP," U.S. Senate Select Committee on Equal Education Opportunity, 92d Cong., November 4, 1971, 9856.

45. William Grant, "Busing to Be Reality Tuesday in Pontiac," *Detroit Free Press,* September 5, 1971.

46. Toni Jones, "Donald: I Like the School All Right," *Detroit Free Press,* September 8, 1971.

47. Frank Angelo, "Mixed Feeling on Pontiac Busing," *Detroit Free Press,* September 13, 1971.

48. Maryanne Conheim, "Why She Chose Busing: A Mother's Decision," *Detroit Free Press,* September 9, 1971.

49. "As Our Readers See It: Is Busing the Best School Solution?" *Detroit Free Press,* September 11, 1971.

50. Ibid.

51. William Grant, "The Media and School Desegregation," in *School Desegregation: Making It Work,* ed. Robert Green (East Lansing: College of Urban Development, Michigan State University, 1976).

52. "Antibusing Housewife Planning to Walk 600 Miles," *Reading Eagle* (Reading, Pennsylvania), March 16, 1972.

53. *ABC Evening News,* March 15, 1972, VTNA.

54. "Antibusing Marchers Pay Brief Visit to City Today," *Evening Independent* (Massillion, Ohio), March 30, 1972.

55. Self, *All in the Family,* 122–123.

56. "Busing Protestors Don't Like District," *Weirton Daily Times* (Weirton, West Virginia), April 4, 1972.

57. "Antibusing 'Army' in Carroll," *Times-Reporter* (Dover, Ohio), March 31, 1972.

58. Mary Beth Haralovich, "Sit-Coms and Suburbs: Positioning the 1950s Homemaker," in *Private Screenings: Television and the Female Consumer,* ed. Lynn Spigel and Denise Mann (Minneapolis: University of Minnesota Press, 1992), 110–141; Lynn Spigel, *Make Room for TV: Television and the Family Ideal in Postwar America* (Chicago: University of Chicago Press, 1992).

59. "'Mad Mamas' Continue Busing Protest March," *Winchester Evening Star* (Winchester, Virginia), April 19, 1972.

60. "Mothers Begin Walk to Back Antibusing," *Cumberland News* (Cumberland, Maryland), March 16, 1972.

61. "Antibusing Walkers Go; Not All A OK," *Journal News* (Hamilton, Ohio), April 1, 1972.

62. "Ordinances Block Rally for Mrs. McCabe," *Altoona Mirror* (Altoona, Pennsylvania), April 5, 1972.

63. "Antibusing Walker," *Cumberland Evening Times* (Cumberland, Maryland), April 15, 1972.

64. "Sore Feet Slow March's End," *Kingsport Times* (Kingsport, Tennessee), April 27, 1972.

65. "Walking Mother Doesn't Relax Her Antibusing Drive," *Daily Review* (Hayward, California), April 28, 1972.

66. "'Mad Mamas' Continue Busing Protest March."

67. *CBS Evening News,* April 27, 1972, VTNA.

68. The three networks broadcast different portions of this part of McCabe's speech: *ABC Evening News,* April 27, 1972, VTNA; *CBS Evening News,* April 27, 1972; and NBC Nightly News, April 27, 1972.

69. As historian Michelle Nickerson notes in her study of 1950s Southern California, "Conservative women have for decades been repackaging housewife populism to meet the political exigencies of their times." Michelle Nickerson, *Mothers of Conservatism: Women and the Postwar Right* (Princeton, NJ: Princeton University Press, 2012), 169.

70. "Women Busing Marchers Leave Home Problems Behind," *Chicago Tribune,* March 20, 1972. For other mentions of tensions between Irene McCabe and her husband, see "Housewife Still Preaching Her Antibusing Message," *Joplin Globe* (Joplin, Missouri), December 26, 1971; and "Antibusing Housewife Planning to Walk 600 Miles," *Reading Eagle* (Reading, Pennsylvania), March 16, 1972.

71. Dow, "Spectacle, Spectatorship, and Gender Anxiety," 153–154.

72. Hank Burchard and Claudia Levy, "Busing Foes Gather in City, Climaxing Lengthy Marches," *Washington Post,* April 28, 1972; Hank Burchard, "Crowd Disappoints Antibusing Leader," *Washington Post,* April 30, 1972.

73. *CBS Evening News,* April 27, 1972.

74. Burchard and Levy, "Busing Foes Gather in City, Climaxing Lengthy Marches."

75. "House Passes Resolution of Tribute for Mrs. McCabe," *Ludington Daily News* (Ludington, Michigan), May 10, 1972; Al Washington, "McCabe Honor Deplored by Local Urban League," *Baltimore Afro-American,* May 27, 1972.

76. Burchard, "Crowd Disappoints Antibusing Leader."

77. "She Begins Long Walk to Capitol," *Daily Review* (Hayward, California), March 15, 1972.

78. As scholar Thomas Keenan has argued, these "images, information, and knowledge will never guarantee any outcome, nor will they force or drive any action." Thomas Keenan, "Publicity and Indifference (Sarajevo on Television)," *PMLA* 117 (January 2002): 114.

79. Jody Carlson, *George C. Wallace and the Politics of Powerlessness: The Wallace Campaigns for the Presidency, 1964–1976* (New Brunswick, NJ: Transaction Books, 1981), 133–179; Dan Carter, *The Politics of Rage: George Wallace, the Origins of the New Conservatism, and the Transformation of American Politics* (New York: Simon & Schuster, 1995), 415–450; Edmund Kallina Jr., *Claude Kirk and the Politics of Confrontation* (Gainesville: University of Florida Press, 1993), 168–183; Dean Kotlowski, *Nixon's Civil Rights: Politics, Principle, and Policy* (Cambridge, MA: Harvard University Press, 2001), 15–43; and Jeremy Mayer, *Running on Race: Racial Politics in Presidential Campaigns, 1960–2000* (New York: Random House, 2002), 96–122.

80. There were also two marches in support of desegregation in Boston in 1974, drawing a total of 14,500 people. See Jeanne Theoharis, "'I'd Rather Go to School in the South': How Boston's School Desegregation Complicates the Civil Rights

Paradigm," in *Freedom North: Black Freedom Struggles outside the South, 1940–1980,* ed. Jeanne Theoharis and Komozi Woodard (New York: Palgrave Macmillan, 2003), 139.

81. "Antibusing March Leader Lashes Out at Governor," *Traverse City Record Eagle* (Traverse City, Michigan), May 8, 1972.

82. "Irate Members Charge Misuse of NAG Funds," *Argus-Press* (Owosso, Michigan), February 24, 1973.

83. "McCabe Quits after Rival Factions Battle," *Ludington Daily News* (Ludington, Michigan), February 21, 1973.

84. "Busing Foe Enters Race," *New York Times,* June 13, 1974.

85. Louise Day Hicks, a leader of Boston antibusing group Restore Our Alienated Rights (ROAR), served one term in the U.S. House of Representatives (1971–1973) and was twice elected to Boston's city council. Bobbi Fielder, a leader of suburban Los Angeles antibusing group Bustop, served in the U.S. House of Representatives from 1981 to 1987. On Hicks, see Ronald Formisano, *Boston against Busing: Race, Class, and Ethnicity in the 1960s and 1970s* (Chapel Hill: University of North Carolina Press, 2003); J. Anthony Lukas, *Common Ground: A Turbulent Decade in the Lives of Three American Families* (New York: Vintage, 1986); and Theoharis, "I'd Rather Go to School in the South." On Fiedler and busing in Los Angeles, see Daniel Martinez HoSang, *Racial Propositions: Ballot Initiatives and the Making of Postwar California* (Berkeley: University of California Press, 2010), 91–129.

86. "Busing Foe Fades from Limelight," *New York Times,* May 21, 1973.

87. "Marching Mothers McCabe Cheered," *Traverse City Record Eagle,* January 15, 1973.

88. "Seventh Anniversary of Busing Passes Quietly," *Argus-Press* (Owosso, Michigan), November 1, 1978.

89. "Busing Foe Fades from Limelight."

90. Author interview with Tony Simuel, February 16, 2013.

91. "As We See It: Graduation Flashbacks," WTTW (Chicago), 1977, University of Georgia Peabody Awards Collection Archive.

92. Author interview with Simuel.

CHAPTER 7

1. *Eyewitness Exclusive: The School Bus Issue,* KPIX (San Francisco), 1968, University of Georgia Peabody Awards Collection Archives (hereafter UGA).

2. *Eyewitness Exclusive: The School Bus Issue.*

3. *Eyewitness Exclusive: The School Bus Issue.*

4. Quoted in Paul Miller, "The Interplay of Housing, Employment and Civil Rights in the Experience of San Francisco's African American Community, 1945–1975 (PhD diss., Temple University, 2008), 281.

5. "Exposing Busing Opponets *[sic],*" *Cleveland Call and Post,* April 22, 1972.

6. National Association for the Advancement of Colored People Legal Defense and Education Fund, "It's Not the Distance, 'It's the Niggers': Comments on the Controversy over School Busing," May 1972, 2.

7. "Assembly Okays Antibusing Bill," *Baltimore Afro-American*, August 5, 1969.

8. Stanley G. Robertson, "L.A. Confidential: What's Ahead in 72?" *Los Angeles Sentinel*, December 30, 1971.

9. "Jordan Asks Nixon for Summit Meetings with Blacks," *Pittsburgh Courier*, November 25, 1972.

10. Frank Stanley, "Busing Issue Nothing More Than White Rage," *Chicago Defender*, September 4, 1971.

11. See Ian Haney López, *Dog Whistle Politics: How Coded Racial Appeals Have Reinvented Racism and Wrecked the Middle Class* (New York: Oxford University Press, 2014).

12. "'Paying Southern Debts' Says Shirley," *New York Amsterdam News*, April 4, 1970.

13. Whitney Young, "A Letter to Jim Crow," *Los Angeles Sentinel*, September 10, 1970.

14. "The National Election," *Norfolk Journal and Guide*, November 4, 1972.

15. "Jordan Asks Summit," *Pittsburgh Courier*, August 12, 1972; "Urban League Chief Fears US Headed for Apartheid," *Norfolk Journal and Guide*, December 23, 1972.

16. "10 Black Lawyers at Justice: Congress Should Reject Busing Bills," *Washington Post*, April 25, 1972.

17. "The Law vs. the Mob," *New York Amsterdam News*, November 9, 1974.

18. Michael Petit, "Black Cong. Fear Return to Separate but Unequal Schools," *Cleveland Call and Post*, March 18, 1972.

19. "Busing Trick to 'Protect' Bias," *Chicago Defender*, September 14, 1971.

20. "Whites Were Not Against Busing Then . . . ," *Norfolk Journal and Guide*, September 20, 1975.

21. "The Busing Farce," *Baltimore Afro-American*, September 20, 1969.

22. "Southerners Stand Up," *Baltimore Afro-American*, February 7, 1970.

23. Stanley G. Robertson, "L.A. Confidential: Who Created 'Fear and Dismay'? *Los Angeles Sentinel*, February 19, 1970.

24. "N.C. Negroes Fighting School Closings," *Washington Post*, November 15, 1968. On the Hyde County protests, see David Cecelski, *Along Freedom Road: Hyde County, North Carolina, and the Fate of Black Schools in the South* (Chapel Hill: University of North Carolina Press, 1994).

25. Gil Hoffler, "Pupils Scold Board for Crestwood 'Phase-out,'" *Norfolk Journal and Guide*, May 22, 1971.

26. Southall Bass III, "Inquiring Reporter," *Norfolk Journal and Guide*, April 25, 1970.

27. "Students Protest Crestwood High School Phase Out," *Norfolk Journal and Guide*, March 28, 1970.

28. Bass, "Inquiring Reporter."

29. "HEW Says Crestwood Phase Out Bias-Based," *Norfolk Journal and Guide,* April 25, 1970.

30. "The School Muddle," *Norfolk Journal and Guide,* April 18, 1970.

31. Bass, "Inquiring Reporter."

32. "The School Muddle."

33. "Saving Booker T.," *Journal and Guide,* July 1, 1972.

34. Cecelski, *Along Freedom Road,* 9.

35. Barry Malone, "Before Brown: Cultural and Social Capital in a Rural Black School Community, W. E. B. Dubois High School, Wake Forest, North Carolina," *North Carolina Historical Review* 85, no. 4 (October 2008): 443–444.

36. George Metcalf, *From Little Rock to Boston: The History of School Desegregation* (New York: Praeger, 1983), 92.

37. "Saving Booker T."

38. Gil Hoffler, "Crestwood Battle Lost; Shift Black Principals," *Norfolk Journal and Guide,* June 19, 1971.

39. Hoffler, "Crestwood Battle Lost; Shift Black Principals."

40. John Smith and Better Smith, "For Black Educators: Integration Brings the Axe," *Urban Review,* no. 3 (1973): 7–9.

41. "2 Educators Rap Busing Edict," *Chicago Defender,* April 21, 1971.

42. Vernon Jordan, "To Be Equal: Black Teacher, Goodbye," *Norfolk Journal and Guide,* June 30, 1973.

43. Cecelski, *Along Freedom Road,* 8.

44. Smith and Smith, "For Black Educators," 7.

45. Children's Defense Fund, *School Suspensions: Are They Helping Children?* (1975), 63.

46. Children's Defense Fund, *Children out of School in America* (1974), 124, 130.

47. Children's Defense Fund, *School Suspensions,* 64.

48. Children's Defense Fund, *Children out of School in America,* 134.

49. Children's Defense Fund, *Children out of School in America,* 133.

50. Children's Defense Fund, *School Suspensions,* 14.

51. Children's Defense Fund, *School Suspensions,* 64

52. Walter Robinson, "Boston School Suspensions: The Racial Disparity," *Boston Globe,* June 17, 1975.

53. Children's Defense Fund, *School Suspensions,* 14.

54. "Diversity in Gary," *New York Times,* March 14, 1972; Angela Parker, "Black Parley Comes Out against Busing," *Chicago Tribune,* March 13, 1972.

55. From the mid-1960s through the mid-1970s, CORE articulated a consistent position in favor of black community control of education over school integration and "busing." See "CORE Seeks Harlem School Board," *New York Amsterdam News,* September 14, 1968; Simon Anekwe, "Fund Eyes Schools in North," *New York Amsterdam News,* May 1, 1971; "CORE Issues Antibusing Statement as Boston School Violence Continues," *Los Angeles Sentinel,* October 24, 1974.

56. Thomas Johnson, "Black Delegates Seek More Contacts," *New York Times,* March 19, 1972; Frank Stanley, "Where Do We Really Stand on Busing?" *Chicago Defender,* April 8, 1972.

57. Lucille Younger, "Rip Busing Vote at Convention," *Chicago Defender,* March 14, 1972.

58. Herbert Denton, "Blacks Vote against Busing," *Washington Post,* March 13, 1972; Parker, "Black Parley Comes Out against Busing."

59. Roger Wilkins, "Gary, the Schoolbus and Mr. Nixon," *Washington Post,* March 21, 1972.

60. Ethel Payne, "After Gary, What?" *Chicago Defender,* March 14, 1972.

61. Paul Houston, "Black Views against School Busing Surface," *Los Angeles Times,* March 17, 1972.

62. "Diversity in Gary," *New York Times,* March 14, 1972.

63. Don Oberdorfer, "School Issues in Landslide," *Washington Post,* March 15, 1972.

64. "Nixon on 'a Question Which Divides Many Americans,'" *Washington Post,* March 18, 1972.

65. "Black Convention Draws Brickbats," *Los Angeles Sentinel,* March 30, 1972.

66. Ethel Payne, "Gary Bus Vote Part of Plot?" *Chicago Defender,* March 28, 1972; Ethel Payne, "Behind the Gary Busing Resolution," *Pittsburgh Courier,* April 1, 1972.

67. Frank Stanley, "Where Do We Really Stand on Busing?" *Chicago Defender,* April 8, 1972.

68. "Hatcher Reviews Parley of Blacks," *New York Times,* March 16, 1972.

69. Eric Wentworth, "Black Caucus Affirms Its Support for Busing," *Washington Post,* March 16, 1972.

70. "Black Convention Adopts Compromise," *Hartford Courant,* March 13, 1972.

71. Wentworth, "Black Caucus Affirms Its Support for Busing."

72. Ethel Payne, "So This Is Washington," *Pittsburgh Courier,* April 8, 1972.

73. "Busing Gets OK from Black Unit," *Chicago Tribune,* April 11, 1972.

74. Parker, "Black Parley Comes Out against Busing"; "Busing Gets OK form Black Unit."

75. "Channel 13 Will Air Batten-Ivie Film on Gary," *New York Amsterdam News,* April 15, 1972.

76. Doris Eastman Harris, "Smothers . . . New Voice of a Silent Majority," *Malakoff News,* October 2, 1970.

77. Paul Sweitzer, "Difficult Campaign Looms, Says Independent Speaker," *Sun* (Flagstaff, Arizona), September 8, 1972; Charles Powers, "Black Adds Voice to White Busing Foes," *Los Angeles Times,* September 10, 1975.

78. "Parents Opposing Busing Picket Court, President," *Avalanche Journal* (Lubbock, Texas), October 29, 1971.

79. "Parents Opposing Busing Picket Court, President."

80. *NBC Nightly News,* February 26, 1972, NBC Universal Archives.

81. "Protestors in Fight as Busing Foes Meet," *New York Times,* February 27, 1972.

82. "Busing, an American Dilemma," *Newsweek,* March 13, 1972, 21.

83. CBS, July 13, 1972.

84. Charles Powers, "Black Adds Voice to White Busing Foes," *Los Angeles Times,* September 10, 1975; "Protesters Slow Delivery of Boston Globe," *Galveston Daily News* (Galveston, Texas), June 23, 1975.

85. "4,500 in Boston Assail Busing, Federal Judge," *Los Angeles Times,* December 16, 1974.

86. Charles Powers, "Black Adds Voice to White Busing Foes," *Los Angeles Times,* September 10, 1975.

87. David Brudnoy, "Black Antibusing Sentiment," *Orange County Register* (Santa Ana, California), May 2, 1977.

CHAPTER 8

1. Muriel Cohen and James Worsham, "Boston Schools Open Today with Desegregated Classes," *Boston Globe,* September 12, 1974.

2. *ABC Evening News,* September 12, 1974, Vanderbilt Television News Archive (VTNA).

3. *NBC Nightly News,* September 12, 1974, VTNA.

4. *CBS Evening News,* September 12, 1974, VTNA.

5. Doris Graber, *Mass Media and American Politics* (Washington, DC: Congressional Quarterly Press, 1980), 225.

6. Sasha Torres, *Black, White, and in Color: Television and Black Civil Rights* (Princeton, NJ: Princeton University Press, 2003); Aniko Bodroghkozy, *Equal Time: Television and the Civil Rights Movement* (Urbana: University of Illinois Press, 2012).

7. John Herbers, "Fear of Busing Exceeds Its Use," *New York Times,* May 28, 1972.

8. *ABC Evening News,* January 9, 1975, VTNA.

9. *CBS Evening News,* December 1, 1971, VTNA.

10. *ABC Evening News,* December 1, 1971, VTNA.

11. *CBS Evening News,* April 14, 1971, VTNA.

12. *ABC Evening News,* September 9, 1974, VTNA.

13. *CBS Evening News,* September 9, 1974, VTNA.

14. *ABC Evening News,* September 9, 1974, VTNA.

15. *NBC Nightly News,* September 11, 1974, VTNA.

16. *CBS Evening News,* December 11, 1974, VTNA; *NBC Nightly News,* December 16, 1974, VTNA.

17. *ABC Evening News,* January 8, 1975, VTNA.

18. *NBC Nightly News,* August 15, 1975, VTNA.

19. *NBC Nightly News,* September 8, 1975, VTNA.

20. Todd Gitlin, *The World Is Watching: Mass Media in the Making and Unmaking of the New Left* (Berkeley: University of California Press, 2003), 7.

21. *ABC Evening News,* January 8, 1975, VTNA.

22. *NBC Nightly News,* December 11, 1974, VTNA.

23. William Chapman and William Claiborne, "Ford Decries Boston School Busing Order," *Boston Globe,* October 10, 1974.

24. J. Michael Ross and William Berg, *"I Respectfully Disagree with the Judge's Order": The Boston School Desegregation Controversy* (Washington, DC: University Press of America, 1981), 243.

25. *Morgan v. Hennigan,* 379 F. Supp. 144 (1974).

26. *Morgan v. Hennigan,* 379 F. Supp. 146.

27. Massachusetts Advisory Committee to the United States Commission on Civil Rights, "Discrimination in Housing in the Boston Metropolitan Area," December 1963, 50, 20.

28. *NBC Nightly News,* October 15, 1974, VTNA.

29. *CBS Evening News,* December 11, 1974, VTNA.

30. *NBC Nightly News,* October 15, 1974, VTNA.

31. *NBC Nightly News,* August 31, 1975, VTNA.

32. *Morgan v. Hennigan,* 379 F. Supp. 46.

33. *Morgan v. Hennigan,* 379 F. Supp. 69.

34. Lily Geismer, *Don't Blame Us: Suburban Liberals and the Transformation of the Democratic Party* (Princeton, NJ: Princeton University Press, 2014).

35. Ronald Formisano, *Boston against Busing: Race, Class, and Ethnicity in the 1960s and 1970s* (Chapel Hill: University of North Carolina Press, 1991), 135.

36. Ernest Holsendolph, "More Cities to Integrate Schools," *New York Times,* September 1, 1975.

37. Doyle McManus, "L.A. Police Ready Contingency Plans as Busing Day Approaches," *Los Angeles Times,* August 13, 1978.

38. *Caution: Children on Board,* WAVE (Louisville, Kentucky), 1975, UGA.

39. *Desegregation: A Tale of Four Cities,* WFAA (Dallas, Texas), 1975, UGA.

40. *Both Sides of Busing,* WKYC (Cleveland, Ohio), 1976, UGA.

41. *Busing: The Green Light,* KNXT (Los Angeles, California), 1978, UGA.

42. *The Ride to Integration,* WTHR (Indianapolis, Indiana), 1985, UGA.

43. U.S. Civil Rights Commission, "Desegregating the Boston Public Schools: A Crisis in Civic Responsibility," August 1975, 203.

44. *Probe: A Southern Perspective on School Busing,* WLBT (Jackson, Mississippi), 1975, UGA.

45. *NBC Nightly News,* September 7, 1975, VTNA.

46. Henry, Hampton, Judith Vecchione, Steve Fayer, Orlando Bagwell, Callie Crossley, James A. DeVinney, Madison Davis Lacy, et al. *Eyes on the Prize: The Keys to the Kingdom, 1974–1980* (Alexandria, VA: PBS Video, 2006).

47. James Green, "In Search of Common Ground: A Review Essay," *Radical America* 20, no. 5 (1987): 56; Ruth Batson, *The Black Educational Movement in*

Boston: A Sequence of Historical Events (Boston: Northeastern University School of Education, 2001), 19–20.

CONCLUSION

1. Jack Thomas, "Nineteen Years Later, School Integration Is Still Just a Goal," *Boston Globe,* September 2, 1973.

2. Commission on Civil Rights, "School Desegregation in Ten Communities," June 1973, 3–4.

3. Jennifer Hochschild and Nathan Scovronick, *The American Dream and the Public Schools* (New York: Oxford University Press, 2004), 34.

4. *Board of Education of Oklahoma City v. Dowell,* 498 U.S. 237, 238 (1991).

5. *Freeman v. Pitts,* 503 U.S. 467, 468 (1992).

6. *Missouri v. Jenkins,* 515 U.S. 70 (1995).

7. Hochschild and Scovronick, *The American Dream and the Public Schools,* 35.

8. *Parents Involved in Community Schools v. Seattle School District No. 1 et al.,* 551 U.S. 701 (2007).

9. *Parents Involved in Community Schools v. Seattle School District No. 1 et al.* See also Ansley Erikson, "The Rhetoric of Choice: Segregation, Desegregation, and Charter Schools," *Dissent* (Fall 2011): 41–46.

10. Alana Semuels, "The City That Believed in Desegregation," *Atlantic,* March 27, 2015, www.theatlantic.com/features/archive/2015/03/the-city-that-believed-in-desegregation/388532/.

11. Gary Orfield, *Dismantling Desegregation: The Quiet Reversal of Brown v. Board of Education* (New York: New Press, 1997), 17.

12. U.S. Congress, House of Representatives, Subcommittee on Civil and Constitutional Rights of the Committee on the Judiciary, 97th Cong., 1st sess., November 19, 1981, 614; Orfield, *Dismantling Desegregation,* 17.

13. Orfield, *Dismantling Desegregation,* 16.

14. Hochschild and Scovronick, *The American Dream and the Public Schools;* Amy Stuart Wells, *Both Sides Now: The Story of School Desegregation's Graduates* (Berkeley: University of California Press, 2009); Gary Orfield and Erica Frankenberg, "Brown at 60: Great Progress, a Long Retreat and an Uncertain Future," *The Civil Rights Project,* May 2014, 37–40.

INDEX

A page with a figure or figures is indicated by *"fig."* following the page number.

ABC (American Broadcasting Company):
Agnew, Spiro and, 149–150; as author
resource, 19; Boston and, 190, 194–95,
195–96, 197; Chicago busing and,
72–73, 75; Civil Rights Act (1964)
violation and, 194–95; Hicks, Louise
Day and, 83–84; Kirk, Claude and, 103,
105, 107; McCabe, Irene and, 142,
145–48, 157, 159, 163*fig.;* Nixon, Richard
and, 115, 136; Parents and Taxpayers
(PAT) (New York City) and, 24, 27*fig.;*
production decisions and, 13; research
lack and, 14

Abner, Willoughby, 56, 228n12

Adabo, Jean, 23

Agnew, Spiro, 13, 101, 106, 116, 121, 149–150

Alabama: busing and, 174; civil rights
movement and, 10, 14; de facto segregation and, 127; desegregation and, 8, 104;
freedom of choice school legislation
and, 52, 110–11; governors meeting and,
102; Hood, James and, 106, 207; Jones,
Vivian Malone and, 106; judicial oversight and, 210; *Montgomery Advertiser*
(newspaper), 11; Rosa Parks and, 2;
Sixteenth Street Baptist Church bombing, 77; Sparkman, John and, 50–51;
University of Alabama integration, 207.
See also Wallace, George

Albert, Carl, 138*fig.*

Alcott Parent-Teacher Association
(Pontiac, Michigan), 155

Alexander v. Holmes (1969), 103, 122–23

Alinsky, Saul, 58

Alioto, Joseph, 170

Allen, James, 122

Allin, Lyndon (Mort), 116

Altschuler, Glenn, 240n10

American Jewish Congress, 43

American Party, 187–88

An American Dilemma (Myrdal), 8

Anderson, Alan, 228n12

Andry, Inez, 168–170, 171–72

Annenberg, Walter, 240n10

antibusing activists, 11–12, 164, 170, 186,
187–88, 199, 246n1. *See also* individuals

antibusing amendments, 1, 28, 52, 96–100,
110–13, 134, 157, 158, 163*fig.*, 165

antibusing legislation, 5, 52, 100, 110

antibusing protests: Chicago and, 70–75;
Labor Day March (Pontiac, Michigan),
145–46, 147*fig.;* legislation and, 5;
National Association for the Advancement of Colored People (NAACP) and,
170; news media and, 11, 179; New York
and, 56; Nixon, Richard and, 131; television and, 13–14, 145–46, 147*fig.*, 155,
164, 192–94, 197, 198*fig.*, 209; white
parents and, 11–12, 24–26, 46–47,
144; women and, 152. *See also* mothers'

Boston School Committee *(continued)*
Fourteenth Amendment violation and the, 199; Garrity, W. Arthur and the, 199–200; Metropolitan Council for Educational Opportunity (METCO) and the, 90; *Morgan v. Hennigan* (1974) and the, 7, 84, 199; Operation Exodus and the, 88, 90; racial discrimination and the, 128, 180; Racial Imbalance Act (1965) and the, 78, 85, 91; segregated schools and the, 194. *See also* Boston; Hicks, Louise Day; school desegregation (Boston)

boycotts. *See* school boycotts

Brady, Phil, 199

Brennan, William, 128

Breyer, Stephen, 210–11

Brinkley, David, 130

Brock, William, 158, 161

Brooklyn (New York), 37, 42, 49, 96. *See also* Bedford-Stuyvesant (New York City)

Brooklyn's Parents' Workshop, 42

Brown, Linda, 2

Brownsville (New York City), 29

Brown v. Board of Education of Topeka (1954): *Alexander v. Holmes County* (1969) and, 122; Brown, Linda and, 2; busing and, 212; Chicago and, 55; civil rights movement and, 4; Clark, Kenneth and, 30, 31; Florida and, 103; House Joint Resolution 620 (H.J. Res. 620) and, 111; Nixon, Richard and, 121–22, 126, 129; northern violation of, 7; school desegregation (New York City) and, 31–32; taxpayer rights and, 26

Brudnoy, David, 187

Buchanan, Pat, 13, 116, 135, 149

Buffalo (New York), 210

Burger, Warren, 118, 123, 125, 126, 129–130, 140

Burnside Elementary School (Chicago), 58–59

busing: ABC (American Broadcasting Company) and, 72–73; "As We See It" (television) and, 166; black communities and, 18, 154–56, 170–75, 180, 183, 184, 188–89; Boston and, 3, 29, 82–85, 87–88, 174, 192–93, 197–200; Chicago and,

70–76; Civil Rights Act (1964) and, 51–52, 95, 103; extremism and, 21, 35–36, 121–22; Glendale-Ridgewood (Queens) (New York City) transfer plan and, 39–41; intact busing, 91; Kirk, Claude and, 16, 95–96, 101, 108, 164, 238n60; Metropolitan Council for Educational Opportunity (METCO) and, 90, 203; moratorium on, 114–15, 134, 136, 139, 172, 174, 182–83; myths and, 15; National Black Political Convention and, 181–84; news media and, 3, 5, 12, 14, 18, 29, 33–34; New York and, 15, 16, 28–29, 33, 34–36, 39–41, 52–53, 93, 111; Nixon, Richard and, 1, 17, 101, 113, 114–15, 118, 130–141, 182–83; as northern de jure segregation remedy, 7; one-way busing, 40*fig.*, 74, 90, 91, 212; politicians and, 3, 4, 5, 15, 16–17, 92, 93–96, 109, 164, 170, 172; Pontiac (Michigan) and, 7, 11–12, 13, 29, 145–46, 154–56, 192; racism of debate on, 172–75; San Francisco Board of Education and, 168–170; school desegregation and, 2, 3, 6, 35–36, 82–84, 87–90, 192, 193, 212; Smothers, Clay and, 18, 171, 185–89; *Swann v. Charlotte-Mecklenburg Board of Education* (1971) and, 129–133, 140; television and, 11, 13–14, 88–89, 95, 133, 150, 192, 204–8, 209; term appearance of, 33; two-way, 90, 203; Wallace, George and, 95, 114, 135, 164. *See also* antibusing amendments; busing frame; Hicks, Louise Day; Kirk, Claude; McCabe, Irene; Nixon, Richard

"Busing Foe Fades from Limelight" (*New York Times*), 165–66

busing frame: black communities and the, 170, 180, 183, 184, 189; Boston and the, 18, 78, 83, 91, 192–93; Clark, Kenneth on the, 35; Hicks, Louise Day and the, 89*fig.*, 91; news media and the, 3, 5, 12, 83, 89*fig.*, 170–71, 175, 180, 189, 209; politicians and the, 170; school desegregation and the, 4, 35–36, 91, 170–71, 192–93, 212

"Busing Gets OK from Black Unit" (*Chicago Tribune*), 184

Committee for Parents of Transported Pupils (Saint Louis), 91

Committee on Education and Labor (House of Representatives), 179

Common Ground: A Turbulent Decade in the Lives of Three American Families (Lukas), 19–20

Concerned About Louisville's Mood (CALM), 204

Concerned Parents (Pontiac, Michigan), 246n1

Congress. *See* U.S. Congress

Congress of Racial Equality (CORE): busing and the, 170, 181, 183–84, 186; Coordinating Council of Community Organizations (CCCO) and the, 59; Dennison, Mary and the, 183–84; education control and the, 170, 253n55; Innis, Doris and the, 25; Innis, Roy and the, 170, 181, 182*fig.*, 183, 186; Operation Exodus (Boston) and, 87; school boycotts (New York City) and the, 43, 45–46; Willis, Benjamin and the, 59

Conheim, Maryanne, 150

Connecticut, 99

constitutional amendments, 52, 157. *See also* antibusing amendments

Conyers, John, 186

Coons, John, 63, 66

Coordinating Council of Community Organizations (CCCO), 54–56, 59, 61–62, 64, 66, 67, 68

CORE (Congress of Racial Equality). *See* Congress of Racial Equality (CORE)

court ordered school desegregation, 1, 3, 5, 7, 8, 29, 190, 192, 204

Cox, Edward, 178

Coxey's Army march (1894), 157

Cradle, Johnnie Mae, 176

Craig, Winston, 36

Cramer, William, 49–50

Crawford v. Los Angeles Board of Education (1982), 100, 175

Crespino, Joseph, 104

Crestwood High School (Virginia), 168, 176, 178

Crisis (journal), 57

Cronkite, Walter, 13, 103–4, 149, 159*fig.*, 196

Crouch, Tom, 132

Dahmer, Vernon, 138–39

Daley, Richard J., 15–16, 55–56, 62–63, 67–68, 70, 76, 99, 117

Dallas (Texas), 13, 149, 179, 205

Davidson, Jack, 109

Davis, Donald, Sr. and Jr., 154–55. *See also Davis v. School District of City of Pontiac* (1970)

Davis, Dwight, 177

Davis, Milton, 59

Davis, Sadie, 154–55

Davis v. School District of City of Pontiac (1970), 7, 152–55

Dawson, William, 228n12

Deacons for Defense and Justice, 86–87

de facto segregation: Baldwin, James on, 6; Boston and, 8, 77–78, 80–81, 84; Chicago and, 55, 66, 67, 69, 127; Civil Rights Act (1964) and, 27–28, 49–50, 51, 111; *Davis v. School District of City of Pontiac* (1970) and, 153; de jure–de facto dichotomy, 6; housing discrimination and, 3–4; Lassiter, Matthew on, 214n21; myth of, 8; New York City and, 32; Nixon, Richard and, 101, 113, 118, 123, 126–29, 130, 153; northern school desegregation and, 3–4, 6, 51; *Parents Involved v. Seattle* (2007) and, 210–11; politicians and, 96; Shagaloff, June on, 7; Stennis amendment and, 100

de jure segregation: Boston and, 7; Chicago and, 55, 69; Civil Rights Act (1964) and, 111; *Davis v. School District of City of Pontiac* (1970) and, 7, 152; de jure–de facto dichotomy, 6; Lassiter, Matthew on, 214n21; Michigan and, 7, 140; *Missouri v. Jenkins* (1995) and, 210; Nixon, Richard and, 101, 113, 117, 118, 123, 126–29, 153; *Parents Involved v. Seattle* (2007) and, 210–11; politicians and, 96; Stennis amendment and, 100; U.S. Department of Health, Education, and Welfare (HEW) and, 69, 98

Delaney, Steve, 149

Delaware, 210

freedom of choice, 39, 42, 52, 73, 85, 97, 98, 103, 110–11, 120
Freeman v. Pitts (1992), 210
Fuchs, Lawrence, 82
Fuqua, Carl, 57, 228n12

Galamison, Milton, 15, 25, 36, 39, 42, 43, 45–48, 87
Gallup polls, 100, 182
Garret, Clarence, 177
Garrity, W. Arthur: Boston and, 190, 193–94, 194–95, 196, 199–200, 202–3, 208; *Common Ground: A Turbulent Decade in the Lives of Three American Families* (Lukas) and, 19; *Morgan v. Hennigan* (1974) and, 7, 84, 180, 199–200
Garvey, Marcus, 78–79
Geer, Stephen, 103
Geismer, Lily, 203
Georgia, 8, 26, 52, 100, 110–11, 149, 172, 174
Gibson, Charles, 196
Gitleson, Alfred, 6–7, 100, 124, 126, 175
Gitlin, Todd, 197
Glendale-Ridgewood (Queens) (NYC) transfer plan, 39–41
Gloria, Leopoldo, 204
Goldberg, Arthur, 136
Goldwater, Barry, 16, 93–94
Goode, Mark, 135
Goodman, Andrew, 138–39
Graber, Doris, 191
Graham, Billy, 125
Grant, William, 156
grassroots antibusing protests, 145, 150, 152, 161
grassroots educational traditions, 169
Green, Edith, 16, 95
Green, Richard, 204
Greenberg, Gary, 122
Greensboro (North Carolina), 132
Green v. County School Board of New Kent County (1968), 103
Griffin, Robert, 158
Griswold, Erwin, 129, 130
Gross, Calvin, 42
Grossvogel, David, 240n10
Gunning, Rosemary, 46–48, 87

Hager, Robert, 196, 197, 201
Halberstam, David, 20, 101–2
Halsey, Margaret, 45
Hamer, Fannie Lou, 86–87
Harlem (New York City), 29–30, 37–38, 43, 45–46. *See also* Congress of Racial Equality (CORE)
Harlow, Bryce, 116–17, 125–26
Harris, Cheryl, 222n7
Harrisburg (Pennsylvania), 133
Hart, Philip, 120–21, 165
Hartford (Connecticut), 91
Hatcher, Richard, 184
Hatchett, Elbert, 154, 170–71
Hauser, Philip, 58, 61, 63
Havinghurst, Robert, 63
Hawkins, Augustus, 126–27
Height, Dorothy, 184
Heineman, Ardith, 165
Henderson, Lloyd, 176
Hesburgh, Theodore, 2, 111, 122, 209
Hicks, Louise Day: ABC (American Broadcasting Company) and, 83–84; Boston schools and, 3, 16, 77–78, 80–81, 82–84, 87–88, 91; *Common Ground: A Turbulent Decade in the Lives of Three American Families* (Lukas) and, 19; *Morgan v. Hennigan* (1974) and, 84; mothers' march (McCabe) (1972) and, 161; neighborhood schools and, 77, 83; news media and, 194; political career of, 83, 91, 165, 251n85; Racial Imbalance Act (1965) and, 78, 82, 91; San Francisco Board of Education and, 169–170
Hirsch High School (Chicago), 61
H.J. Res. 620 (House Joint Resolution 620), 52, 110–12, 134, 157, 163*fig*. *See also* Lent, Norman
Hodgson, James, 137–38
Hoffman, Julius, 58
Holland, Spessard, 51
Holland Evening Sentinel (newspaper), 142
Holley, Edward DeLeyatte, 176
Holmes, Peter, 179
Hood, James, 106, 207
Horn, Stephen, 5, 209
House Education and Labor Committee, 67

House Joint Resolution 620 (H.J. Res. 620), 52, 110–12, 134, 157, 163*fig. See also* Lent, Norman
housing discrimination: Boston and, 88, 90, 200, 203; Chicago and, 73; de facto segregation and, 3–4; federal policies and, 101; Kerner Commission report and, 9; New York City and, 29–30; politicians and, 26; Pontiac (Michigan) and, 153
housing patterns, 127–28. *See also* de facto segregation
Houston (Texas), 13, 179
Howe, Harold, 70
Howell, A. J., 176
Huggins, Nathan Irvin, 12, 144
Human Events (newspaper), 123
Humphrey, Hubert H., 16, 65–66, 94–95, 115, 136
Hunt, Richard, 196, 201
Huntley-Brinkley Report (television), 10
Hyde Park (Massachusetts), 193, 194

Illinois, 28, 58, 67, 181. *See also* Chicago
"Increasing Desegregation of Faculties, Students, and Vocational Education Programs" (report), 70
Indiana, 26, 28, 66, 182*fig.*, 205–6, 210. *See also* National Black Political Convention
Indianapolis (Indiana), 205–6, 210
Innis, Doris, 25
Innis, Roy, 170, 181, 182*fig.*, 183, 186, 188, 189
intact busing, 91
Integrated Education (journal), 64
Intergroup Committee on New York Public Schools, 30, 32
"It's Not the Distance, 'It's the Niggers'" (NAACP report), 114, 172
Ivie, Ardie, 184

Jackson, Ellen, 16, 84, 85–90, 144
Jackson, Gregory, 106, 194, 195, 196, 197
Jackson, Jesse, 170, 184
Jackson, Robert, 148
Jacksonville (Florida), 210
Jaffa, Henry, 94

Jansen, William, 29–30, 31, 32, 34–36, 42
Jarrett, Vernon, 75
Javits, Jacob, 50, 53, 95, 96
Jim Crow laws, 6, 31, 43, 62, 77–78, 93, 111, 173, 191
John Birch Society, 187–88
Johnnene, Fran, 199
Johnson, Lady Bird, 68
Johnson, Lyndon: Chicago schools and, 15–16, 55, 68, 69, 117; Goldwater, Barry and, 94; Model Cities legislation and, 96; Nixon, Richard and, 115; school desegregation and, 120, 121; U.S. Department of Health, Education, and Welfare (HEW) and, 121
Johnson, Nicholas, 9
Jones, Vivian Malone, 106, 207
Jordan, Vernon, 172–73, 175, 178
judiciary branch, 117–18, 121, 123, 187. *See also* U.S. Department of Justice; U.S. Supreme Court
Justice Department. *See* U.S. Department of Justice

Kallina, Edmund, Jr., 109
Kansas City (Missouri), 7
Kaplan, Nathanial, 37, 38
Katzenbach, Nicholas, 49
Kaufman, Irving, 6
Keating, Kenneth, 50
Keith, Damon J., 7, 145, 152–53, 246n1
Kelly, Chris, 191, 201
Kemmitt, Edward, 169
Kennedy, Edward, 195–96
Kennedy, John F., 49, 94, 115
Kennedy, Robert F., 16, 94
Kentucky, 13, 35–36, 164, 185, 204–5, 210–11
Keppel, Francis, 66–67, 68, 69, 70
Kerner, Otto, 9, 67
Kerner Commission, 9
Keyes v. School District No. 1, Denver (1973), 128, 153
Kiernan, Owen, 81
Kiernan Commission, 81, 82
Kiesling, Herbert, 137
Kiley, Robert, 206
Kincaid, Jim, 157
King, Coretta Scott, 122

Nixon, Richard *(continued)*
schools and, 101, 124, 127, 130, 173; news
media and, 13, 17, 115–17, 133, 136; northern vs. southern school desegregation
and, 101, 127, 128; Panetta, Leon and, 7;
racial imbalance and, 113, 118–19, 120;
racism and, 136, 184; Safire, William
and, 101; school desegregation and, 36,
101, 112–13, 116–129, 133, 173; Southern
Strategy and, 120–21, 127; Stennis
amendment and, 128, 243n70; *Swann v.
Charlotte-Mecklenburg Board of Education* (1971) and, 124–25, 129–133; television and, 115, 116, 133, 134–36, 138, 143,
164; Texas and, 120, 131–32; U.S.
Congress and, 114, 119, 134–35, 136–37,
138*fig.,* 139, 182–83; U.S. Department of
Health, Education, and Welfare
(HEW) and, 17, 112–13, 117, 118–19,
120–21, 122, 124, 128–29, 131–32, 139–
140; U.S. Department of Justice and, 17,
112–13, 114, 117, 121, 122, 124, 128–29,
136, 138–140, 153; U.S. Supreme Court
and, 118, 123, 129–130, 132, 136–37;
Wallace, George and, 114, 118, 134, 136;
Washington Post (newspaper) and,
114–15, 122, 125, 138–39, 174, 184
Nixon administration. *See* individuals;
Nixon, Richard
Norfolk Journal and Guide (newspaper), 19,
173, 175, 176, 177
North Carolina, 2–3, 119, 132, 176, 177, 209.
See also Charlotte-Mecklenburg schools
Northeastern University, 20
Northern Student Movement (civil rights
group), 86
northern vs. southern civil rights: Chicago
and, 54, 69; Civil Rights Act (1964)
and, 50, 52; Malcolm X on, 45–46; news
media and, 9, 11, 21, 44–45, 195; *New
York Times* on, 44, 45; Ribicoff, Abraham on, 99; Stennis, John on, 98–99;
Title VI (Civil Rights Act) and, 65–66;
U.S. Department of Health, Education,
and Welfare (HEW) and, 69
northern vs. southern school desegregation:
antibusing and, 3; anti-HEW measures
and, 96; Civil Rights Act (1964) and, 4,

28, 51; de jure–de facto dichotomy and,
6; *Human Events* (newspaper) and, 123;
news media and, 21; Nixon, Richard
and, 101, 127, 128; Parents and Taxpayers
(PAT) (New York City) and, 48;
Pasadena (California) school case and,
104; school desegregation (New York
City) and, 32
Northshield, Shad, 150
Northside Center for Child Development
(New York City), 30
Novak, Robert, 68–69, 120, 132–33

Office of Civil Rights (OCR), 179
O'Hara, James, 95, 97
Ohio, 28, 49, 95, 157, 172, 179, 205, 210
Oklahoma, 138*fig.,* 210
Oliphant, Thomas, 138
one-way busing, 40*fig.,* 74, 90, 91, 212
open enrollment policies, 39–42, 44, 85,
194, 195. *See also* Operation Exodus
(Boston)
Operation Exodus (Boston), 85–90, 192,
194
Operation Transfer (Chicago), 57–58
Orfield, Gary, 5, 211
Osborne, Ray, 109

Page, Ray, 67
Pan-Africanism, 169
Panetta, Leon, 7, 123–24
Parents Against Forced Busing (Florida),
110
Parents and Taxpayers (PAT) (New York
City), 23–29, 46, 48, 52, 87, 93
Parents Committee for Better Education
(New York City), 37, 43, 45–46
Parents in Actions Against Education
Discrimination (New York City), 37
Parents Involved v. Seattle (2007), 111,
210–11
Parents' Workshop for Equality in New
York City Schools, 39, 43, 45–46
Parker, Mike, 205
Parks, Paul, 80, 82, 199
Parks, Rosa, 2, 12, 144
Pasadena (California), 104, 128, 131, 204,
209

Stennis amendment, 98–100, 104, 128, 243n70
Stewart, Potter, 118, 140
Student Nonviolent Coordinating Committee (SNCC), 10, 30, 86–87, 172
Student Pushout: Victim of Continued Resistance to Desegregation, The (Southern Regional Council), 179
student transfers, 3–4, 23, 39–40, 60–61, 195. *See also* Operation Exodus (Boston)
student transportation, 2, 125, 131, 214n20. *See also* busing
Sullivan, Neil, 85
suspensions, pushouts of black students, 18, 171, 179–180
Swann v. Charlotte-Mecklenburg Board of Education (1971), 111, 129–133, 140, 178
Sweatt v. Painter (1950), 38
Sweeney, Al, 91

Tampa (Florida), 209
taxpayer rights, 73, 222n8. *See also* Parents and Taxpayers (PAT) (New York City)
Taxpayers Council of the Northwest Side (Chicago), 71
Taylor v. Board of Education of City School District of City of New Rochelle (1961), 6, 38–39, 58
Teachers for Integrated Schools (Chicago), 59
television: antibusing protests and, 13–14, 145–46, 147*fig.*, 155, 164, 192–94, 197, 198*fig.*, 209; Associated Press (AP) and, 14; "As We See It," 166; bias of, 12–13, 106, 143; black communities and, 208, 217n41; *Black Journal*, 173–74; Boston and, 13, 18, 84, 171, 190–210; busing and, 11, 13–14, 88–89, 95, 133, 150, 192, 204–8, 209; civil rights and, 9–11, 170; Egly, Paul on, 12; *Eyes on the Prize* and, 208; Fairness Doctrine (FCC) and, 12, 46–48; *51st State, The*, 184; *Frank McGee Report*, 87–89; Goldwater, Barry and, 94; Kirk, Claude and, 101, 102, 103–10; McCabe, Irene and, 17, 143, 144–152, 156–164, 166; National Action Group (NAG) and, 143; Nixon, Richard and, 115, 116, 133, 134–36, 138, 143, 164; Operation Exodus (Boston) and, 87–89;

Parents and Taxpayers (PAT) (New York City) and, 23–24, 25*fig.*; Pontiac (Michigan) and, 154, 155, 156; production decisions and, 13–14; racism and, 8–9; research lack and, 14; San Francisco Board of Education and, 168; school desegregation and, 11, 14, 46–48, 156, 192; segregation policies and, 10–11; Smothers, Clay and, 188; South Boston, Charlestown and, 193, 200–204; "Southern Perspective on School Busing in Boston, A," 206; violence and, 196; white backlash and, 144; women and, 247n9. *See also* ABC (American Broadcasting Company); Boston; CBS (Columbia Broadcasting System); NBC (National Broadcasting Company); network news; news media
Tennessee, 35–36, 52, 110–11, 125, 149, 158, 161, 166, 179, 185
Texas: Austin School Board, 131–32; black student suspension rates and, 179; Boston busing and, 205; Dallas, 13, 149, 179, 205; McCabe, Irene and, 149; Nixon, Richard and, 120, 131–32; Tower, John, 118–19, 132; violence and, 35–36. *See also* Johnson, Lyndon
Theobold, John J., 41
Thomas, Clarence, 111
Thurmond, Strom, 26, 102, 103, 118–120, 121, 123
Time (magazine), 83
Title I of the Elementary and Secondary Education Act of 1965, 137
Title IV (Civil Rights Act) (1964), 4, 28, 51, 111
Title VI (Civil Rights Act): antibusing amendments and, 97; Chicago and, 15–16, 54–56, 65–70, 117; federal enforcement of, 98; Federal funds denial and the, 230n49; northern vs. southern civil rights and, 65–66, 69; school segregation and, 15
"Title VI: Southern Education Faces the Facts" (*Saturday Review*), 55
Tower, John, 118–19, 132
Trilling, Leon, 90
truth squad mothers, 58, 144

Tucker, Charles, Jr., 155
Tucker, Lem, 196
TV Guide (magazine), 116, 240n10
two-way busing, 90, 203

United Concerned Citizens of America
(UCCA), 185
United Parents Associations of New York
City, 31, 43
United Press International (UPI), 14, 159
University of Alabama integration, 207
University of Georgia, 19
University of Mississippi, 106, 207
University of Notre Dame, 2, 111
Urban League. *See* National Urban League
Urla, Joe, 166
U.S. Commission on Civil Rights: Boston
and the, 190; busing and the, 15, 209;
Chicago and the, 63; Coons, John and
the, 66; Hesburgh, Theodore and the, 2,
111; Horn, Stephen and the, 5, 209;
Kiley, Robert and the, 206; Nixon,
Richard and the, 122, 133; school deseg-
regation and the, 209
U.S. Congress: busing and the, 95, 114; civil
rights legislation and the, 49; Daley,
Richard J. and the, 68; Hauser, Philip
and the, 61; mothers' march (McCabe)
(1972) and the, 157, 158, 161, 162; Nixon,
Richard and the, 114, 119, 134–35, 136–
37, 138*fig.*, 139, 182–83; Reagan, Ronald
and the, 211; Title VI (Civil Rights Act)
and the, 65; U.S. Department of
Health, Education, and Welfare
(HEW) and the, 97–98. *See also* antibusing amendments; Civil Rights Act
(1964); House Joint Resolution 620
(H.J. Res. 620); individuals
U.S. Department of Health, Education,
and Welfare (HEW): anti-HEW measures and, 96–100; "As We See It" (television) and the, 166; black educators
and the, 178; Boston and the, 192,
194–95; Chicago and the, 15–16, 54–56,
65–70, 75, 76, 96, 99, 117; Crestwood
High School (Virginia) and the, 176;
Johnson, Lyndon and the, 121; Lambda
Corporation and the, 137; Nixon,

Richard and the, 17, 112–13, 117, 118–19,
120–21, 122, 124, 128–29, 131–32, 139–
140; Panetta, Leon and the, 7, 123–24;
Quigley, James and the, 66; Richardson,
Elliot, 131; school desegregation and the,
15, 176; Title VI (Civil Rights Act) and
the, 98; U.S. Department of Justice:
Chotin, Arthur and the, 138–39; Finch-
Mitchell statement and the, 121; Florida
and the, 103; lawyer resignations and
the, 114–15, 122, 139, 174; Nixon, Richard and the, 17, 112–13, 114, 117, 121, 122,
124, 128–29, 136, 138–140, 153; Reagan,
Ronald and the, 75, 211; school desegregation and the, 211; school district
discrimination and the, 124
U.S. House of Representatives, 27, 91, 165,
179, 251n85
U.S. Justice Department. *See* U.S. Department of Justice
U.S. News and World Report (magazine),
120
U.S. Office of Education, 54, 55, 119, 122
U.S. Supreme Court: *Alexander v. Holmes
County* (1969), 103, 122–23; *Board of
Education of Oklahoma City v. Dowell*
(1991), 210; *CBS v. Democratic National
Committee* (1973); *Freeman v. Pitts*
(1992), 210; *Green v. County School Board
of New Kent County* (1968), 103; *Keyes v.
School District No. 1, Denver* (1973), 128,
153; Kirk, Claude and, 103, 104; *Milliken
v. Bradley* (1974), 17, 118, 140, 153, 210;
Missouri v. Jenkins (1995), 210; National
Association for the Advancement of
Colored People (NAACP) and the, 121;
Nixon, Richard and the, 118, 123, 129–
130, 132, 136–37; *Parents Involved v.
Seattle* (2007), 111, 210–11; Rehnquist,
William and the, 94; school desegregation and the, 4–5, 119; *Swann v. Char-
lotte-Mecklenburg Board of Education*
(1971), 129–131, 178; taxpayer rights and
the, 26; Thomas, Clarence and the, 111;
United Concerned Citizens of America
(UCCA) and the, 185. *See also Brown v.
Board of Education of Topeka* (1954);
individual Justices

Program for School Improvement and, 76; resignation of, 61, 70; school desegregation and, 61, 63–64, 76; school transfers and, 60–61; Title VI (Civil Rights Act) and, 66–67, 68; *Washington Post* (newspaper) on, 68–69; *Webb v. Board of Education of the City of Chicago* (1963) and, 58; "Willis Wagons" and, 59

Wilmington (Delaware), 210

Winship, Thomas, 19

WKYC (NBC), 205

WLBT (television), 206

women: antibusing protests and, 152; black mothers, 37, 58, 75, 144, 168, 170; housewife populism and, 250n69; Parents and Taxpayers protest march (NYC) and, 23; white mothers, 12, 28, 29, 51, 144, 168. *See also* mothers' march (McCabe) (1972); *individual women*

Women's National Press Club, 124

Women's Strike for Equality, 147

Wood, Clifton, 178

Woodlawn Experimental Schools Project (Chicago), 178

Woodlawn Organization (Chicago), 58, 59, 144

WTHR-TV (NBC), 205–6

WTTW (television), 166

Young, Whitney, 173

Ziegler, Ronald, 121, 123, 130, 132, 134

Zuber, Paul, 37, 38–39, 57–58

9 780520 284241